Bollywood and Globalization

Bollywood and Globalization

Indian Popular Cinema, Nation, and Diaspora

Edited by
Rini Bhattacharya Mehta and Rajeshwari V. Pandharipande

ANTHEM PRESS
LONDON · NEW YORK · DELHI

Anthem Press
An imprint of Wimbledon Publishing Company
www.anthempress.com

This edition first published in UK and USA 2011
by Anthem Press
75-76 Blackfriars Road, London SE1 8HA, UK
or PO Box 9779, London SW19 7ZG, UK
and
244 Madison Ave. #116, New York, NY 10016, USA

© 2011 Rini Bhattacharya Mehta and Rajeshwari V. Pandharipande
editorial matter and selection; individual chapters © individual contributors

The moral right of the authors has been asserted.

All rights reserved. Without limiting the rights under copyright reserved above,
no part of this publication may be reproduced, stored or introduced into
a retrieval system, or transmitted, in any form or by any means
(electronic, mechanical, photocopying, recording or otherwise),
without the prior written permission of both the copyright
owner and the above publisher of this book.

British Library Cataloguing in Publication Data
A catalogue record for this book is available from the British Library.

Library of Congress Cataloging-in-Publication Data
Bollywood and globalization : Indian popular cinema, nation, and diaspora / edited by
Rini Bhattacharya Mehta and Rajeshwari V. Pandharipande.
p. cm.
Includes bibliographical references.
ISBN 978-0-85728-782-3 (pbk. : alk. paper)
1. Motion pictures–India. 2. Motion picture industry–India. 3. Motion pictures
and globalization–India. 4. Culture in motion pictures. I. Mehta,
Rini Bhattacharya. II. Pandharipande, Rajeshwari V.
PN1993.5.I8B592 2011
791.430954–dc22
2011016244

ISBN-13: 978 0 85728 782 3 (Pbk)
ISBN-10: 0 85728 782 6 (Pbk)

TABLE OF CONTENTS

Acknowledgements   vii

Notes on Contributors   ix

Chapter One
Bollywood, Nation, Globalization: An Incomplete Introduction   1
Rini Bhattacharya Mehta

Chapter Two
Sentimental Symptoms: The Films of Karan Johar
and Bombay Cinema   15
Sangita Gopal

Chapter Three
Is Everybody Saying 'Shava Shava' to Bollywood Bhangra?   35
Anjali Gera Roy

Chapter Four
Bollywood Babes: Body and Female Desire in the Bombay Films
Since the Nineties and *Darr*, *Mohra* and *Aitraaz*: A Tropic Discourse   51
Purna Chowdhury

Chapter Five
Globalization and the Cultural Imaginary: Constructions of
Subjectivity, Freedom & Enjoyment in Popular Indian Cinema   75
Gautam Basu Thakur

Chapter Six
Rang De Basanti: The Solvent Brown and Other Imperial Colors   93
Manisha Basu

Chapter Seven
Between *Yaars*: The Queering of *Dosti* in Contemporary
Bollywood Films   111
Dinah Holtzman

Chapter Eight
Imagined Subjects: Law, Gender and Citizenship in Indian Cinema   129
Nandini Bhattacharya

Chapter Nine
'It's All About Loving Your Parents': Liberalization, Hindutva
and Bollywood's New Fathers   145
Meheli Sen

Notes   169

Select Bibliography   195

ACKNOWLEDGEMENTS

Our first vote of thanks goes to Indranil Mitra, without whose cordial encouragement and urgent reminders we may not have finished putting this collection together. We are grateful to the contributors who devoted their precious time and endured the long process of publication with graceful patience. We also thank Tej Sood and others in the London office of Anthem Press, for their prompt help in production.

NOTES ON CONTRIBUTORS

Manisha Basu is Visiting Assistant Professor in the English Department at the University of Illinois, Urbana-Champaign. Her research interests are in postcolonial studies, literary theory, global literatures, religious fundamentalisms, literary secularisms and vernacular modernities. She has published with journals such as *Theory and Event* and *Postmodern Culture* and is currently working on a book manuscript tentatively titled *Fathers of a Still-born Past: Hindu Empire, Globality, and the Rhetoric of the Trikaal*.

Gautam Basu Thakur is a doctoral student of Comparative Literature at the University of Illinois. His research areas include nineteenth century British & Indian (Bengali) literature and postcolonial studies; critical theory; Freudian-Lacanian psychoanalysis; media, culture, and the modern state. He is currently working on his dissertation *Scripting Anxiety, Scripting Identity: Indian Mutiny, History, & Colonial Imaginary, 1857–1911*, which studies the affective impact of the 'Indian Mutiny' on British and Indian cultural consciousness. He has published articles on the Austrian filmmaker Michael Haneke in *New Cinemas* (2007) and *Psychoanalysis, Culture, Society* (2008) and is co-editor of *(Re)-Turn: A Journal of Lacanian Studies*.

Nandini Bhattacharya is Associate Professor of English at Texas A&M University and an affiliate of the Women's Studies and Film Studies programs. Her fields of expertise are South Asia studies and Indian cinema, transnational feminisms, feminist theory, and gender and colonialism. From 2003–2006 she served as chair of the Department of Women's and Gender Studies at the University of Toledo. In 2006 she published a second book with Ashgate Press on transnational consciousness of gender and racial identities evolving within slavery, colonialism and connoisseurship in the late eighteenth century transatlantic world. She is now finishing a book on Indian cinema as mediation of the classic political binary known as the nation-state.

Purna Chowdhury was a Lecturer in Comparative Literature at Jadavpur University, Kolkata, India from 1989 to 1995 and is currently Professor of English at Heritage College, Quebec, Canada. Her research interests include culture Studies, colonial and post-colonial discourse and women writing from India. She is a peer reviewer for *Postcolonial Text* and the author of *Nation, Rushdie and Postcolonial Indo-English Fiction* (Edwin Mellen, 2007) and 'Refiguring Modernity in the Postcolonial Space: A Reading of Gender, Nation and Modernity in Sara Suleri's *Meatless Days*' in *Rethinking Modernity* (New Delhi: Pencraft International 2005).

Sangita Gopal is Assistant Professor of English at the University of Oregon. Her publications include: Co-editor (with Sujata Moorti) *Global Bollywood: Transnational Travels of the Song-Dance Sequence*, University of Minnesota Press (Forthcoming, 2007); Monograph: *Post-Nuptial Contracts: Conjugality and Nationalism in South Asian Literature and Film*; 'The Look in Ruins: Naipaul's The Enigma of Arrival and the Dialectics of Seeing' in *South Asian Review* 26: 1 (2005); 'Hindu Being, Hindu Buying: Hindutva Online and the Commodity Logic of Late Nationalism' in *South Asian Review* 24: 1(2003), 161–179; 'Home Pages: Immigrant Subjectivity and Cyberspace' in *Globalization and the Humanities: Field Imaginaries, Virtual Worlds and Emergent Subjectivities*, Ed. David Li, Hongkong: Hongkong University Press, 2003, 212–231; and 'Sex Outside: Postcoloniality and Ethnosexual Queerness' in *Journal of Commonwealth and Postcolonial Studies* 10:1 (2003), 11–33.

Dinah Holtzman is a PhD candidate in Visual and Cultural Studies in Rochester, NY. She is a film programmer at George Eastman House and an assistant editor at *Afterimage: Journal of Media Arts and Cultural Criticism*. 'Save the Trauma for your Mama: Kara Walker, the Art World's Beloved,' a chapter from her dissertation *Illnesses of Love: Portrait of the Artist as Melancholic Cannibal*, appears in *Revisiting Slave Narratives II*.

Rini Bhattacharya Mehta is Visiting Assistant Professor in Comparative and World Literature at the University of Illinois, Urbana-Champaign. Her research interests include nationalism and religious fundamentalism, the cultural politics of globalization, the Indian diaspora, and Indian cinema as local/national/global cultural production. She has published articles on the politics of religion in nineteenth and early twentieth century Bengal and is currently working on an anthology of South Asian literature, a manuscript on nineteenth century Indian nationalism's revisiting of the Indian past, and a co-edited volume on Partition.

Rajeshwari V. Pandharipande is Professor of Linguistics, Religion, and Comparative Literature at the University of Illinois, Urbana-Champaign. She served as director of the Program for the Study of Religion (2002–2005), and was selected as an associate by the Center for Advanced Study in 1987, 1993 and 2007. In 2008 she received the title of Distinguished Teacher/Scholar – the highest honor granted by the University. She teaches courses on Hinduism, Hinduism in the US, and Hindi literature. She has published numerous books, including a collection of her original Hindi poems, and more than 60 research articles and chapters.

Anjali Gera Roy is a Professor in the Department of Humanities of Social Sciences at the Indian Institute of Technology, Kharagpur. She has recently co-edited with Nandi Bhatia a volume of essays entitled *Partitioned Lives: Narratives of Home, Displacement and Resettlement* (Delhi: Pearson Longman 2008) on the Indian Partition of 1947. Her book on Bhangra's global flows *Bhangra Moves: From Ludhiana to London and Beyond* (Aldersgate: Ashgate 2009) is in development. She investigated the relationship between global musical flows and diasporic identity formation on a Senior Research Fellowship of the Indo-Canadian Shastri Institute in 2007 and is now researching the Bollywood's transnational flows at the Asia Research Institute National University of Singapore.

Meheli Sen is Assistant Professor of Media and Cinema Studies at DePaul University's College of Communication. Sen's primary research area is post-independence popular Hindi cinema; she is interested in how the filmic registers of genre, gender and sexuality negotiate specific moments in India's troubled encounters with modernity and more recently, globalization. Her work has been published in journals such as *The Journal of the Moving Image* and *South Asian Review*.

Chapter One

BOLLYWOOD, NATION, GLOBALIZATION: AN INCOMPLETE INTRODUCTION

Rini Bhattacharya Mehta

Bollywood, or Bombay Cinema, or Indian Entertainment Cinema went global in 1995, with Aditya Chopra's *Dilwale Dulhaniya Le Jayenge* (The True of Heart Will Win the Bride). *DDLJ*, as the film came to be called (in the 1990s' style of abbreviating long Bollywood titles), outperformed *Maine Pyaar Kiyaa* (I Have Loved, 1989) in the box office which in its day had outperformed the long-time record-holder *Sholay* (Flames, 1975). In *DDLJ*, the Non Resident Indian (the NRI), hitherto portrayed in Hindi films as the marginal outsider with affected speech and behavior was redeemed and validated as not just a possible Indian national subject, but possibly one of the best. This film had a storyline highly unusual for its time. Baldev Singh, a Punjabi storeowner in England returned to India to marry off her daughter Simran to a native Indian Punjabi. The daughter had already had a brief romantic encounter with a Punjabi British man named Raj, and was determined to marry him. But Raj, who then followed Simran and her family to India, would marry Simran only if she was 'given away' in the 'traditional Indian way,' by her father Baldev Singh. Baldev's impression of Raj from a brief encounter was that of an irresponsible individual with no sense of 'tradition,' someone who was just not 'Indian enough'. But as the narrative unfolded, Raj proved his 'worth' and Indian-ness to Baldev, 'won' the bride, and the film ended with the newly-weds returning to England, as Indians as they ever were. The film broke several established Bollywood models; the men rather than the women were projected as guardians of 'tradition' and 'honor' (albeit Simran – the woman – was still locus of the struggle as well as the prize to be won), and it was the male hero who had to atone and toil to make up for his brief youthful misgivings. Covering two continents, the drama as it unfolded was visually and verbally 'Indian'; it was openly vocal about Indian values and customs, in spite of the fact that the major protagonists lived their lives in England. Moreover, the NRI was not required to return to India and stay there – and this was the twist that made it for *DDLJ* – the NRI could remain NR and be the 'I,' that is, Indian. Kuljit – the Indian Punjabi groom chosen by Baldev for his daughter – was portrayed as an opportunist crook, as he and his entire family perceived of his arranged marriage with Simran as a way to climb the social ladder. At one point, Kuljit verbally reveled in his aspirations of living a hedonistic life in England – his cherished destination of personal freedom without responsibility.

The significance of *DDLJ* in setting the new trend for the depiction of a new form of 'identity' in the global and the national context cannot be overstated. This film is specifically relevant to this anthology because if there is a narrative that several of the essays in this book claim, it is that of the 'Return of the Nation.' Nation, despite not having gone away anywhere, has come back with a vengeance in globalized India. What has diminished radically is the 'postponement' of assertion and gratification. The Nation in post-global India is an overwhelming 'now.' Not necessarily here, but now. Since the reconfiguration of the Third World as a geopolitical entity in the new world system, India as an archetype of non-Western nation-state in this system has renegotiated its commodity-value. As the Western news and media have nurtured and projected India's turn of the millennium image as an emerging super-power, a force to be reckoned with, a 'democratic,' tamable alternative to red China, the official and unofficial ideological apparatuses in India have reflected and embellished the image, to be perpetuated at home and out in the world. One of the significances of Bollywood lies in its self-positioning as an unofficial ideological apparatus.

In addition to drawing out Bollywood into the 'global', *DDLJ* also created a neo-nationalist imaginary. Using the time-honored comic trope of the wedding of young lovers as the denouement, *DDLJ* built itself upon the spectacle of the 'ritual' itself, following on the footsteps of another blockbuster that preceded it by a year. Sooraj Barjatiya in *Hum Aapke Hai Kaun* (Who I Am To You, 1994) – abbreviated as *HAHK* – had tried and tested successfully the formula of 'celebration', by making the family (in this film, a transparent signifier for the nation) an all-rounded unit, subsuming complexities of all kinds under the aegis of a benevolent patriarchy. The 'celebration' itself is highlighted as both the foundation and centerpiece of the narrative, and as Virdi describes, 'the protracted wedding celebration maximizes the pleasure in ritualized articulations of filial and sexual tensions through folk songs, dance routines…'[1] The obsessive underscoring of 'family' in an isolated, almost fetishized form in *HAHK* echoed and mirrored a parallel ideological phenomenon: the jingoist militant nationalism that the 'war and terrorism' films perpetuated. The patriotic Non-resident Indian, the content family, and India's 'just war' against terrorists and enemy-states formed a three-pronged cultural agenda for a post-cold war, neo-liberal, resurgent nationalism.

From India to India Inc.

Whether we choose to read Indian Cinema as 'social history' or not, the 'social history' of Indian Cinema has been intricately bound with that of the nation. The current, new Bollywood is the face of post-global India, and any attempt at comprehending the enormity of its social, cultural, political, and economic significance calls for a revisiting of India's postcolonial decades prior to globalization. During the cold war, India had embraced and led the Non-aligned Movement, a political alliance of African and Asian nation-states that had refused to subscribe to or be enlisted by either the USA or the USSR. Jawaharlal Nehru's vision of India was radically different from Gandhi's in terms of its relationship with development and industrialization, but nevertheless followed an overall pacifist and reconciliatory attitude towards global politics. But while the Indian government cultivated a progressive, image of itself in the international arena, and was frequently labeled as a 'socialist' state, it was continually crippled by an enormous burden of intra-national problems, which it handled alternately with dismal inefficiency and with ruthless operatives. To the critics, the postcolonial Indian nation-state was a caricature of its promises. As seen from the magic realistic view of Salim Sinai (the narrator and chief protagonist of Salman Rushdie's *Midnight's Children*) on the fabled midnight of freedom from two hundred years of colonial rule, India woke not to the much-advertised dream of freedom, but to the nightmare of a chaotic and repressive nation-state. The postcolonial Indians, the 'midnight's children,' were doomed to suffering and failure.

The reality of the first four decades of the Indian nation-state is too complex to summarize. While rapid industrialization and federally controlled plans based on the Soviet model were envisioned and implemented under Nehru, most leftist movements advocating extensive land reforms and democratization of resources were either explicitly suppressed or carefully co-opted by the behemoth central government. The British imperial bureaucracy (originally put in place by the East India Company) was retained almost fully, to check the growth of indigenous capitalist ventures and liberal reform movements and curb political dissent. While the British imperial bureaucracy benefitted the British Raj, India's postcolonial bureaucracy became both the means and the end, and mockingly came to be called as the 'Permit Raj' or the 'License Raj,' a reference to the Kafkaesque system of regulations that apparently curbed the growth of wealth and capital. In spite of the progressive, secular, and left-leaning rhetoric perpetuated by Nehru and his party in the political programs, his quasi-socialist mixed economy did little to alleviate the historical injustices to the disenfranchised poor and/or the lower castes. Projecting an enlightened left-leaning image to the world, Nehru and after him, Indira Gandhi, did all to prevent leftist interventions in and critiques of economic processes. The contradiction between India's international and national politics in the first four decades of its nationhood is simply staggering. Between 1969 and 1971, Indira Gandhi used military and paramilitary might to suppress and dissipate brutally the Naxalite movement, named after Naxalbari in Northeastern India (that was the first site of the group's conflict with the local landowners). At the same time, Indira Gandhi procured the support of the USSR, sent the Indian Army into East Pakistan, and played a 'heroic' role in liberating East Pakistanis from their oppressive Pakistani government to form the new nation-state of Bangladesh. The rhetoric of 'development' espoused by the Nehru-Gandhi dynasty and the interim governments invited long-term damages to environment and socio-polity that far outshone the elusive short-term gains. The 'Green Revolution' in the Northwestern state of Punjab and the Narmada Valley Dams Project in central India are two oft-discussed examples.

It was in the 1990s that India's protective economic politic of the cold war era gave way to liberalization, embracing a new market economy envisioned by Rajiv Gandhi and implemented under Narasimha Rao's government. The economic change was coeval with the parallel rise of Hindu nationalism in its most virulent form, India's revival of its nuclear program, and military encounters with nuclear-armed Pakistan. The changed economic policies of the Indian government allowed investment of foreign capital, establishment of manufacturing or service centers, many of them in Secure Economic Zones or SEZs. A new class of workers, better-paid than ever, flourished in renewed realms of consumption, carrying the bourgeois consumerist ambition to new levels. At the same time, villages lost their dwindling infrastructures, their access to clean drinking water, and agricultural bank loans, thus creating a wave of poverty and destitution that have been described as unprecedented by critics of globalization as varied as Arundhati Roy, P. Sainath, and Vandana Shiva.

The specter of 'India Incorporated' that became part of global political parlance in the 21st century was in the making throughout the 1990s, and Indian Popular Cinema underwent profound changes in that decade. In retrospect, the 'transition' of the 1990s proved to be a productive period for Bollywood, as it coordinated and re-arranged its various generic orientations to adapt to an increasingly neo-liberal attitude towards economics and culture. Besides 'naturalizing' the free-floating Non-resident Indian as an essentialist cultural signifier, Bollywood popularized various capital-driven phenomena in India, including basketball (the game and the brand merchandise associated with it) and Valentine's day, opening up the market for new 'cultural' merchandise. Interestingly, it was Bollywood again that popularized regional parochial Indian traditions like 'karva chaut' and 'dandiya' among pan-Indian audiences, and turned them into cultural capital. The greeting cards industry that up until the 1990s was limited to Christmas, New Year, and Birthdays, began mass-marketing cards and merchandises for the Indian festivals, many of them printed in Indian languages. Brand names (mostly global, such as Nike, Adidas, Diesel etc.) were displayed on-screen unabashedly for the first time in the 90s, and by the turn of the century, all awkwardness related to product-advertisement was gone, and the display of imported/global brands appeared seamless. While Indian markets were flooded with brands which were up until the 1980s available only illegally, the proliferation of cable television brought images of the world, India's view of it and vice versa, to an audience progressively eager to catch the next train to global capital. The mood of advertisements and product placements in television programs moved away from a contrived 'old world elegance' to an equally contrived 'ethnic chic,' catering to the viewership an image of affluence previously unimaginable. In a significant number of post-global Bollywood films, affluence rising out of globalization and India's presumed role in it became the diegetic signifier for national value or pride.

However contrived or believable the new image of India is, many of the questions that the postcolonial Indian nation-state faced in the era of the Cold War and the Non-aligned movement still remain valid and extremely relevant in public discourses. The juggernaut of state bureaucracy, the conflict between interests of the state and private capital ownership, and the postcolonial nation's continued struggle to follow the developmental paradigm have retained a core problematic that cannot be classified as anything but 'national.' To use Frederic Jameson's expression, there is still a 'geopolitical unconscious,' despite the 'disappearance of specifically national' culture and its 'replacement, either by a centralized commercial production for world export' or by 'mass-produced neotraditional images.'[2] But the newly arrived corporate media (Fox, Sony, CNN) in post-global India – in an amazing retracing of the steps of the only federally owned and operated media up until the eighties – has contributed to the democratization of the airwaves, instead leading to a literal drowning of legitimate political discourses on the ground. The corporate news-channels both represent and cater to the ambitions and political niches of the upper middle-class post-global India, a niche where 'anti-government' or 'anti-populist' may actually mean 'anti-people.' And Bollywood has emerged in the recent years as a great ally of this corporate media. In her

Critique of Postcolonial Reason, Gayatri C. Spivak had directed our attention to a 'certain postcolonial subject' who recoded the 'colonial subject' and appropriated the Native Informant's position.'[3] It is possible to stretch Spivak's conjecture to cover the global entertainment industry, and see in Bollywood's new discourse the advent of a popular cultural and more mercenary avatar of that 'new subject.' With the increase in the travelling power of Bollywood's merchandise, with the widening of commerce and the buyer, a power of place has been divested on the seller; and identity or self-expression has become a predominantly jouissant celebration. As Kaushik Bhaumik suggests, the new post-global melodramas of Bollywood have 'taken to emphasizing the lyrical as an occult yet substantial presence constructed both as a universalist modernist project and as an alternative to the Western modern.'[4]

Not surprisingly, it was in the era of globalization that Bollywood cinema entered the Cinema Studies discourses, with an increasing number of courses offered not only in Film/Media or Cultural Studies programs but in literature curricula as well. The turning point in Indian Cinema Studies owes its impetus to the postcolonial moment in literary and cultural studies, inaugurated according to most scholars by Edward Said's *Orientalism* (1978). Until the 1980s, critical work on Indian cinema was limited to iconic figures such as Dadasaheb Phalke, Satyajit Ray, Shyam Benegal and a few others. The biographical and critical works on the few auteurs known to the Western world via their presence in the film festivals at Cannes, Berlin, and Moscow followed an isolationist and individualist approach in that there was little or no intellectual involvement with the broader cultural and political milieu that these auteurs belonged to, and often drew from. It would be only in the late 1980s that Indian commercial cinema came to be counted as a 'valid' cultural product, an episteme worthy of the attention of the Anglo-American academia. Since the later eighties, the categories and terminology associated with postcolonial and cultural studies have permeated critical discourses on popular Indian cinema. Predictably, nation has been an integral part of the critical discourses. Sumita S. Chakravarty, writing the first significant critical volume on Indian Mainstream Cinema had chosen to use Nehru's *The Discovery of India* (1933) as the repository of national syncretism and synthesis, and showed how Indian Cinema interacted with both the 'cultural-national' project (of Discovery) and the Nehruvian socialist/liberal vision of the nation-state. In her 'Conclusion,' Chakravarty called 'Indian entertainment cinema' the 'mistress' to a 'master narrative,' 'Indian national identity.' Jyotika Virdi, writing on classical Bollywood about 15 years after Sumita S. Chakravarty, chose to highlight 'nation' in the title and content of her book (*The Cinematic ImagiNation*). In the period between the publication of Chakravarty's book and Virdi's, more than a dozen significant single-author as well as edited books, and at least one significant journal on South Asian Popular Culture have contributed considerably to the scholarship on Indian commercial cinema.

Re-turn of the Nation

In order to gauge the significance of *DDLJ* as a new paradigm, it is necessary to turn our gaze on the paradigm that it displaced. In 1970, a quarter century before *DDLJ* was released, a film with the transparent title East and West (*Purab aur Pashchim*) took the cliché of the supposedly spiritual, chaste, morally superior 'East' and the materialistic, corrupt, and sexually degenerate 'West' to a simplistic extreme rarely attained in Bollywood. The hero, played by Manoj Kumar at the height of his fame and fortune, had the even more transparent name 'Bharat' (one of the Sanskrit names for the Indian subcontinent), the son of a martyred freedom fighter who travels to England. The expatriate Indians in England whom Bharat meets emulate the English as ardently as they eschew Indianness in any form. It is to these deracinated expatriates that Bharat directs his lectures on the greatness of India. Bharat's essentialist messages on India and his patriotic rantings are ineffectively confronted by the Londoner Indians' equally essentialist generalizations regarding 'Western' culture. The plot is complicated by his falling in love with the 'beautiful but Westernized' Preeti, played by Saira Banu. In order to be Bharat's bride, Preeti eventually has to travel to India, unlearn 'Western values' and embrace 'Indianness' and the story has a predictable and happy ending.

I refer to this film because of its rarefied presentation in a single package of a wide range of ideological generalizations regarding the existential rift between the 'East' and the 'West,' that has been underlined in numerous Bollywood films in the pre-global era. Interestingly, Bollywood cinema did neither imagine nor invent the East/West binary; it simply clothed a pre-existing body of discourse in kitschy garb. The discourse on nation and its cultural politics originated in the nineteenth century when nationalism evolved out of what Partha Chatterjee has called the 'point of departure' of the colonized from the agreement with the colonizer's civilizational discourses, the latter laden with the rhetoric of enlightenment universalism but dubious in practice. In most postcolonial readings of Indian history, the urge to define 'home' as the domain of culture and identity – and to protect and separate it from the 'world' which was controlled by the colonizer – has been identified as the foundational act of cultural nationalism. The essentialist schism between the world and the home, as representative of two irreconcilable cultural spheres was first cultivated in the Indian literature(s), notably in the novel, but a kitschy version of it permeated Indian Cinema from its early days. In a large majority of these representations, the 'West' did not need to be a geographical presence; it was effective and powerful enough as a vague cultural signifier. The 'bad women' in popular films have frequently been 'Westernized vamps,' for example: the signifying markers being short hair, consumption of cigarettes and alcohol, revealing Western attire etc. The 1989 blockbuster *Maine Pyaar Kiyaa* (I have loved) that created a new record at the box office revived the 'traditional Indian good woman' vs. 'Westernized vamp' binary with a vengeance in its most simplistic form. Its presentation of this binary made this film uncannily similar to an earlier blockbuster: *Shree 420* (Mr. Fraud, 1955).

The oversimplification of class, gender and cultural differences within the traditional comic trope in mainstream Indian cinema finds a brilliantly apt turn of phrase in 'epic melodrama,' the expression Ashish Rajadhyaksha uses to illustrate the dominant narrative form in classical Bollywood. In the general world of melodrama, the boundaries and contrasts are drawn deeper and brighter by excesses, and in classical Bollywood, culturally loaded signifiers pointing to such concepts as nation-ness, womanhood, tradition, and benevolent patriarchy have played a momentous role. At its oversimplified best, the 'West' or 'Westernization,' as stated above has been used frequently as a signifier for a set of cultural values or functions. Likewise, the 'city' (as opposed to the 'village') has often stood for debauchery, heartbreak, corruption, and immorality. A real village was not always needed to perpetuate the romantic generalizations like 'simplicity,' innocence, virtue etc. The Bombay pavement dwellers in *Shree 420*, for example, were villagers at heart, living in an island of innocence in the ocean of greed teeming with black-marketeers, money launderers, gamblers, small and big-time thieves and crooks. A parallel in the context of the representation of the NRI world would be an essential Indian-ness residing in the hearts of expatriates. In *Pardes* (An Alien Land, 1997), the heroine Ganga (named after the 'sacred river' that flows from the Himalayas in the northwest into the Bay of Bengal in the east), who has just arrived from India, finds home in a tiny room of her prospective father-in-law's mansion in California where the old grandmother of the family worships deities familiar to Ganga.

A phrase as useful to students of Bollywood as Rajadhyaksha's 'epic melodrama' is 'feudal family romance,' Madhava Prasad's designation for the dominant textual form of the popular Hindi cinema of the 1950s and the 1960s. 'Feudal family romance' in the context of classical Bollywood can be very briefly described as a process of linear progression from patriarchal status quo to a definite or indefinite rebellion/conflict and then finally to a resolution where patriarchal authority is restored with minor diachronic change. According to Prasad, several variations of this structure thrived during the 70s and the 80s, without the basic form getting altered in any way. The 'feudal family' part of the definition contains a tacit or explicit exchangeability between the family and the nation (or any community that can stand in for the nation, e.g. the village of Ramgarh in *Sholay*): the family with its (mostly Hindu) patriarchal distribution of power, and the nation with its ideological and repressive apparatuses, schools and colleges, police and the court etc. There are occasional films where 'feudal family' stands against the nation. *Qayamat Se Qayamat Tak* (From Doomsday to Doomsday), an 'off-beat' film (it was strategically marketed so) is one of the memorable examples. Ajanta Sircar in her insightful essay on *Qayamat* has commented on the timeliness of the resurrection of the pseudo-feudal family ethic in the background of economic liberalization. The symbolic interchange between 'family' and the 'nation' has continued to be explored in various ways through every decade and phase in Bollywood's rich history. However, if 'nation' returns with a vengeance in post-global Bollywood, so does 'family.' Intra-familial conflicts, like intra-national conflicts have faded into the background, and the unquestioned acceptance of patriarchy has become more and more prevalent. Films with diasporic contents such as *Kabhi Khushi Kabhie Gham* have propagated an extreme yet immensely successful formula of patriarchal control over post-global modernity and have pushed Bollywood's ideology to the far-right. With the advent of this modernized neoliberal patriarchy, the 'feudal family romance' has been saved from its natural death and has been replaced merely by a post-global version of itself.

The Song as a Cloak

If 'feudal family' and 'nation' have existed in perfect harmony through the decades, the modus operandi of 'romance' – the last component of Prasad's formulation – has been trickier. Given the censor board's official and unofficial ban on any 'un-Indian' display of affection, namely and most (in)famously the 'kiss,' what could the boy and the girl do when they met? To protect 'Indian culture' from 'foreign expressions and impurities' they could do only one thing: they sang a song. In several successful films, pre-marital (or extra-marital) sex is an effect of either intoxication, or an accidental opportunity, or a temporary lapse of judgment, or the combination of two or all of the above, the situation frequently presented through a song. In Shakti Samanta's *Aradhana* (Love is Worship, 1969) the male and the female leads – Arun and Vandana – are caught in a thunderstorm and are forced to spend the night together in a room. The prospect of a man and a woman being in the same room without societal/familial surveillance turns out to be inherently dangerous. After they are obliged to shed their wet clothes, a slightly hesitant Vandana clad in a towel leads the equally hesitant Arun to bed, and the camera moves to cover the flickering flames in the fireplace. A song plays in the background in which a male voice, speaking of his enchantment with the beauty of the woman, warns himself against a moral error. Arun and Vandana are briefly seen as silhouettes, embracing. The 'morning after' finds them awkward towards each other, as they realize the major step they have in their relationship; they had taken their marital vows in a temple earlier and they promise to announce their marriage to the world soon. But Arun is killed in an accident; and Vandana, finding herself pregnant leaves home and lives a life of anonymity and poverty, gives their son Suraj up for adoption and becomes a servant to stay close to Suraj. When Suraj is about twelve, he strikes and inadvertently kills the man who attempts to rape his mother. Vandana pleads guilty for the crime her son committed, and goes to prison for 14 years. When she is released, her son has grown up to be a pilot, and she feels she has been able to fulfill her and her dead lover's dream of a future. The title of the film literally means 'worship,' and both the title and the motif of 'sacrifice' evoke tradition in multiple ways and yet successfully markets the film as a romantic 'hit.'

'Sacrifice' has a particular dynamic with (patriarchal) 'tradition' in the Indian context. The story of the (finite and purgatory) suffering of the woman who gives in to temptation and/or circumstances has been an integral part of Indian literary imagination beginning from at least the classical Sanskrit period. The archetype is Shakuntala in (Kalidasa's classical Sanskrit play *Shakuntala and the Ring of Recollection*) who consummated an improvised marriage with the king Dushyanta, and the lovers suffered for years before they could be reunited. It is worthwhile to mention that the narrative of Shakuntala that Kalidasa had inherited from the existing literary tradition (especially from the Sanskrit heroic epic *Mahabharata*) had neither the suffering nor the woman's deference to the idea of fate. Shakuntala in the *Mahabharata* is a rustic, independent woman, and she argues vehemently for her rights when the king pretends to have not recognized her. Kalidasa had to invent and introduce several narrative factors to vindicate the king and tame the rustic woman of the forest. Most memorable women characters of the classical and post-classical Sanskrit literature and all the other later literatures in the vernaculars have been molded on the 'reformed' ('*sanskrit*') demure woman who is completely at home with patriarchal tradition and the burden of virtue and suffering imposed on her by it. Another example from pre-modern Indian literary tradition is Sita, the wife of Rama, the hero of the other Indian epic *Ramayana*. In Valmiki's heroic epic which is arguably a pre-classical text Sita showed reasonable resistance, anguish and anger when faced with injustices brought upon by machismo, patriarchy, and tradition; but she is reformed and recast into a weeping martyr in classical, medieval, and most of the later renderings of the Rama narrative. Under the influence of colonial modernity, this suffering woman – who understands and has internalized patriarchy so well that she never complains – is further merged with the 'woman in the house' of post-enlightenment bourgeois society. Popular Indian Cinema has consistently used the resultant 'ideal Indian woman' – productive, uncomplaining, kind, pragmatic, equally at home with Indian tradition and colonial (and postcolonial) modernity – as the ultimate backup, representative of a cultural state of equilibrium that at times could serve as a signifier for either family, society, or the nation.

The role of the song-and-dance factor in the representation of sexuality and sexual acts is enormous. The fact that romantic pair sings (or lip-syncs) a song while it could actually be physically intimate has sustained (and still does) Bollywood's sibling industry, that of playback music. The extra-diegetic song enhances the suggestive yet minimal physicality of the 'love scenes' with poetic innuendos, but also ultimately sterilizes them; because ultimately nothing happens in full-view, and whatever happens outside our view is only narrated or merely suggested. The power of the song to sterilize the 'love scene' and to push any 'action' out of the frame is unassailable. A particularly interesting example of this is Raj Kapoor's *Bobby* (1971) in which Raj and Bobby – the teenager hero and heroine – find themselves in a room in a desolate location, and embark upon a song about the wonderful possibilities that the opportunity of being shut in a room together might bring: 'Hum tum ek kamre mein bandh ho, aur chaabi kho gaye' (What if we were locked in a room, and key was lost). It is nothing less than a philosophical conundrum that after they have arrived at the opportune time and place, all they can do is sing about that exact opportunity in other times and places. Marketed as a paean to teenage love, *Bobby* thus carefully circumvents the issue of sexual contact, and there is an obvious cultural logic (no matter how juvenile or trivial in retrospect) to the progression of that non-union to the happy ending of the film (in contrast with the union resulting in disaster in *Aradhana*). In *Julie* (1975) – a film with stronger sexual content – the teenage heroine and the slightly older hero actually engage in sexual intercourse while a song plays in the background: '[male voice] *It na bhi door mat jaao, ki paas aana mushkil ho*; [female voice] *Itna bhi paas mat aao, ki door jaanaa mushkil ho...*' (do not go so far that it is so hard to get close; do not come so close that it is hard to move away). Predictably, complications and suffering follow.

Such concordance between the 'song and dance' element and the depiction of sexuality has arguably been the most intriguing idiosyncrasy of Indian popular cinema. In classical Bollywood (1950s and 60s), the song was often a stand-in for the sexual act, filled with references and suggestions of things not presented diegetically. What is presented within the diegetic space is a highly stylized set of gestures and movements, instantly acceptable and recognizable to the seasoned viewer, but a curious enigma to the outsider. Whether the stylized presentation actually sublimates the 'sexual' or enhances it by means of tantalization is anybody's guess. The stylization of the Bollywood song-and-dance finds its best description in Salman Rushdie's *Midnight's Children*, where Rushdie brilliantly depicts an entire range of innovative stylizations for displaced sexual behavior, emphasizing primarily the mystique of the Bollywood 'kiss':

> Pia kissed an apple, sensuously, with the rich fullness of her painted lips; then passed it to Nayyar, who planted, upon its opposite face, a virilely passionate mouth. This was the birth of what came to be known as the indirect kiss – and how much more sophisticated notion it was than anything in our current cinema; how pregnant with longing and eroticism! The cinema audience (which would, nowadays, cheer raucously at the sight of a young couple diving behind a bush, which would then begin to shake ridiculously – so low we have sunk in our ability to suggest) watched, riveted to the screen, as the love of Piya and Nayyar, against a background of Dal Lake and ice-blue Kashmiri sky, expressed itself in kisses applied to cups of pink Kashmiri tea; by the foundations of Shalimar they pressed their lips to a sword…as they mouthed to playback music…[5]

What is remarkable therefore is not the suppression or the sublimation of desire but the stylization that is Bollywood's gift to World Cinema. The fact that Bollywood has always been self-conscious of this particular form of stylization is apparent to any aficionado: a number of films take their titles from phrases of popular songs from earlier films, films have featured songs that evoked earlier songs and sequences, and a number of post-global films have used old Bollywood songs to evoke nostalgia and strangely enough, a pan-Indian culture. In *Ek Duje Ke Liye* (Made for Each Other, 1981), the hero Vasudevan who cannot speak Hindi woos the heroine Sapna with a song made out of a string of titles of older Hindi films, and in the more recent *Dil Chahta Hai* (What the Heart Wants, 2001), Sameer and Pooja – one of the three couples – watch a Hindi film in a theater. As a song and dance sequence commences, they feel themselves mirrored in a retro song filmed in black and white, evoking some of the well-known romantic pairs from the 60s, 70s, and the 80s.

Outside of Bollywood, Mira Nair's *Mississippi Masala* (1991) evoked Bollywood music as a signifier in a starkly remarkable way. Ugandan soldiers harassing Kinu – an Indian expatriate woman on her way out of Uganda – rummage through her luggage, and stumble across a cassette player. Kinu switches the player on, and the music that plays is a song from Raj Kapoor's 1955 film *Shree 420* (Mr. Fraud): 'My shoes are Japanese,/ My trousers English,/ My red hat is Russian,/ But my heart is Indian.' Gibreel Farishta in Rushdie's controversial novel *Satanic Verses* (1988) too sings this song during his descent on London. Nair's *Mississippi Masala* is undoubtedly one of the most elegant and nuanced depictions of the politics of homeland and exile, and the use of this song adds poignancy and complexity to central question in the film. Kinu and her husband Jai had claimed Uganda to be their homeland, but Idi Amin's government claimed the African nation in the name of 'black Africans,' thus turning Indian settlers into foreigners who must leave the country and forfeit their property. What shall the viewer make of Jay and Kinu's claim that they were actually Indians at heart, their 'foreign' attire and appearance only a grand cosmopolitan masquerade? Or is Bollywood the easiest marker for nationalist nostalgia in a nation of linguistic, cultural, and religious multitudes? After all, another 'diasporic' film of the *Mississippi Masala* era – Gurinder Chadha's *Bhaji on the Beach* (1993) – evoked Bollywood (especially the song and dance feature) as a trope for romantic nostalgia. Within Bollywood, a number of films since the late 1980s have used older Bollywood songs diegetically – the characters singing a few lines or dancing to the tune of an easily recognizable older song – and the trend continues. A number of cable channels in India play current and older songs from Bollywood in a loop which allows the song videos to live a life of their own, apart from and beyond the life cycle of the films to which they belong. Quite a few song videos in the post-global (and hence post-MTV) years are custom-made for television (not merely lifted directly from the films) so that they can be disseminated as independent music videos. Music industry, cable television networks and Bollywood thus interpellate the complex relationship between production and consumption.

Bollywood and India in the World

The post-global influx (and travel) of multinational capital and cultural apparatuses has had a visible effects on Bollywood. The regional avatars of syndicated television shows such as 'Who Wants to be a Millionaire,' 'Big Boss' and 'Indian Idol' have involved Bollywood stars and starlets, and the growth of post-global media in India has been invariably linked to Bollywood in one way or the other, as mentioned earlier. New factors such as the recently begun but immediately popular India International Film Festival in London, the current or planned drama schools owned by Bollywood personalities, the availability of Bollywood fare in Europe and the USA via satellite channels, and the renewed prevalence of Bollywood in the popular cultural imaginary of the Indian diaspora continue to sustain the most successful industry that ever existed in India. From 2007 onwards, erratic yet promising (from the vantage point of venture capitalism) alliances with Hollywood have surfaced; *Saawariya* (Beloved, 2005) was the first Hindi film to be produced entirely by a Hollywood-based film studio. In 2009, Shahrukh Khan became the first Bollywood star to present an award at the Golden Globe Awards Ceremony, and A. R. Rahman won two Oscars for his musical compositions for Danny Boyle's *Slumdog Millionaire* (2008).

Whether Hollywood's nod to its 'other' at the Golden Globe is the world finally waking up to Bollywood (as Shahrukh Khan interpreted) or a subtle and indirect 'hello to opportunity' (as most scholars and critics of globalization would perhaps read it), it remains to be seen. The cameo appearance of 'Bollywood' in Boyle's *Slumdog Millionaire* – owing to the film's 'surprising' and overwhelming success – has in fact made 'Bollywood' reach out to more viewers that Bollywood films themselves could ever venture. The results of the future encounters and collaborations between Europe, Anglo-America and Bollywood are difficult to predict. The same observation can be made of the scholarship on Bollywood. Realistically speaking, the institutional fate of postcolonial discourse and media/cultural studies as they have thrived since the 1990s is uncertain, and in the midst of global economic instability and crisis it is difficult to imagine most shapes of things to come in the academia. The future configurations of global politics and its relationship with multinational capital will undoubtedly cast its shadow on both cultural production and the critical apparatus that lends an unrelentingly observant eye to it. Bollywood has arrived, so it seems, at the global capital, and at Campustown, USA. What happens next is anybody's guess.

Chapter Two

SENTIMENTAL SYMPTOMS: THE FILMS OF KARAN JOHAR AND BOMBAY CINEMA

Sangita Gopal

Indian film historian Ashish Rajadhyaksha had once famously and perhaps apocryphally quipped that all Indian films may be divided into two categories – Bombay cinema and Satyajit Ray – the former a cinema for the masses, the latter an art cinema of limited commercial appeal of which Satyajit Ray was the great exemplar. More recently, this mass-class/commercial-art binary is being re-written by the popular press, and by fans and bloggers as 'hat-ke' versus 'KJo.' 'Hat-ke' literally means 'off-center' and 'KJo' is short for the Bollywood Director Karan Johar. These terms name divergent tendencies in Hindi cinema in the last decade and as such can shed light on the disintegration of film form and the segmentation of movie publics currently ongoing in the film industry. 'Hat-ke' refers to a growing body of films that are made on smaller budgets by new production corporations like Adlabs, Pritish Nandy Communications and UTVfilms. They feature lesser-known stars and match formal innovation with utterly contemporary – often risky – subject matter. The 'hat-ke' film usually plays well in the multiplexes in India's many urban centers and is favored by a younger, cosmopolitan spectator.[1] Though more commercially oriented than art cinema, 'hat-ke' films share the vision of the art film movement that attempted to capture reality more authentically by creating an alternative to the mass product emanating from the industry in Bombay. In other words, they bear a morphologic affinity with what Rajadhyaksha calls the 'Ray' film. But what about the second term in this new pairing: 'KJo?' If Satyajit Ray named a certain tendency in Indian cinema, what trend does 'KJo' serve as shorthand for? What, in turn, is its relation to the category it is displacing – Bombay cinema? What light can the 'KJo' film shed on the seismic changes that the Indian film industry has been undergoing since the 1990s – changes that have led to the transformation of popular Hindi cinema into Bollywood? In short, how does an enquiry into the 'KJo' film help us track what cinema scholars in recent years have termed the Bollywoodization of Hindi cinema?

Johar's reputation rests on three films of which he is the director – *Kuch Kuch Hota Hai* (Something Is Happening, 1998), *Kabhi Khushi Kabhie Gham* (Sometimes Happiness, Sometimes Sadness, 2001, aka *K3G*) and *Kabhi Alvida Na Kehna* (Never Say Goodbye, 2006, aka *KANK*) and a fourth *Kal Ho Na Ho* (If Tomorrow Comes, 2003, aka *KHNH*) of which he is the writer-producer. Though *Kal Ho Na Ho* was directed by Karan Johar's former assistant Nikhil Advani, it is fair to say that his close association with all aspects of this film and the strong aesthetic and thematic links *Kal Ho Na Ho* bears to the other three films directed by Johar merits its nomination as a 'KJo' product. This slim cinematic output apart, Johar's other claim to media fame is a very popular TV talk show 'Koffee with Karan', now in its last season, that features witty fast-paced interviews with film personalities. Other than starting with the letter 'K' (a superstition the director shares with his friend, TV producer Ekta Kapur whose Balaji Telefilms is credited with revolutionizing soap programming in Indian television and who like Johar is addicted to the letter K)[2], Karan Johar films are always fronted by Shahrukh Khan, India's most globally-renowned male actor, and some combination of the top stars of the past decade including Kajol Devgan, Rani Mukherjee, Preity Zinta, Saif Ali Khan, Hrithik Roshan, Kareena Kapoor, legendary actor Amitabh Bachchan, his wife Jaya Bachchan and their son Abhishek. They boast big budgets, gorgeous production values and carry cheesy subtitles like 'It is all about loving your parents.' Whether set in a summer camp the likes of which do not (yet) exist in India (*Kuch Kuch Hota Hai*) or against the kind of magnificent Manhattan skyline seen only in the movies (*Kal Ho Na Ho* and *Kabhi Alvida Na Kehna*), the 'KJo' film explores the lives and loves of the rich and the beautiful and is driven by melodramatic plots, extravagant emotions and fabulously picturized song-dance sequences. In brief, the 'KJo' film assembles many of the features that we associate with post 1970s popular Hindi cinema – melodrama, elaborately staged musical numbers, fairy-tale endings and a big starcast – and then proceeds to exaggerate these features, making big, glittering films that return their weight in gold at the box-office, particularly the overseas box office comprised of diasporic Indians in the UK, United States, Australia and to a lesser extent Fiji, Trinidad and the middle east. How well have these films fared in the diasporic market? The top two spots in an all-time list of overseas blockbusters belong to *Kabhi Alvida Na Kehna* (445 million rupees) and *Kabhi Khushi Kabhie Gham* (365 million rupees) while *Kal Ho Na Ho* (267 million) and *Kuch Kuch Hota Hai* (227 million) come in at numbers 10 and 11.[3] But if we look at top earners between the period 2000 and 2009 domestic and foreign combined, *Kabhi Khushi Kabhie*

Gham comes in at 7, *Kabhi Alvida Na Kehna* at 18 and *Kal Ho Na Ho* at 24 while *Kuch Kuch Hota Hai* ranks at 18 in All Time Earners[4] suggesting that Johar's films do not fare quite as well nationally. Clearly, the overseas box office belongs to 'KJo,' ironically recalling the record run of Ray's *Pather Panchali* at the famed Fifth Avenue Cinema in NYC.

In order to analyze the heuristic 'KJo'/ 'Hat-ke', we must see that what is at stake is no longer a historical distinction between the masses and classes, or between art and commercial cinema as referenced by Rajadhyaksha's categories but rather two different approaches towards the transformation of popular Hindi cinema and its publics.[5] If the 'hat-ke' film jettisons the old form altogether and is addressed to an emergent subject – the domestic cosmopolitan – the 'KJo' film supposes a different public – the nostalgic diasporic – and employs a different aesthetic strategy (codification) to stage a departure from Hindi popular cinema. As such, both trends mark minority positions within the multiplicity that is contemporary Indian cinema where the most significant development has been class-based market segmentation, regional fragmentation and the rise of the genre picture.[6] These minority positions might be caricatured as follows. So while the 'hat-ke' film is trying to break with commercial Hindi cinema by introducing new form and fresh content, the 'KJo' film appears to be doing more and more of the same.[7] So if Hindi films are notoriously long, the 'KJo' film is even longer; if the relation of Hindi cinema to reality is weak, the 'KJo' film intensifies this artifice; if Hindi cinema is star-driven; the 'KJo' film is star crazy; if the fragmented form of Hindi cinema enabled it to connect with adjacent economies like music and fashion, the 'KJo' films strengthens this dispersal and activates multiple revenue stream by turning itself into an intermedial phenomena; if the Hindi cinema sought to conquer the nation, the 'KJo' film is set on world domination and so on and on. The lines moreover are sharply drawn – thus the cinephilic blog 'passionforcinema' is frequently referred to as a 'KJo-free zone' and acclaimed 'indie' film directors Vishal Bharadwaj and Anurag Kashyap have weighed in against the 'KJo' brand of film-making as detrimental to good cinema while Karan Johar asks that there be room in the industry for all kinds of films including the genre to which he lends his name[8] and the hundreds of responses on his blog daily from places as distant as Morocco and Peru reminds us once again of 'KJo's' global brand equity.[9]

From Interruption to Attraction

Yet Karan Johar is by no means the first director to deliver overseas blockbusters. The legendary successes of Rajashri Films' *Hum Aapke Hain Kaun* (Who Am I to you?, 1994, hence *HAHK*) directed by Sooraj Barjatya and

Yashraj Films' *Dilwale Dulhaniya Le Jayenge* (The True of Heart Will Win the Bride, 1995, hence *DDLJ*), directed by Aditya Chopra brought home to the Bombay film industry the vast potential of the diasporic market and ever since the non-resident Indian audience has been actively cultivated by the Bombay film industry. While the circulation of Hindi cinema in the Indian diaspora and in many parts of the world is not a new phenomenon,[10] such circulation was unorganized, informal, sporadic – fed by a desire for the homeland and its culture or by Hindi films accidently arriving in and connecting with viewers in transitional societies. The industry itself did not pay much attention to these overseas networks. However, starting in the mid-1990s, the industry became alert to the revenue potential of this market. Now it is a common occurrence for big-budget movies to be released simultaneously in upwards of 50 screens in the US while Hindi movies often feature in the top 10 in the UK box office. This new and extremely lucrative market is also diegetically solicited by films set in the West featuring lead characters who are non-resident Indians or NRIs and the films thematize through family and romance the relation of the diaspora to the homeland. This trend, as scholars have frequently noted, coincided with the liberalization of the Indian economy, the rise of new forms of cultural nationalism which reimagined the relation between the nation-state and its capital-rich diaspora and the spread of new media technologies including satellite television that radically globalized India's mediascape.[11] The widespread use of the term Bollywood to refer to Bombay-based Hindi popular cinema owes much to this trend and the concomitant opening up of the nation and its cinema to the world.

As even this brief survey reveals, there are at least two movements of cinema implied in the term Bollywoodization.[12] One refers to film's immersion in a media ecology including branding etc and the other is an active cultivation of the overseas market. In each case the term Bollywood signals a shift from the object that was Bombay cinema – whether we understand the shift to be a dispersal of the cinematic object and its assembling with other practices and commodities or whether we interpret the term more narrowly to refer to a film product created for overseas consumption which would also imply a form of branding.[13] On both counts, the category 'KJo' seems to epitomize the process of Bollywoodization, a process that intensifies and turns into capital the inherent and informal tendencies of Bombay cinema. 'KJo' as brand name is a case study in diffusion (TV, stage shows, awards ceremonies, fashion, video games, comic books and the even the university lecture tour) while the 'KJo' film presents the conventions and industrial modes of Bombay cinema as a set of 'attractions' – melodrama, song-dance sequences, stars, dialogues – that adds visual and affective value to a product whose underlying narrative principles adhere quite closely, as I shall show, to the Hollywood model. Taking the lead from scholars who have noted the importance of Karan Johar to the Bollywood canon, let us now turn to examine in greater detail the 'KJo' films' conversion of the protocols of the Bombay 'masala' movie into 'film effects' which by turning the form of Hindi cinema into a set of reproducible codes simultaneously marks its own break with the form.[14]

This 'general' form that arguably held its own into the 1980s is clearly quite distinct from the internally coherent narrative that we associate with classical Hollywood cinema that strives to represent a recognizable world – what Bordwell calls the story world – populated by believable figures and asks that the spectator identify with the reality onscreen.[15] Thus in a compelling reading of the form in Hindi cinema, Lalitha Gopalan, playing off of Tom Gunning's concept of a 'cinema of interruptions' has suggested that the Bombay popular product is best viewed as a 'cinema of interruptions' that does not so much preserve an older presentational mode of representation as it disrupts narrative linearity towards other ends.[16] If these interruptions mark a localization of global norms, does the 'KJo' film in fact reverse this formula by attempting to globalize the local which might account for their great success overseas? If Bombay cinema, as Tejaswani Ganti has so perceptively shown, had a long history of taking Hollywood films and indigenizing them according to its norms, does the 'KJo' film in fact move in the opposite direction to sentimentally evoke the narrative techniques and aesthetic modes of Bombay cinema – tableau framing, frontality, the interval – within a film form effectively structured by the protocols of Hollywood?[17] If the textual heteronomy of Hindi cinema according to Prasad et all enabled it to present the 'new' without endangering a conservative ideology, the 'KJo' film's retention (and exaggeration) of the formal elements of Bombay cinema seems oriented to memorializing the old.[18] Thus the conventions of Bombay cinema become the means for staging culture as spectacle – songs that showcase Hindu rituals, weddings, etc – but even more crucially they provide nodes of intensity and excess.[19] In other words, Bombay cinema's narrative conventions function as 'attractions' that commemorate and codify the features of this cinema and therefore prove particularly attractive in a diasporic context.[20] In Karan Johar's words, they are 'one big Indian joyride with good looking faces, in good looking clothes, saying beautiful things and preaching the right morals to their children.'[21] As such, it is a transitional genre – one that neutralizes the shock of transformation by tarrying with the superseded forms and turning them into valuable souvenirs but like any transitional genre, it is temporally finite. In the remainder of the essay, I will turn to Karan Johar's conversion of the some of these thematic tropes and narrative conventions of Hindi cinema including melodrama, frontality and the tableau. I will make my case by demonstrating how Johar's revival of the 'family film' accomplishes this dual task – while the family enables him to establish a relationship to history (as well as connect to a new audience base in the diaspora), the thorough re-coding of the form and function of the family also enables us to grasp the new formation that the 'KJo' film connotes.

The Value of Family

The opening up of the diasporic market to Hindi cinema – i.e. Bollywoodization – coincided with the release of a number of films thematically focused on the family. As we have seen above, *Hum Aapke Hain Kaun* (Who I Am To You, 1994) and *Dilwale Dulhaniya Le Jayenge* are landmark events in this regard and all 'KJo' productions to date have retained this emphasis on the family. Romantic couple formation continues to be, as it has always been, at the center of these films, but we notice, as well, a new emphasis on inter-generational co-operation, what Moinak Biswas in a vivid phrase has called a 'romance with patriarchy.'[22] The 'social' or in Prasad's words the 'feudal family romance' has traditionally had a conservative conclusion whereby the couple – though romantically constituted – had to be incorporated into the governing ideology of the *khandaan* or extended feudal family. This usually took the narrative form of reconciliation between the hero and the patriarch. As discussed above, the textual heteronomy of Hindi commercial cinema might be viewed as a formal solution to the problem of accommodating individual desire with social norms, modernity with tradition etc. The 1970s marked the exhaustion of the social as a master genre and a concurrent diversification of the film product. The 'big' films of the decade – Ramesh Sippy's *Sholay* (The Flames, 1975), Yash Chopra's *Deewar* (The Wall, 1975) and Chandra Barot's *Don* (The Don, 1978) show new traits including an affinity for Hollywood genres like the Western and the gangster movie, greater technological finesse including a more propulsive camera, the increased use of zoom and telephoto lenses, a sophisticated use of background sound, parallel editing and special effects. If stars, especially Amitabh Bachchan in his reprisal of the 'angry young man' – a working class hero who fights injustice through violent and criminal means – continue to grow in influence, this decade is also marked by the rise of name-brand directors with recognizable styles like Ramesh Sippy, Prakash Mehra, Manmohan Desai, Yash Chopra and the scriptwriting duo Salim-Javed.[23] These new developments however are not accompanied by a substantial formal shift, though it might be argued that during the 1970s and into the 1980s when cinema's dominance is seriously threatened by television, the heterogeneous form of Hindi commercial cinema ossifies into formula.[24] This decade is also characterized by the rise of a 'middle cinema' focused on the vicissitudes of couple formation in a comedic or dramatic vein. These films, addressed to an emerging urban middle-class eschewed melodrama, were often women-centered, socially progressive and director-driven. This and the emergence of a state-sponsored art cinema as I have indicated above are important precursors to the contemporary 'hat-ke' film.[25]

The resurgence of the family melodrama in the mid-1990s is therefore particularly remarkable given that it follows two decades – the 1970s and 1980s – when the representation of family values and romantic conjugality was in a state of flux across a spectrum of films. While 'couple formation' was a relatively minor note in action-oriented blockbusters, in romantic hits like K Balachander's *Ek Duuje Ke Liye* (Made for Each Other, 1981) and Mansoor Khan's *Qayamat se Qayamat Tak* (From Doomsday to Doomsday, 1988) transgressive lovers chose death over reconciliation with an authoritarian patriarchy.[26] Not only middle cinema but even mainstream films like Yash Chopra's *Silsila* (The Affair, 1981) and Esmayeel Shroff's *Thodisi Bewafai* (A Small Betrayal, 1980) and comedies like B R Chopra's *Pati, Patni aur Woh* (Husband, Wife and Other, 1978) charted the risky territory of incompatibility, infidelity and divorce. The emergence of the female avenger figure in films liken Chandra's *Pratighaat* (The Revenge, 1987) and Raj Kumar Santoshi's *Damini* (1993) and 'KJo's' favorite hero, Shahrukh Khan's unconventional star turn as a schizophrenic stalker in films like Yash Chopra's *Darr* (Fear, 1993) and Abbas-Mastan's *Baazigar* (The Gambler, 1993) all bear witness to a film scene where the pleasure and promise of romantic love and the power of the family to regulate its members, especially women, `of them wrestle with it as 'interruptions' or 'paranarratives' are attenuated, strenuously rationalized or nominally present.[27] Even as in *DDLJ*, the braveheart Raj goes from London to Punjab to gain the consent of the father of the bride though the bride herself is willing (at her mother's urging) to elope, other directors like Mani Ratnam and Ram Gopal Verma were giving us distinctly unfamiliar family relations. While Mani Ratnam isolates and fully invests (even over-invests) in the sovereignty of the romantic couple in films like *Roja* (The Rose, 1992), *Bombay* (1995) and *Dil Se* (From the Heart, 1998) where the couple, if anything, is hyper-nucleated, in the films of Ram Gopal Verma, the family disappears altogether.[28] As opposed to the gangster of old, who took to a life of crime to avenge his family, the eponymous hero of Verma's film materializes in Gangland Bombay, literally out of nowhere and films like *Bhoot* (Ghost, 2003), directed by Ram Gopal Verma and *Ek Hasina Thi* (There Was A Beautiful Girl, 2004), directed by Sriram Raghavan, strain credulity by featuring such radically unmoored protagonists.[29]

Thus the recuperation of the family in the 'KJo' film runs counter to tendencies in Hindi cinema in the previous decades nor is it the only or even the most dominant trend in its own time. How then do we explain this love affair with the family in the Karan Johar film even while elsewhere, Hindi cinema has been engaged with challenging or entirely circumventing the power of the family? Most critics insightfully link the centrality of the family film to the active solicitation of a diasporic audience, since the ideology of the undivided Indian family links the nation to the diaspora.[30] They argue that 'family values' neutralize the threat of globalization while simultaneously reflecting an increasingly sectarian Hindu politics. I would like to supplement such accounts by suggesting the following: a focus on the family evokes a sentimental relation to the historical deployment of this theme and trope in Hindi cinema even as the 'KJo' film thoroughly reinvents what and how a family means and works. Further, this reinvention of the family must be tracked alongside his conversion of Hindi film form into 'attractions' embedded in a narrative technique that is strictly Hollywood.

Let us begin by considering Johar's own family ties. He belongs to a group of young directors like Aditya Chopra and Farhan Akhtar all of whom come from 'filmi' families. Thus Johar is the son of veteran Bollywood producer Yash Johar while Chopra and Akhtar also have famous fathers – the director Yash Chopra and famed scriptwriter and lyricist Javed Akhtar. The film industry in India (and now increasingly in Hollywood) has always functioned like a family business. The decline of the studio system in the 1940s led to a radical disintegration of the three sectors of the film industry – production, distribution and exhibition. The production end passed into the hands of independent producers who make films on an ad hoc basis – outsourcing and then reassembling the various components – with the star functioning as the one steady source for attracting finance. Thus Madhava Prasad has noted while this mode of production is capitalist it is not fully rationalized such that 'precapitalist ideologies in which relationships based on loyalty, servitude, the honor of the *khandan* (clan) and institutionalized Hindu religious practices' structure relationships within the industry, the production process and the cultural content of cinema.[31] Karan Johar's description of how the Bombay film industry functions in comparison with Hollywood seems to echo Prasad, 'In our film fraternity, relationships are stronger than contracts.... We've been nurturing these equations for years, and we do it sans agents and managers and assistants. Those of us lucky to be raised within the industry have the word of our fathers, our siblings, and those friends that might as well be family. We're small, and we may bicker, but we've sat in each other's living rooms, and we've built this industry to what it is.'[32] This blogpost is addressed to foreign media giants with 'their big corporate presentations' and their 'pie charts' who seek to do business with Bollywood, 'We might be a little old fashioned in our pitches, but we make films because the nation's heart thumps for it. Appeal to that sentiment, and understand our culture. Employ people who understand this about us, as an industry, and as a country. We're emotional, and we're more connected than you'd think, but we have our patterns. Try to understand who we are as an industry, what works for us and more importantly, for our audiences.' What 'KJo' identifies as unique to the Bollywood mode of production is indeed social relations modeled on the family, business dealings structured by sentiment and he draws a figurative relation between the sociology of the industry, audience expectation and the content of cinema. This familial mode of functioning, Johar stresses must be reckoned with as Indian cinema globalizes, for it has not only historical value but renders fiscal advantage. Ravi Vasudevan has traced the long history of this link between a diegetic investment in the creation of a joint family and industry's own use of this metaphor to enhance its social legitimacy, especially in times of crisis. He notes the correlation between the figurative use of the family in a 1940s film like *Kismet* to resolve social contradictions and the industry's own self-representation as a family at a time when one industrial mode was yielding to another. Thus actress Devika Rani referred to the vertically integrated studio Bombay Talkies founded by herself and Himanshu Rai as a 'big, happy family' though this studio would not survive the depredations of new forms of speculative capital overtaking the film industry and the star – so long attached to the studio – would soon abandon these loyalties and turn himself into a free agent.[33] But the same figure – family – could now describe a new model – the independent producer-star relation. We must view 'KJo's' invocation of the family in a similar light – as having referential and normative value. It describes an industrial scenario controlled by a few powerful families such that they determine the type of all social relations but this figuration of the industry as family also provides social, and in the case of Johar, global legitimacy to a certain mode of production even as it is undergoing transformation. A recent study of the industry has revealed that there is an ongoing partial shift in this mode of production with greater horizontal integration of the sectors of distribution, marketing and exhibition, while the creative product still remains largely in the control of specialized production companies. As of 2005, 90 per cent of all films and the top 30 earners between 2003 and 2005 were thus produced.[34] The authors note that the main trend seems to be towards an industry model based on alliances that take advantage of scale economies in distribution and financing while retaining the creative and managerial advantages of small firms in production.[35] This model continues to be profitable because it is based on tight social networks such that 'business relations among different roles in film projects (scriptwriters, actors, producers, directors, and so on) are, ceteris paribus, likely to be influenced by family relations and other types of strong ties in India than in film industries located in countries with other national institutional fields, such as Hollywood. Business relations may hence to a relative high extent rely upon trust than upon contracts.[36] At the same time, the authors note that in a rapidly evolving environment with many new entrants into the field, these production companies have had to professionalize, investing in management, process and planning. Companies like Johar's Dharma Productions and Yashraj Films have emerged as market leaders because they have taken the strengths of the family model and successfully refunctioned it to meet the new professional standards taking hold in the industry.

The 'KJo' film, I argue, is engaged in a similar project of reform. While the family's capacity to evoke sentiment and establish historical continuity is preserved, the 'KJo' film also significantly rethinks the family. This takes the most immediate form of a disappearance of society and the state and a retreat into the family as the only staging ground of action. As such, 'KJo''s characterization of the industry as family as well as the content of these 'domestic dramas' seem to reprise what we have called the 'social' or in Prasad's words, the 'feudal family romance' which did not need 'the kind of integrated production process' which is necessary when narratives are 'particularistic, focused on chunks of the real.'[37] Prasad links the aesthetic dominance of this heteronomous form to a social totality where the feudal family is still in power and the modern, sovereign individual (who is also a citizen) is yet to emerge. Though the law was 'formally' vested in the postcolonial Indian state, the feudal family continued as an alternative locus of power. Thus to give Prasad's vivid example, the police in these films always arrive too late. Justice is meted out according to the laws of the feudal family but the actual incarceration of the criminal is performed by the state. If the Indian state kept Bombay cinema at a distance, refused to grant it industry status and thus access to institutional finance, imposed a punitive entertainment tax on film and functioned as a censoring body, popular cinema remained vested in the ideology of the feudal family and its favored mode - melodrama. Prasad views the heterogeneous form of Hindi cinema and its weak investment in realism as an aesthetic symptom of this attachment. But the force of the family in the 'KJo' film as I shall show below is quite weak for there is a shift in emphasis from the family as an absolute power that abrogates to itself a law that is beyond its jurisdiction to the family as a transmitter of values. Its coercion is affective rather than legal or economic.

For one, these films valorize the father's love rather than his authority and there is an odd reversal of generational priorities. The old do not oppose the desires of the young, but rather facilitate them. Thus the widower-hero Rahul's (Shahrukh Khan's) mother in *Kuch Kuch Hota Hai* conspires with his 8-year old daughter to orchestrate a romantic liaison between Rahul and his best friend from college Anjali (Kajol). Rahul's father-in-law assists her in this task. The grandmothers in *Kabhi Khushi Kabhie Gham* initiate a chain of events that reconciles an autocratic father Yash (Amitabh Bachchan) to the son Rahul (Shahrukh Khan) that Yash had once cast out. In *Kabhi Alvida Na Kehna*, the adulterous Maya's (Rani Mukherji) father-in-law, Samarjit (aka 'Sexy Sam' played again by Bachchan) upon discovering her affair with Dev (Shahrukh Khan) urges that she leave his son, Rishi (Abhishek Bachchan – Amitabh's son in real life), so that all concerned might move on and make new lives for themselves while Dev's mother, Kamaljit (Kirron Kher) opts to stay on with her daughter-in-law Rhea (Preity Zinta) when the couple separates. In *Kabhi Alvida Na Kehna*, though the parents are the first to learn about Dev and Maya's affair, they do not publicize the news – rather the adulterous couple make a joint decision to break off their impossible relationship and confess all to their respective spouses. The parents, though present, are not the enforcers of morality.[38]

Parents, including fathers, with the possible exception of Yash in *K3G*, are hardly the irascible authoritarian figures of the feudal family romance. The child's right to make a romantic choice and the romantic choices of children are mostly encouraged and supported which signals, if anything, a weakening of the family as a locus of alternative fiscal and ideological power. Affective rather than material ties structure family life and emotional attachments modify and regulate filial hierarchies. Thus Dev who is an ill-tempered father in *Kabhi Alvida Na Kehna* has to be disciplined by the end of the film while familial dysfunction in *Kal Ho Na Ho* is resolved as the members learn to communicate more openly. Moreover, these ties – suddenly contingent in a globalized world order that demands and rewards mobility – have to be ritually and gesturally affirmed.[39] Thus the 'KJo' film is littered with hallmark moments - hugs and kisses between parents and children, affections expressed through cards, stuffed toys, privatized handsigns, nicknames, family-centered song-dance sequences, a mise-en-scène cluttered with photographs and, perhaps most importantly, frequent exhortations to be more expressive. Thus Rahul's mother in *Kuch Kuch Hota Hai* advises Anjali to speak her heart while Sexy Sam in *Kabhi Alvida Na Kehna* regrets not showing his love while he still had time. Dev and Maya almost give up on a future together by concealing their true situations from one another while Yash, the father, in *Kabhi Khushi Kabhie Gham* imperils the unity of his family for ten long years by not showing his affections while his wife, Nandini (Jaya Bachchan) makes things right by breaking her silence. Interpersonal communication is not only a highly-prized ethic in the world of 'KJo,' but the 'KJo' film is replete with scenes of role-playing such that characters access affects and effects through iterative performance.

This is especially the case with regard to heterosexual couple formation. If romantic love versus the arranged marriage had been the two opposing norms of conjugality in Indian cinema, serial monogamy emerges here as a third option. Romantic love in the 'KJo' film is as much about desire as circumstance, relationships can be managed and love can happen at first or subsequent sight. Thus in *Kuch Kuch Hota Hai*, Rahul and Anjali are best friends and though Anjali falls in love with Rahul, at this stage, for him she is just one of the guys. He gives his heart to the alluring outsider, Tina. The broken-hearted Anjali disappears. In the meantime, Rahul and Tina (Rani Mukherji) marry but Tina dies at childbirth. Eight years pass and Rahul and Anjali meet again but this time she – long-haired and feminine – is the alluring outsider, and Rahul falls in love with her. So, though Anjali does not get her love at first, she gets him at last. In *Kal Ho Na Ho*, we start out with a triangle where Aman (Shahrukh Khan) and Naina (Preity Zinta) love each other, Rohit (Saif Ali Khan) loves Naina but she thinks of him as her best friend. Aman is dying so he wants to make sure that Naina finds happiness with someone who loves her. So, he teaches Rohit how to make Naina fall in love with him – 'chhe din, ladki in' ('six days and the girl is yours) – and she does! Rohit and Naina marry and go on to live a long happy life. The film, told in flashback concludes with Naina telling her daughter (à la Rose in the 1997 blockbuster *Titanic*) that while Aman was her first love and she will never forget him, it is Rohit she now loves. In the typical Hindi film triangle, a first love always emerged to threaten the hard-earned contentment of a subsequent relationship or a triangle could only be resolved spatially, as one party left the scene usually as a result of death or sacrifice. Here, Naina might not marry the man she loves but she falls in love with the man she marries. She is allowed to love twice. In *Kabhi Alvida Na Kehna*, Dev and Maya, both in unhappy marriages, act upon their desire for one another by pretending that each is the other's spouse. This performance frees them up to express their relationship needs and anxieties and better prepares them for their love affair. Thus while romantic longing might not meet its mark at first, it will do so at last.

This reinvention of the family as liberatory (and liberal) space and the emergence of serial monogamy are central to the refunctioning of the social that the 'KJo' film engages in. Critics have repeatedly drawn attention to the 'look' of the 'KJo' film – the addiction to designer labels, the immaculate interiors, the beautiful people, urban milieus from which all dirt, crime, poverty has been excised such that even a congested neighborhood in New Delhi like Chandni Chowk looks as it might in a heritage calendar. If cinema, particularly commercial cinema, has always been adept at inciting desire through a display of bodies and commodities, the 'KJo' film fully harnesses the technological potential of cinema to immerse spectators in a consumerist utopia. This liberation into the world of things in Karan Johar's cinema has been justly read in connection with India's transition to free-market capitalism in the 1990s and the sudden flow of images and commodities into a nation whose economy since independence had been partly socialist and whose media, including cinema, fairly regulated. The focus on the family has been viewed as a counter-movement, one that manages the destabilizing potential of capital by locating it in the closed space of the upper-class, upper-caste Hindu home while appealing at the same time to a wealthy Indian diaspora who desire just such a harmonious union between capital and culture. It is true that the 'KJo' film features Oxford-returned mini-skirted Indian girls (Tina in *Kuch Kuch Hota Hai* for instance) who sing pitch-perfect Hindu hymns and other such paragons of flexible citizenship who skillfully navigate the flows and disparate spatio-temporalities of globalization. The mode of subjection in the 'KJo' film is allied to liberalization discourse that as Mankekar has pointed out was viewed as 'freeing the creative and productive energies of the people.'[40] Equally striking is this new relation between generations and the emergence of the subject through performance. It is as such a biopolitical project that brings into being emergent social relations – relations that do not so much reflect reality as construct them. Thus for instance, when Johar was asked why he chose to set *Kabhi Alvida Na Kehna* in New York despite his claims that his theme – adultery – reflects a growing social reality in India, he responded that he needed to show Dev and Maya conduct their love affair – unhindered and unobserved – in public spaces and an Indian setting would not allow this. The New York milieu, in other words, was dictated by his pedagogic project of bringing the adulterous couple out into the open so that he could explore the vicissitudes of their relationship – something as yet impossible in India. This spatio-temporal mismatch between the emergent subject and a recessive milieu provides us another way to think of the disappearance of the social in the 'KJo' film. If the families in 'KJo' films – unmoored in any social reality – seem unreal that is entirely appropriate since he is imagining modes of being and belonging whose time has not yet come. Here, the family does not so much impose its values, but is rather thoroughly re-valued.

Sentimental Symptoms

If the old are not enforcers of the law but facilitators of desire, the young, in effect, have nothing to rebel against. Rather than opposing tradition since it no longer wields any real power, the young invest it with sentiment. Thus they don ethnic gear and dance at festivals, perform rituals and mimic gestures that memorialize tradition from a vantage that is utterly contemporary. It would appear then that the generations rather than beings at odds accommodate each other. What then is the use of melodrama in the world of 'KJo' that in Hindi film traditionally represented the clash between law and authority, good and evil, past and present? Though Johar makes ample use of melodramatic plotting (all his films have 'ticking clock' finales), acting style, and cinematography, this view of the subject as flexible and of the self as managerial substantially diminishes the need for melodrama which as a mode relies upon the inability of protagonists to act upon their desires or express themselves owing to adverse circumstance or social interdictions.[41] In the typical Hindi film melodrama, conflict usually arises because time is out of joint and all manner of external misfortune is visited upon the good. The moral order is restored when the tides turn and time rather than obstructing virtue, makes it visible. The hero has little to do except be unstintingly heroic and the villian's change of heart is both necessary but unconvincing. Thus time, rather what Linda Williams has identified as the temporal dialectic between 'just in time' or 'too late,' is the narrative engine of a melodrama.[42] But in the world of Karan Johar it is never too late. While chance is an important narrative device (the films thrive on coincidences), failed communication, the inability to express or act upon one's feelings equally drives melodrama in the 'KJo' film. Though this expressive blockage is circumstantial, it is also indicative of a certain cultural logic. Let us look at some examples.

My first example is from *Kabhi Khushi Kabhie Gham* that seems the most reactionary of 'KJo' films. The patriarch Yash, for all his new-fangled ways, is an unreconstructed autocrat who casts out his son Rahul for marrying a lower class girl against his will. But Rahul, who leaves home and the family business and immigrates to the UK, not only survives but actively thrives. It is very clear that the family wields merely emotional power over its members. The allegiance that Rahul owes his father is underwritten not by necessity but by affect. The once-whole family is remembered through photographs that play a prominent role in the mise-en-scène. The opening sequence, saturated with sentimental iconography, is a montage of photos alternating with fragments of video that play scenes from Rahul's happy childhood alerting us at once that the film to come will in fact document the disintergration of this family. In the older melodrama, emotional excess speaks to a structure of power (at least this is how melodramatic emotion has been theorized via a repressive hypothesis), here emotion represents a particular relation to the past, an excess that cannot entirely be contained by the rationalities of the present. Thus when Rahul finally returns home after a decade, Yash asks his forgiveness and chides Rahul for having taken such an extreme step at a parent's words spoken in anger. Yash has to learn that the affective family is also surprisingly contingent. It does not endure but has to be affirmed so while a few angry words can sunder a family, gestures of love can make it whole again. Family is coded with a new form of value.

Melodrama's capacity to monumentalize sacrifice is activated by the 'KJo' film though in fact, the situations do not rationally demand such sacrifices. Thus in *Kuch Kuch Hota Hai*, when Anjali is on the brink of getting-together with Rahul, her fiancée Aman arrives thus delaying this outcome; in *Kabhi Alvida Na Kehna*, Maya, despite her misgivings, does not call off her ill-advised marriage to Rishi because a chance meeting with a stranger convinces her that friendship is as good a reason to marry as love. The younger generation in the 'KJo' film do not 'yet' feel entitled to treat romantic love as a sovereign value and act upon their desires but feel rather the pressure of older modes of being that valued renunciation over enjoyment, familial (and social) obligations over personal fulfillment. They experience these outmoded affects and that sustains melodrama but these affects are not demanded by the narrative but in excess of it. Let us consider this instance from *Kuch Kuch Hota Hai*. When Rahul and Anjali meet again, he is widowed but she is engaged. However, it is clear that the man she is engaged to, Aman (Salman Khan), has no real expectation that she loves him. Rather, he jokes that she will prove a runaway bride. Nor does her family pressure her to marry Aman, rather her mother appears skeptical about Anjali's commitment. So, why does Anjali refuse to break it off though the circumstances are hardly compelling? She does so to give Aman the chance to release her from this obligation recalling the heroic sacrifice that was the resolution of many a Hindi film triangle. Johar's staging of this ticking clock finale recalls an older economy of desire in Hindi cinema and is, as such, a purely formal homage in a film that otherwise subscribes to a radically altered economy of desire.

In the light of such hesitations, it is especially significant that the call to free oneself of this logic is issued by the older generation. In each instance, the narrative resolution also entails access to this more expressive mode.[43] Thus the tomboy Anjali in *Kuch Kuch Hota Hai* has to own up to her feelings for Rahul, Yash in K3G has to express his love, Maya has to cure her repression. In every case the family and an extended kin network – parents, spouses, siblings, parents-in-law – authorize these transformations. Whereas the family in Bombay cinema wielded a juridical power that rivaled that of the state and the protagonist typically shuttled between these poles (that we may also gloss as tradition and modernity), in the 'KJo' film, the family is not the arbiter of a (despotic) law that the individual either submits to or needs to escape to become fully sovereign, but a cultural resource and an affective milieu that enables the self-actualization of its members. At the same time, the older figuration of the family and conjugality in Hindi cinema is aesthetically memorialized – through song and dances, melodrama, and even duration. During an era of shrinking film-length, the 'KJO' film is at least three hours long, often longer. In her most recent book on Chinese cinema and globalization, Rey Chow has specified the sentimental '*as an inclination or disposition towards making compromises and towards making do with even – and especially – that which is unbearable* may best be described as a mood of endurance.'[44] She goes on to theorize sentiment '… as a vaguely anachronistic affect whose mere survival points to another mode of attachment and identification – and whose non-contemporaneity stands in mute contrast to global visibility.' Taking my lead from this compelling reading of sentiment as an accommodation of older modes of filial power and piety, I suggest that we view 'KJo's' so-called 'romance with patriarchy' as a sentimental stance towards the modes and affects of another time. Paradoxically, this stance is taken not by the older generation but by the younger one. It is an excess of feeling – in Chow's phrase 'a form of intensity' – towards the old. We must therefore view 'KJo's' exaggeration of the formal features of Hindi cinema as a sentimental symptom that commemorates the superseded aesthetic even while his films fully assimilate the narrator system of Hollywood.[45]

Out of Time

Such thematic re-functioning of generational relationship and conjugality – I have argued above – is accompanied in the 'KJo' film by an intensification of the aesthetic effects of Hindi cinema. These effects memorialize the form of Hindi cinema - its styles and techniques of narration. They function as 'set pieces' in a narrative schema that cleaves quite closely to the protocols of Hollywood. Let us consider two instances where stylistic features of Hindi cinema are both referenced and re-coded. The first is from *Kabhi Khushi Kabhie Gham*. This sequence occurs towards the midpoint of the film – a few minutes prior to the interval. It is part of the long flashback that comprises most of the first half of the film where the grandmothers are recounting to Rohan the circumstances under which his older brother Rahul left home a decade ago. Here Yash who has arranged a marriage between Rahul and Naina, the daughter of a business associate learns that his son is in love with Anjali, a girl from the wrong side of the tracks. The first part of this 4 minute 22 second sequence comprises of 18 shots and activates the 'high style' of the Bombay melodrama to represent this face-off between two of Bollywood's biggest stars – Amitabh Bachchan and Shahrukh Khan. Tracking close-ups punctuate 360 degree panning shots and a thundering background score accompanies this confrontation between father and son – the one channels 'parampara' (tradition), while the other espouses 'pyar' (love). The opening two-shot sequence introduces us to the principals and then we cut to a high angle that constructs a tableau of father and son along a sharp diagonal. The tableau as Ravi Vasudevan has argued 'displays interruptive, interventionist functions in the flow of scenic construction…the function of this spatial figure is to encode a socially and communally defined address.'[46] This opening tableau reminds us that we are the familiar territory of Hindi film melodrama where the forces of desire and love oppose each other – a compositional template most recently reprised in Aditya Chopra's *Mohabattein* (Loves, 1998) featuring the same actors. The next segment made up of an alternating series of pans and close-ups ramps up the melodrama as Yash berates Rahul for being unmindful of his family name while Rahul claims that love knows no reason. Our sympathies are clearly with Rahul for his reactions in close-up shape our response to Yash's unreasonable class prejudice. But from around shot 18, the sequence shifts gear as Yash begins to express disappointment rather than rage at his son's 'failing.' This group of 7 shots commences with a shot of Yash where the camera moves ever so slowly upwards and Yash appears forlorn and diminished, Bachchan's resonant baritone modulating downwards. What follows are a series of rapid shot-reverse shots that undercut our former attachment to Rahul's point of view, until by shot 25 Yash sinks down into an armchair, tired and dejected. We now view him in profile in the extreme foreground in a deep shot where Rahul appears blurred in the background. This composition in depth, rack-focused, stands in marked contrast to the tableau that opened the sequence for it does not 'relay' a transcendent meaning (law versus desire) but rather asks to be read immanently, in the context of the particulars of the story world. And what are those particulars? Rahul is Yash's adopted son and thus Yash's charge that Rahul has failed to act like a 'Raichand' takes on a special resonance. We must read Rahul's abjection to the father's will – he agrees to give up Anjali – not as a capitulation to patriarchal power per se but rather the psychic reflex of a child who has sworn allegiance to his adoptive family. Shot 26 is a flashback to the 8-year old Rahul, who learns that he is adopted and then folds his hands in respect before his 'new' father. It is this promise that Rahul makes good on in the final shot as he submits to Yash in a gesture that graphically recalls the flashback we have just seen.[47] Though the scene begins by reprising a classic conflict in a melodramatic mode familiar to the audience from countless Hindi films, it shifts to a more realist register as the framework moves from a sociology to a psychology of the family. Yash and Rahul's confrontation is no longer allegorical but rather embedded in a particular history. This move from the family as necessary to the family as contingent is underscored by a stylistic shift from Hindi film melodrama to Hollywood style realism.

In our second example from *Kabhi Alvida Na Kehna* we notice a similar conversion of the techniques of Bombay cinema into film effects that add intensity to a narrative structured by the conventions of Hollywood. The lovers Dev and Maya suffer no social or circumstantial constraints – adultery here is driven not by the mistreatment of one spouse by another or even by the return of a past lover but rather by the nature of the people involved – Dev who cannot connect with the upwardly mobile Rhea especially after he is unmanned by an accident and Maya who entered into a marriage based on care rather than romantic love. Events are ordered by motivation and psychology – Dev and Maya form a connection because Dev is unhappy in his marriage and Maya is clearly not in love with the man she is about to marry. These preconditions are quite economically conveyed in the opening sequences. Why Maya speaks so openly and frankly to a stranger and a male at that is openly acknowledged and explained away – sometimes it is easier to talk to strangers than to friends – they are free to speak the truth. And what does Dev tell Maya when she expresses concern that if she bases her marriage on friendship there is always the danger that she might fall in love after she is married? He responds that if she does not look for love, she will not find it. But even as he constructs for her this voluntarist version of human action – an ethic of selfcontrol/selfsacrifice in essence, it is clear that in the very course of this exchange – the play of looks, body language and flirtatious wordplay – love has arrived unbidden to derail such an ethic. Consider the scene itself – two people in a bench in a garden that is absolutely empty, placed frontally in relation to the camera. Though this framing graphically evokes the convention of frontality in Indian cinema, it is a citation merely. If frontality in Indian cinema has been theorized as instituting spectatorial relations quite at odds with voyeurism, this is indeed a private scene.[48] The fourth wall is firmly in place and the characters are speaking only to each other. Moreover, the camera is very unobtrusive and the editing seamless. The camera is placed at eye level and the sequence comprises relatively long takes alternating with brief interludes of shot-reverse shot. It starts out as a midshot and moves ever so imperceptibly closer to the principles, never quite achieving a close-up. In brief, the sequence plays out naturalistically with almost no dramatic emphasis thus activating the scopic drive. The conversation comes to a close as Dev urges Maya to hurry up and get married. As they part from each other they exchange names and the film makes its first direct allusion to Bombay cinema as Dev mimics the distinctive speaking style of his celluloid namesake, actor Dev Anand. Almost on cue the apparatus shifts gear and the framing and editing become much more stagey. First the camera pulls back and up to an overhead shot of the two figures parting and the background score plays the instrumental section of the title song. This overhead shot of two figures walking away from each other (which will function as a visual leitmotif in the film) alternates with a rhythmically edited shot reverse shot of Dev and Maya looking back at each other even as the overhead camera and the traditional authority that it relays demands that they part. The overhead shot functions like a tableau conveying in a congealed form the social mandates that demand that a married man and a woman on the eve of her wedding have no right to be flirting with each other. This exact composition will return to remind us of this mandate when midway through the film, Dev declares his love for Maya (this time in an empty train station in the middle of the night) and Maya is in no position to deny that she loves him too. But unlike that first time, when Dev and Maya walked away from each other, this time Maya ignores the injunction of the tableau and runs towards Dev in an agonizingly long sequence.

It is by now almost a truism that the ordering of events and actions in the Hindi film melodrama is not driven by motivational logic of a psychological-realist kind but rather characters perform actions that will enable the plot to move forward and take its many twists and turns. Since the narrative drive of an externalized form like the melodrama is the initial disturbance and final restitution of the moral order, there is no real suspense in a melodramatic narrative, there is no unexpected character-driven reversals or projections of action either. Thus the tableau performs such an important function in the melodrama – it consolidates the moral order that the action will fulfill. But Maya disrupts the tableau – and takes an action based on her own unique experiences that will run athwart traditional morality. Like in the scene from *Kabhi Khushi Kabhie Gham* described above, the transition from an older cultural logic to a newer one occurs via a flashback. Maya recalls key moments with Dev and her husband Rishi, but as these scenes from the first half of the film playback, she reprocesses them and then decides to go with her lover. We witness, in other words, a cognitive remapping that enables Maya to break through one set of habits and emerge into another. What we diegetically experience as Maya's individual agency is also a cultural transformation.[49]

If melodrama was the aesthetic mode best suited to capture the face off between law and desire, tradition and modernity – these antinomies are no longer narratively necessary in the world of 'KJo'. His project, as we have seen, puts into place a new kind of family and new modes of subjectivity that are less agonistic, more self-actualizing. We must consequently view his activation of the melodramatic mode and his use of micro-narrational techniques like the tableau and frontality as a memorialization of the older form of Hindi cinema and the social relations they embody. They are the relics of another time – valuable souvenirs – that evoke sentimental affects and add value at the box office. However, as we saw in the examples above, they also have to make way for a mode of narration that is more Hollywood than Bombay cinema. As such, the 'KJo' film is a transitional object that lingers awhile with a cinematic form whose time is up. Perhaps the most vivid instance of this is the strange timeline of *Kabhi Alvida Na Kehna*. The film breaks in three parts. The first segment is 16 minutes long and occurs on March 21, 2002 (Dev precisely dates it for us). Dev and Maya meet for the first time. They part. She gets married, he has an accident that partially cripples him and ends his career as a football player. The second commences 4 years later, in 2006 and lasts for almost 150 minutes. Dev and Maya meet again, have an affair, decide to break it off, confess their transgressions to their respective spouses who throw them out. But they do not get together – rather each lies to the other that they have been forgiven for after all 'family is family.' So they go their separate ways. The third segment where Dev and Maya are reunited is about 20 minutes long occurs three years later – i.e. in 2009, three years after the release of the film in 2006! This might very well be one of those continuity lapses that Hindi cinema was notorious for. Alternately, the untimely ending lends itself to a different reading. We might view it as another melodramatic set piece – a sentimental gesture to the disappearing moral and aesthetic universe of Hindi cinema. The lovers are reunited in a 'nailbiting' climax at a train station, aided by their exes – Rishi and Rhea – who have now moved on and rebuilt their lives. So why does the film need this interval of 3 years, during which we witness onscreen the lovers pining for each other to the accompaniment of the title song whose lyrics translate 'never say goodbye?' This flashforward is motivated by the 'KJo' films' nostalgia for the cultural logic of Hindi cinema. Infidelity remains a risky subject in Hindi cinema. In *Kabhi Alvida Na Kehna*'s most illustrious precursors – *Silsila* (The Affair, 1981) and Mahesh Bhatt's *Arth* (Meaning, 1982) – marriage vows are broken under extenuating circumstances. Even a recent spate of 'hat-ke' films like Amit Saxena's *Jism* (Body, 2003), and Anurag Basu's *Murder* (2004) and *Life in a...Metro* (2007) rationalize infidelity by featuring lonely women trapped in dysfunctional marriages. But Dev and Maya's actions are motivated only by desire – they are each 'soulmates' and their spouses, Rhea and Rishi hardly deserve this humiliation! So three years must pass, during which Rishi and Rhea rebuild their lives and Dev and Maya's emotions are lyrically mediated by song. Song and the 'ticking clock finish' in a train station draw on the melodramatic codes of Hindi cinema to metamorphose the adulterous couple into romantic lovers who have paid their dues in time and tears so that the audience can now root for their union! At the same time, 'KJo' renders such a coda virtual by setting it in the future. It is a happy ending that is out of time.

To conclude then, the 'KJo' film, qua category, presents a distinct stance to the cinematic past and selectively mines certain strains within it and this, as I have shown, is a crucial way in which the 'KJo' film breaks with Bombay cinema. For not only does this archival relation to Bombay cinema turn it into a historical object but the 'KJo' film also evokes the thematic tropes and aesthetic protocols of Hindi cinema, only to transform them. We have traced this through the 'KJo' films' multiple iterations of the 'family' – as theme, as aesthetic, and as metaphor for Bombay cinema's mode of production, as a new source of value, as a relation to social and cinematic history. If the 'hat-ke' film is marked by its addiction to the new, the 'KJo' film invents a new relation to the old.

Chapter Three

IS EVERYBODY SAYING 'SHAVA SHAVA' TO BOLLYWOOD BHANGRA?

Anjali Gera Roy

Theorizing Indian Cinema as a national cinema, film studies have focused on the relationship between popular Hindi films and the Indian nation. Sumita Chakravarty's *National Identity in Indian Popular Cinema: 1947–87* set the trend for a number of texts that viewed Indian popular cinema as a cultural system through which the new nation was imagined. Readings of popular Hindi films by scholars such as Ashish Rajadhyaksha, Madhava Prasad, Ravi Vasudevan and Gayatri Chatterjee have called attention to their nationalistic ideology and to their commitment to the nationalistic drive towards modernity and highlighted the role they played in the formation of the Indian citizen subject.[1] Lately, Hindi Cinema, rechristened Bollywood, has begun to attract attention as a transnational phenomenon. Vijay Mishra, in *Bollywood Cinema: Temples of Desire*, was the first to draw a parallel between the collective experience of reading newspapers creating the sense of belonging to a nation on the one hand and on the other, 'the way in which Bombay Cinema constructs an Indian diaspora of shared cultural idiom.'[2] Whether it was 'a decidedly ideological form' or whether its 'catholicity' was triggered by commerce or not, most studies concur that the simulacra of Hindi Cinema partially facilitated the confirmation, if not the construction, of the Indian nation and Indian modernity.[3] As a consequence, the music of Hindi Cinema, which has evolved its distinctive idiom by blending classical and folk Indian traditions with Western, has acquired the status of national popular music.[4]

The denigration of the Bollywood song and dance sequence as a tested formula to ensure the box office success of a *masala* film has gradually given away to its elevation as the key ingredient in Bollywood's constitutive difference from World Cinema.[5] The song and dance routine has been accorded academic legitimacy through the attention provided to songs and music not only by film scholars but also by creative writers, historians, sociologists and anthropologists.[6]

Rather than being dismissed as fantastic interludes disrupting the progress of the cinematic narrative, songs and dances are now valorized as part of the cinematic grammar through which the signification of meaning takes place in Bollywood creating a new aesthetic for Indian cinema. Following indigenous performance traditions such as Ramlila, *nautanki*, *tamasha* and Parsi theatre that combined several aesthetic modes, the Bollywood song and dance routine is seen as performing a wide range of functions including heightening a situation, accentuating a mood, commenting on theme and action, providing relief and serving as interior monologue.[7] But, as Madhava Prasad shows, it also introduces a new Bollywood language for the representation of the forbidden private within the overarching framework of feudal family romance.[8] Teri Skillman agrees, 'Songs were used to express sentiments that could not be spoken, and when dramatized in film, the body language, covered by the veil of a song, suggested a display of affection, which was forbidden in public.'[9]

While Bollywood music is usually regarded as an independent category of Indian music that has formed the emotional imaginary of the nation, it does not belong to any particular region.[10] 'National popular music' is produced through Bollywood music directors' cannibalization of national classical and popular regional folk music and dance over the years. 'Bambaiya' folk traditions, deterritorialized and decontextualized, have always been made to perform rustic exotica for the imagined urban viewer of Hindi cinema.[11] Like other folk musics, Punjabi folk tunes also gave Hindi cinema several 'hits' beginning with *Khajanchi* (The Treasurer, 1941). The domination of Punjabi tunes and dances in Bollywood might be traced back to the reputation of the Lahore school in pre-Partition Hindi cinema led by Master Ghulam Haider, which was carried over to post-Partition Bombay by O P Nayyar and others.[12] But the naturalization of Punjabi music and dance, for which I use the generic term Bhangra, in Bollywood's song and dance routine in recent Bollywood blockbusters has transformed it into a new Bollywood formula.[13] As the specific differences between diverse Punjabi musical and dance genres have been conveniently eroded in the construction of Bollywood Bhangra, the term has been used here to include other categories of Punjabi music such as *geet*, *qawwali*, *sufiana kalam* and so on.[14]

Bollywood's cooption of ethnic musics normally proceeds by way of their exoticization. In fact, ethnicity is also the largest source of appeal in Bhangra's insertion into the Bollywood code of signification, which proceeds by way of exoticization. Bhangra must essentially be decoupled from its roots in Punjabi harvest ritual to be reinscribed as a formulaic cinematic idiom. Overwriting traditional Bhangra with a Bollywood semiotics of dress, appearance, gestures and bodily movement and sound serves to transform the harvest ritual from its specific ethnic context into a specialized Bollywood lingua understood by all

Indian ethnicities. The privileging of Punjabi wedding song and dance in Bollywood *sangeets* and *shaadis* over other regional rituals has placed a reified *punjabiyat* at the service of Bollywood addressing a nationalist drive towards modernity. Bhangra's insertion into Bollywood's popular cultural space has generated pessimistic mutterings from non-Punjabis as well as Punjabis, one side deploring Bollywood's Punjabi invasion on aesthetic grounds and the other bemoaning the insertion of the Punjabi sacred into popular cultural commerce.[15]

But Bollywood audience's reappropriation of Bhangra from the popular cultural into the folk and communal space raises important issues about signification, spectatorship and community formation in relation to Bollywood and Bhangra texts. Ella Shohat and Robert Stam, arguing that contemporary media shape reality, had stated that 'in a transnational world typified by the global circulation of images and sounds, goods and population, media spectatorship impacts complexly on national identity, political affiliation and communal belonging.'[16] Shohat and Stam's point about the 'cultural variegated nature of spectatorship,' which 'derives from the diverse locations in which films are received, from the temporal gaps of seeing films in different historical moments to the conflictual subject positionings and community affiliations of the spectators themselves' has a bearing upon the way Bollywood audience shape and are shaped by the cinematic experience with an endless, dialogical experience.[17]

This essay locates Bhangra in the Bollywood song and dance formula to examine the cross signification through which Bollywood audience decode the popular cultural text to disrupt its reification of Bhangra and reappropriate it to negotiate issues of tradition and modernity in the context of challenges posed by globalization. In doing so, it engages with the heterogeneous spectator positionings against the ethnographic grid suggested by Shohat and Stam to isolate the tensions in the reception and appropriation of Bollywood Bhangra affected by geographical location, language, age and ethnicity, but mainly by the contexts in which Bhangra texts are received and performed. Its objective in the displacement of character identification in the apparatus to an ethnographic theory of difference is to engage with what Judith Mayne calls 'the tension between cinema as monolithic institution and cinema as heterogeneous diversity.'[18] In privileging categories of social differences, position and social experience to determine relations to the Bollywood film, the essay does not seek to fetishize differences as concrete identities but to identify a politics of spectatorial positions through which Bollywood texts are negotiated.

Bhangra's invasion of Bollywood coincided with Daler Mehndi's arrival on the Indian popular musical horizon.[19] Daler's album *Bolo ta ra ra ra ra* was the first regional music album to make a crossover by registering a record sale of a million copies in Kerala in the deep South. Mehndi made 'Balle Balle' a national catchphrase. The Bollywood 'superstar' Amitabh Bachchan's insistence that Mehndi perform live along with him for *Mrityudaata* (1997), his comeback vehicle in the late eighties, launched Bhangra in Bollywood. Bachchan's patronization of Bhangra continued with *Major Saab* (1998) in the 'sohna sohna' song and his recording in his own voice for Bally Sagoo's *Abby Baby* (1996).[20] By the time he called out 'Everybody say shava shava' in *Kabhi Khushi Kabhie Gham* (Sometimes Happiness Sometimes Sadness, aka K3G, 2001), the entire nation and the diaspora had perfected the art of responding to Bhangra calls. As celebratory and courtship dance, Bhangra has become so naturalized into the Bollywood sonic vocabulary that its specific Punjabi location is forgotten to the point of its insertion into non-Punjabi contexts. While in 'shava shava,' temporarily bridging the gender, age, class was in character with the full-bodied Punjabi patrician he played in *K3G*, Bachchan was also made to dance Bhangra with wife Hema Malini in the 'meri makhna, meri sohniye' number in *Baaghbaan* (The Gardener, 2003). The mandatory Bhangra ritual performed at celebratory moments in popular Bollywood texts has embedded Bhangra so deeply now in the Indian popular cultural vocabulary that its Punjabi specificity does not appear to be an obstacle to its non-Punjabi crossovers.

Music and dance scholars concede that Punjabi song and dance are complex sonic and kinesic genres requiring natural talent and intensive training and are capable of articulating a wide range of emotions or *rasas* (emotions or moods) as any other folk or classical genre. Bhangra aficionados strongly disapprove of Bollywood Bhangra for its disrespectful hybridization of distinctive Punjabi dance genres into a homogenized Bollywood Bhangra dance, to its containment of Bhangra's open and spontaneous movements by Bollywood-style choreography and, most of all, to its dissemination of sexualized moves performed to *ashleel* or vulgar lyrics as Bhangra. In their view, Bollywood Bhangra is a fake copy, a humiliating *naqqal*; it is not Bhangra at all.[21] But to the rest of India, and now to a large part of the Indian diaspora, Bhangra is Bollywood Bhangra.

What is Bollywood Bhangra? Bollywood Bhangra is a made-in-Bollywood genre in which Bollywood actors dance movements choreographed by Bollywood dance trainers, who mix *dhamaal* and *luddi* with disco and break-dance while permitting 'stars' to improvise their own signature movements.[22] Unlike traditional Bhangra, that is governed by elaborate, culturally coded rules of performance, Bollywood Bhangra is a free-for-all dance in which one is legally permitted to make wild noises. These images of leaping, prancing, jostling bodies are then represented as Bhangra and are made to signify the body in pleasure. Due to its misrepresentation by Bollywood, Bhangra has come to signify to Bollywood audience a wild shaking of torso or limbs best performed in an inebriated state.

There is no doubt that Bhangra's dominant *rasa* (emotion evoked) is *hasya* or joy, and it articulates the 'eat-drink-and-be-merry' (*khao piyo mauj karo mitro* in Punjabi) ethic that has traditionally been mapped on the Punjabi body. But Bollywood bowdlerizes it and reduces it to a saleable formula and its signification of the epicurean Bhangra ethic takes place only through a gross violation of Punjabi gestural codes. To stage Bollywood pleasure, females are made to perform male gestures and vice versa; dissimilar dance genres are mixed with one another or display a dissonance with music. Most of all, Bhangra is decontextualized in Bollywood and becomes a 'floating signifier' that may be pasted on any occasion in any setting. Finally, Bollywood, with the exception of Bhangra performed in family settings, isolates erotic pleasure from Bhangra to the exclusion of other forms of pleasure.

Bhangra's decontextualization and hybridization, while retaining its exoticized ethnicity, enable it to perform ethnic celebration as well as romance in non-Punjabi contexts in Bollywood blockbusters. Bhangra's acquisition of the status of the signifier of communal conviviality, family bonding, and mating dance in the Bollywood sonic idiom facilitates its incursion into the national celebratory idiom. Though it might privilege some forms of pleasure over others, Bollywood Bhangra, as celebratory dance, still draws upon the traditional connotations of the Punjabi harvest dance to signify different forms of joy, which I will describe as 'family values', 'hero woos heroine', and 'item number'.[23] Bhangra functions both as family values and courtship dance as well as item number, which depends on its particular location in the Bollywood narrative. Its *bolis* (calls and responses) might equally enact courtship and romance in family settings or a brazen variety of modern Indian sexuality as item number.

One of the main tropes Bollywood Bhangra inscribes is the enactment of family bonding and love. Like the harvest dance, Bollywood Bhangra is also performed at all family gatherings and events and is used to signify filial affection and traditional values. While its lyrical content might be the same as other Bhangra texts, the 'family values' Bhangra may be easily distinguished from other forms of Bollywood Bhangra through its traditional setting and costumes. Having joined Bollywood's iconic images, family values Bhangra now invites instant recognition and recall from its audience like the rain dance or the temple visit. The iconic image consists of a group of dancers of all ages, classes and genders. Male dancers, clad in embroidered *sherwanis* or *kurtas* and colourful stoles around the neck, raise their arms upwards and shake their pelvic muscles; female dancers, dressed in *salwar kameezes*, *lehnga cholis*, and saris, sway their waists. The lead dancer changes depending on the cast. In a Bachchan film, Bachchan himself, flanked by younger Bollywood actors – Shahrukh Khan, Salman Khan, Akshay Kumar or Abhishek Bachchan, is given the honour of leading the dancers and to woo his female lead – Jaya Bachchan, Hema Malini or Kiron Kher – with a Bhangra *boli*. Not only that, Bachchan also gets to dance with the pretty young things – Rani Mukherjee, Kajol, Preity Zinta or Kareena Kapoor – in addition to the 'sexy' female dancers of all complexions forming the group. Shahrukh Khan, Hritik Roshan and Abhishek Bachchan get to dance with Rani, Preity or Kareena only when the elder Bachchan releases them. The rest of the time they must make do with Jaya Bachchan, Hema Malini or Sushma Seth, and even Fareeda Jalal and Zohra Sehgal (*K3G, Veer Zaara, KANK*). If the younger stars are in the starring role, it is the Khans, Kapoors or Khannas who lead the dancers and call out to the heroine, followed by uncles played by Anupam Kher, Alok Nath et al. In both, families gaze lovingly at each other as they dance the Bhangra together; fathers hug sons, brothers hug one another; lovers tease one another as sisters, wives, mothers and aunts look on adoringly. Whether it is a *sangeet* or an engagement, *karva chauth* or *diwali*, families resplendent in silks and gold perform traditional rituals by dancing the Bhangra and singing Bhangra *bolis*.[24] Bollywoodized Bhangra performed at family gatherings have become as naturalized to encode family-togetherness in Bollywood as dancing around trees is to express romantic love. Post-global Bollywood families rarely sing *bhajans* (devotional songs) or perform *aartis* (ritual worship) together as they did in the pre-global past but always dance together irrespective of age, gender, class, or ethnicity to reinforce family togetherness and reaffirm tradition. What bridges 'family values' with Bhangra in Bollywood may be summarized in a single sentence; 'Families which dance together are happy families'. The corollary to this is that the best way of expressing filial love and affirming family values is to dance the Bhangra in ostentatious costumes in ancient *havelis* or modern mansions.

The major change that 'family values Bhangra' documents is the new hedonist ideology of the sixty plus male and the fifty plus female that subverts the self-denying, austere Bollywood elders that persisted as late as the eighties. While the 'Swinging Sam' (*Kabhi Alvida Naa Kehna*) characters that Bachchan has played in the recent years might have been specifically created to accommodate the ageing superstar, Bachchan's new screen persona, embodying the esthetic of pleasure, revises the severe, self-abnegating Bollywood father. With Bachchan, Bollywood fathers do not have to retreat to the Himalayas or Kashi to meditate as they did in the past, but can eat, drink, womanize and be merry. Bollywood's new found hedonism, except when Bachchan plays the disciplinarian, is not restricted to fathers but also percolates to mothers, and even grandmothers. In *Viruddha* (Opposition, 2005), Sharmila Tagore, Bachchan's wife is permitted to confess her weakness for wine, Kiron Kher in *KANK* (2006) is shown to be vain about her figure and loves to dance, in *Kal Ho Na Ho* (Tomorrow May Not Come, 2003), grandmother Sushma Seth is permitted to revive her romance with her village beau Dara Singh, and the irrepressible Zohra Sehgal never misses a chance to dance from *Dil Se* (Straight from the Heart 1998) to *Bend it Like Beckham* (2002).

Bhangra may be danced to articulate different forms of love including that of the patriotic and divine variety. The traditional format of the Bhangra *boli* is that of the praise song in which the singer calls out the attributes of the beloved, homeland or the deity in a plain, homespun idiom. But Bollywood, with the exception of 'aisa des hai mera' in *Veer Zaara* (Veer and Zaara 2004) and 'rang de basanti' in *Rang de Basanti* (Paint It Saffron, 2006), isolates romantic love from Bhangra to the exclusion of other forms of love. Bollywood Bhangra songs today are expositions of romantic love dedicated to the beloved and only rarely to the homeland or to the divine. It was Bhangra's courtship idiom's perfect fit with the Bollywood romance vocabulary that facilitated its adoption as the new Bollywood courtship language.

As Mishra, Prasad and Trivedi have noted, Bollywood traditionally resorted to Urdu poetry, particularly to the *ghazal*, to expound on the beloved's beauty or the theme of romantic love.[25] Unlike Urdu poetry, which offers a means of expressing romantic love in the *ghazal's* gentle melody, Bhangra is an unequivocal, loud, public declaration of adoration. Unlike the metaphoric, allusive, complex rhetoric of Urdu poetry, Bhangra *bolis* achieve their effect through plainspeak and tonality rather than ambiguity and euphemism. Bhangra's difference from Urdu poetry as courtship song in its directness makes it a better match for contemporary plainspeak styles just as its exploitation of tonality rather than semantics for constructing meaning helps it to cross the linguistic divide.

Bhangra lyrics consist of formulaic descriptions of the beloved's beauty, of an object worn by the beloved, or that of the heart being stolen, lost or broken. Whether one puts it down to the constraints of oral formulaic composition or explains it as Punjabi laconicity, Bhangra lyrics might be reduced to a handful of words strung together in various permutations and combinations. Bhangra's lyrical minimalism is taken to ridiculous extremes in Bollywood Bhangra and its repetitive play reduced to repetitive endearments and nonsense loops: *Ik Panjaban/Kudi Panjaban/Dil churake lai gayi/Sohna sohna/Dil mera sona* (*Major Saab*), translated as 'A Panjaban/A Panjabi lass/Has stolen my heart/Oh beautiful/My beautiful heart!'

The most frequently repeated word is the address to the beloved, *sohni* or *sohna*, which transliterates as beautiful. Other repetitive words are *dil*, heart and *ishq*, love. But Bhangra's lyrical minimalism turns out to be its strength in its incorporation into the national romantic repertoire. Much in the same way as the Urdu terms such as *dilruba*, *mehbooba*, or *janeman*, had served as nationally recognizable codes for naming the beloved, Punjabi equivalents for the beloved such as *mahi*, *heer*, *ranjha*, *dholna*, *makhna* have entered the national romantic idiom.

But Bhangra's greatest advantage over the *ghazal* is it's complementing of word and music with the body language of dance. It aural and visual appeal makes it intersect with another nineties' addition to the Bollywood song and dance vocabulary, 'the item number.'[17] Karan Johar's classification of 'shava shava' as an 'item number' inadvertently provides the clue to Bhangra's transition to the field of popular cultural commerce in which Bollywood culture industry is thoroughly entrenched. An item number is a dance sequence of raunchy movements and risqué lyrics with little relation to the plot line, which aspiring starlets use to debut in Bollywood. In keeping with Bollywood's libidinous drive, an item number is normally added on to generate publicity, to guarantee the film's box office success and ensure repeat viewings. Bhangra's intersection with item numbers, originating in their common folk location, is cemented by its insertion into the cinematic narrative as dramatic relief. Like item numbers, Bhangra's inclusion seems to have been initially motivated by the sheer joy of rhythm and movement but without the voyeuristic titillation provided by semi-clad female bodies. The 'presence' of Daler Mehndi prancing about the film frame as the original item number establishes the commonality between the energy and vitality exuded by the rotund Sikh and the 'nubile' females of the item numbers. Gradually, while retaining its conventional virility and vigor, Bhangra gets simultaneously imbricated with the item number's sinuous sexuality through its import of the London or New York nightclub.

The fetishizing male gaze through which the beloved transforms into the object of male adoration may be illustrated through the 'Everybody say shava shava' number in *Kabhi Khushi Kabhi Gham*: *Roop hai tera sona, soni teri paayal* (You are beautiful, so is your anklet); *Hoye, roop hai tera sona sona, soni teri paayal* (You are very beautiful, so is your anklet); *Chhan chhana chhan aise chhanke, kar de sabko ghaayal* (The tinkle of your anklets wound everyone); *Keh raha aankhon ka kaajal, ishq mein jeena marna, yay* (The kohl in your eyes says let's live and die for love).

Once again, the secret of Punjabi courtship dance's appropriation as item number into Bollywood's dance grammar lies in the candour of the *boliyaan* lyrics. Unlike the veiled and suggestive sexuality of the *ghazals*, Bhangra *bolis*' plainspeak results in the expression of adoration for the beloved in coarse peasant masculinity, which lends itself to the item number's raunchy sexuality. The male gaze of the item number, which fetishizes the female object by fixing the camera on exposed female anatomy, draws upon traditional Bhangra *bolis* in which the adoration for the beloved is often fixated on a bodily part or an object worn by the beloved. The generic fetishization of the female object through the imagined feudal, patriarchal male subject of Bhangra in Bhangra *bolis* is exploited in the item number's sexualization of the exposed female body to seduce the male viewer though the same *bolis* might be used to articulate romantic adoration in 'the hero woos heroine' trope.

Bhangra's Bollywoodization could be viewed as an act of desecration perpetrated by the reduction of the Punjabi harvest ritual to a box office formula. The violence of disembedding Bhangra from its specific location in Punjabi family celebrations, the mixing of various Bhangra genres into a typical Bollywood style dance and song routine and converting a participatory rite to a gigantic screen spectacle cannot be denied. But more interesting is the complex dialogue between Bhangra texts and contexts in which the Bollywood formula is given a new twist. This involves several levels of cooption. Bollywood co-opts Punjabi festive music as Bollywood celebratory music, which is reappropriated by its audience as traditional celebratory dance or as new Asian dance music. Bollywood Bhangra, as celebratory music, leads to a reinvention of the traditional Indian corpus through the cross fertilization of various traditions in Bollywood's eclectic, amalgamating space.

Though Bhangra's inclusion in the blockbusters of the 1990s might be explained easily through Bollywood's customary cooption of marketable tunes, it can also be attributed to the change in Bollywood's positioning of the spectator from the national to the ethnolinguistic subject. Despite her poststructuralist reading of the Bombay film's concern with the 'enigma' of (male) subjectivity and the need for the disawowal of fixed nations of identity, Chakravarty disagrees with the view that the Bombay film 'fails' to identify its characters.[26] She maintains that filmic texts use visual codes to situate the hero at best broadly as either Hindu or Muslim, upper class or poor, educated or not while Mishra identifies the hero as distinctly North Indian. A shift in Bollywood's spectator's positioning from the idealized national subject of Hindi cinema to the ethnolinguistic subject may be observed partially as a result of Bollywood's transnationalization, which makes the celebration of *punjabiyat* in the 1990s' Bollywood quite different from its eclectic collage of vernacular genres in the past.

Bollywood's new market segmentation, in which the diaspora is clearly factored, constructs the subject as Punjabi in deference to the Punjabi domination of the diaspora whose body becomes the site for the play of tradition and modernity. It must be pointed out that Punjabi identity or *punjabiyat* has always been inscribed by a certain form of corporeality. Whether in the valorized body of the *vir* or the warrior in Punjabi tradition or that of 'the martial race' in imperialism, *punjabiyat* has always been articulated to materiality. Punjabi identity was ascribed by British imperialism through their inclusion as one of the martial races who were recruited in the imperial army particularly after the rebellion of 1857. The martial races were supposedly the big built, broadshouldered, lightskinned, hardy inhabitants of certain parts of India who were seen as naturally warlike and aggressive in battle and as possessing qualities like courage, loyalty, strength, resilience and industry. But this ascription perfectly fitted the

Punjabi self construction as an industrious, warrior community. The text that set the trend for valorizing an essentialized *punjabiyat* (Punjabi-ness) as rusticity, namely *Dilwale Dulhaniya Le Jayenge* (The True of Heart will take the Bride Away, 1995), is often cited to establish the nexus between NRI capital, the location of the director, Bollywood culture industry and the imagined spectator. Bhangra emerges from the diasporic film's romanticization of rustic authenticity through the image that Mishra labels 'Home and the green, green field of the Punjab.'[27] The valorization of Punjabi peasant values as Indian over others may be attributed to their fitting perfectly into the techno-nostalgia suffered by the diaspora. The association of Punjabis with agricultural prosperity results in the nostalgia for the homeland and its traditions being mapped onto a specifically Punjabi rural imaginary. Not stereotyped Bengali or Tamil intelligence but the caricatured Punjabi peasant kinship structures are reclaimed in nostalgic returns to the face-to-face community of the homeland. Since the publication of Mishra's book, three global films, *Monsoon Wedding* (2001), *Bollywood Hollywood* (2002) and *Bend it Like Beckham* (2002) identify the Indian diaspora in UK, US and Canada as unmistakably Punjabi and specify Indian family values as Punjabi Hindu or Sikh.

But the positioning of the Bollywood subject as ethnolinguistic rather than national in the NRI film is carried over in films intended for home consumption, which also borrow *punjabiyat* to signify family values. As Mishra points out, Bollywood's conscious diasporization, which shifts the ideal spectator from the Indian to the diasporic, which is Punjabi, makes the diaspora the ideal space for the Indian spectator as well.[28] In the 'Hindu Family Values' film, of which *Kabhi Khushi Kabhi Gham* is the prime example, begins the synecdochic mapping of Punjabi bodies and sites onto a national imaginary that continues in *Kal Ho Na Ho*, *Veer Zaara* and *Kabhi Alvida Na Kehna*. While the home audience might not share the diaspora's strong identification with Bollywood as homeland, aspects of the Bollywood media imaginaries are used to perform ritual and culture by urban Indians everywhere. In these performances of ethnicity, Punjabi forms becomes metonymic of the Indianness that is being revived through mediatized images in part as a conscious post national modernist drive to resist the pull of the global. As Ashish Rajadhayaksha explains, the revival of traditional music along with traditional values is part of the conscious export of a commoditized Indian nationalism and a 'feel good' version of 'our culture.'[29]

What happens when the virtual hedonistic body disseminated through Bollywood Bhangra comes into contact with bodies in real places? I am interested in revealing the corporeality of the tensions between terror and pleasure mapped on the Bhangra body in the dialogue between different voices and bodies that Bhangra enables. How does the dissemination of virtual bodies in digital space modulate the kinesthetic and acoustic of the nation compelling real bodies to perform/enter the other by mimicking the other's posture and movement? How does it release the body from its workday stress and articulate it with the body in pleasure of Bhangra?

In order to understand how Bollywood Bhangra mediates in Indian public space, one must grasp the strong audience identification with Hindi cinema, the spillover of reel life into real life and the active participation of viewers in the viewing space that has been noted with respect to Hindi cinema audience. Film studies have emphasized the problematic identification of Indian audience with popular cultural ritual in Bollywood film and television soaps, which has often matched the hold of traditional folk traditions like the epics. *Monsoon Wedding* and *Bollywood Hollywood* illustrate the extent to which Bollywood culture has become internalized in the lives of Indians on the subcontinent as well as the diaspora. Nowhere is Bollywood's impact on the Indian imagination made as evident as in Deepa Mehta's parody of Bollywood conventions in *Bollywood Hollywood*. Sunita Singh alias Sue, passing off as Hispanic, claims familiarity with Indian culture through Bollywood. But Sunita Singh's inability to resist Bollywood idol Akshaye Khanna's (who plays himself in the film) invitation to dance at a party reveals her own infatuation with Bollywood. Similarly, Sunita Singh's father is shown to be in the habit of using Bollywood musical vocabulary to express emotion.

While the commodified productions of locality in market dictated media images needs to distinguished from the production of locality in real contexts, the mediatized reinvention of tradition spills over into the production of everyday life in which Bollywood texts, the star system and ancillary commercial enterprises cannot be ignored. Vimla Patil, a former editor of the popular Indian women's fortnightly *Femina*, notes that wedding rituals such as *mehndi*, *sangeet* or *baraat* have become a privileged site for actualizing Bollywood produced images in the production of a cultural identity within the format of a modern Indian 'everyday life.'

> Even middle class weddings are being celebrated in full Bollywood style, with the enthusiastic brides and their anxious grooms getting jitters over how to dress for each event and ritual. And a list of the events and rituals – as well as the games and shenanigans planned by both parties – show a distinct influence of films made by Karan Johar, Dharmesh and Sunil Darshan, Yash Chopra, Suraj Barjatya, Abbas Mastaan and other well-known wedding-video directors! No longer are there South Indian kalyanams, Maharashtrian lagnas, Punjabi shaadis, Bengali vivahas or Rajasthani lagans! There is only The Great Bollywood Wedding – with its glamour and fun ingredients planned with immaculate attention – which is setting a worldwide trend![30]

The dance revival at family weddings in India can singularly be attributed to Bhangra's nationalization via Bollywood. Bhangra's naturalization as Bollywood dance and its spillover into the concrete reveals an intermeshing of the cinematic and real as star weddings (such as Karishma Kapoor's leading the *baraat* at her cousin Nikhil Nanda's wedding with Amitabh Bachchan's daughter Shweta) or 'star presence' at weddings (Shahrukh Khan at the wedding of Lakshmi Mittal's daughter), the marketing of film-inspired merchandise (Shahrukh Khan's Sherwaani or Kajol's salwaar kameez in *K3G*) becomes inseparable from the production of tradition by individuals in everyday contexts.

Through its Bollywoodization, Bhangra has crossed cultural and linguistic barriers invading the ritual space of other ethnicities. Inherently resistant to adopting ethnic modes, other than their own, diverse Indian ethnicities have received and accepted Punjabi music as Bollywood song as readily as modern Indian women have accepted Punjabi *salwaar kameez* as the national workwear. Inspite of elders' disapproval of what they term 'crass' Punjabi culture, youngsters of other ethnic groups have adopted Bhangra style dancing and singing in their own rituals and celebrations. Like other wedding rituals named by Patil, Bhangra dancing is as likely to be performed today at a Bihari wedding as at the Maharashtrian Ganapati festival or at the Gujarati Navaratri celebration supplementing other forms of singing and dancing in approximation to the The Great Bollywood Wedding or celebration. Thus, Bhangra's Bollywoodization, a cause for great concern to Punjabis, makes it function as a shared code that enables various Indian ethnicities to construct Indian tradition with which it meets or replies to a globalized modernity.[31](Rajadhyaksha 2003)

What is performed in post-global Bollywood Bhangra is not only tradition at weddings and family functions but modernity as well. Bhangra's complementing or substitution of song and melody with the fast beats and 'high energy' body language of dance facilitates its induction as Asian dance music in the rapidly changing club culture. While Bhangra might perform traditional ritual in community functions and festivals, it performs modernity as Asian dance music. Indian youth may be seen dancing to Bollywood Bhangra numbers in the various discotheques and nightclubs that have mushroomed in Indian metro cities and at parties. A different aspect of Bhangra gets appropriated in the performance of Indian youth identities, namely the rhythm and the dance. On the dance floor, Bhangra's ethnic location or ritual location takes second place to its suitability as dance music. To the Indian youth in India and the diaspora, Bollywood Bhangra numbers signify an Indian beat on which they converge to construct their difference from their Western counterparts. As background music in clubs and parties, Bollywood Bhangra is disengaged both from its film and real contexts by youth in constructing youth subcultures. Indian youth have discovered in

Bollywoodized Bhangra an essentialized Indian beat, which they employ to resist global youth culture.

Bollywood's eclectic space enables Bhangra's cross-fertilization with other musical genres and its transmutation into a Bollywood formulaic genre that facilitates non-Punjabi ethnicities' identification with Bhangra. But Bhangra's adoption as Indian culture that other Indian ethnicities might adopt occurs through a simultaneous identification and distancing. Non-Punjabi identification with Bhangra performance in Bollywood film requires a simultaneous dis-identification, a schizophrenic split that might be juxtaposed against the stereotyped representation of *punjabiyat* in other Indian imaginaries. The non-Punjabi spectator identification with the imagined Punjabi subject of the contemporary Bollywood film requires that the spectators recognize themselves in the Punjabi other. The desire for the idealized full-bodied Punjabi male constructed as the Bollywood subject is canceled by the revulsion for the stereotyped depiction of the Punjabi as uncouth peasant. The ambivalence in Bhangra's appropriation by non-Punjabi ethnicities in the construction of a romanticized Indianness comes from a distancing from Punjabi 'crassness' while identifying with the body in pleasure articulated through Bollywood Bhangra.

In order to understand Bhangra's role in the performance of Indian tradition and modernity today, the notion of the subject as divided becomes extremely crucial. According to Hindu philosophy, all life is made of a combination of three *gunas* or qualities, *sattwa* (light), *rajas* (dynamism) and *tamas* (lethargy) and is seen as transcending from *tamas* to *rajas* and to *sattwa*. While each individual might combine these qualities in different degrees, the dominant quality determines a person as *satvik*, *rajasik* or *tamasik*. We must begin with the initial fragmentation through which the integrated self is split into the material and the spiritual and the latter privileged as constitutive of Indianness and materialism inscribed on a particular body in the nation. While most cultures have placed the body and mind in a hierarchical relationship, the traditional balance between the bodily and spiritual was translated in orientalism as a privileging of the spiritual over the material. In the new imperial division, Punjabi, as 'the martial race,' became the sign of the body while the rest of the nation arrogated spirituality to itself. Elaborate the historical context, see comment made earlier. The *satvik* body represented by the ascetic figure of Mahatma Gandhi, which relegated the *rajasik* body of the royals to the background, came to be privileged as the ideal body in Indian nationalism. The martial Punjabi body and the spiritual national body, therefore, were powerful imperial constructs that were thoroughly internalized by the colonized. The Bhangra body in pleasure was made to engage with the ascetic bodies of 'the athletes of self-restraint,' the *yogis*, normalized through orientalist representations of the vedantic corpus in modern India, and through the emaciated body of Mahatma Gandhi in Indian nationalism. Though this model of self-restraint is equally embodied in the 'immaculate' body of Buddha or Vivekananda, Gandhi invented a new corporeal semiotic in which the contours of the *baniya* (merchant) body arrogated the signification attached to the brahmin's body – abnegation and self-control. Gandhi's resignification of the merchant's body, traditionally associated with the quality of *tamas*, through his appropriation of an ascetic code of conduct and lifestyle produced a new nationalist ideology. It is this body that dominates the representation of India as spiritual in post-colonial self-representation. The mapping of the bacchanalian ecstasy on the Punjabi body positions it as a hedonistic alterity to the national ascetic norm. The ascetical attributes of restraint, moderation, abnegation and abstinence are privileged to constitute the nation in the image of the brahmin and the *yogi*, aspects of which different ethnicities appropriate in their self constitution, engendering stereotypes of the artistic Bengali, the simple Gujarati, the austere Maharashtrian, and the intelligent Tamil brahmin.

The Bakhtinian concept of carnivalesque, particularly the deeply positive bodily element of grotesque realism may be used to understand the Bhangra body's role in releasing the national body from the rules of the everyday. The dancing Bhangra body comes to signify to the nation a hedonist philosophy that is in conflict with the professed ascetic ideal constructed through the mind body opposition in Indian thought and culture. Images of the Punjabi body in pleasure disseminated over the national media produce in the spiritual self a strong awareness of the lack of *jouissance* and a desire for the hedonist other. Signifying infinite pleasure forbidden by Law, the Bhangra body presents to the self the joy it excised in the process of the body soul division and the naturalization of the soul as Indian. Through its insertion in popular culture and the sinful nightclub, Bhangra is inscribed by excessive pleasure forbidden by Law. Yet it is the suggestion of excess that is required for the repressed body to be released from the injunction of the Law. The repressed body returns in the image of the Bhangra dancer carrying the promise of all corporeal pleasures including eating, drinking and sexuality. The hedonist Punjabi body, as the other of the national ascetic body, becomes the site of repressed pleasures. Through enacting sounds and body movements of the Punjabi body, the national body attempts identification with the other. The Indian self that has been constituted in opposition to the hedonist ideology of *khao piyo mauj karo* (eat, drink and be merry) now seeks to be its other.

The return of the repressed body is what the dance boom in India in the 1980s and 1990s heralded. The press of bodies on the dance floor makes the bodies of the *yogi* (ascetic) collide with the body of the *vir* (warrior) as well as with that of the lord of misrule. As the *satvik* national body contacts the *rajasik* and *tamasik* bodies signified by contemporary Bhangra, there is a breaking free of the restraints and prohibitions that inhibit the body's movements and pleasures.

As the *rajasik kshatriya* and *tamasic mirasi* body are made to couple with the idealized *satvik* body of abstinence, difference makes contact in this bacchanalian release of the body in pleasure guided by Bhangra sounds and images. It is as if by imitating the gestures and sounds of Punjabi dance, Gujarati, Maharashtrian, Bengali and Kannada difference can enter the Punjabi body, which seems to promise infinite pleasure. Through the contact of these bodies with Punjabi sound and gesture, the repressed body breaks free of all taboos. Through its identification with the leaping, jumping shouting body, the self attempts to repossess the body and the pleasures it promises. Through mimicking the corporeal kinesics of the body in pleasure, the self attempts to appropriate pleasures that body promises and to make itself whole through identification with the hedonist other. Through being like the other, dancing like other, and feeling the other, the self desire to overcome the primal fragmentation.

Thus, Bhangra's cooption in Bollywood implicates it in a field of commerce and it is subjected to the rules of Bollywood marketing. It must consent to its exoticization and 'nativizing' through which it becomes encoded as a signifier of meaning that is essential to the films' marketing be it family values, rusticity, or modernity. But Bhangra audience extracts from the Bhangra texts meanings apposite with or contradictory to the projected meanings for performing Indian tradition and modernity. Through Bollywood Bhangra audience's construction of different forms of community in relation to the Bhangra texts Bhangra once again mediates in the construction of binaries of tradition and modernity enabling Indian culture to reinvent an Indian tradition capable of resisting the threat of Western modernity as globalization.

Chapter Four

BOLLYWOOD BABES: BODY AND FEMALE DESIRE IN THE BOMBAY FILMS SINCE THE NINETIES AND *DARR, MOHRA* AND *AITRAAZ*: A TROPIC DISCOURSE

Purna Chowdhury

The uncontested acceptance of Bollywood as the only available term for conceptualizing the Hindi film Industry in our times and the re-conceptualization of female sexuality in the films produced since the 1990s points towards a symbiotic relationship between the two cultural phenomena. This chapter will draw from the symptoms of the shifting paradigm of (female) sexuality, trying to understand the changed/changing symptoms not only as a dimension of performance, but, also in a larger sense, as a set of relations between the elements internal to the script as well as those which constitute its field: its audiences, its socio-economic structure and its ideological milieu. Approached from this angle, the gender matrix of 'Bollywood' may well offer insights into the changing modalities of Indian national identity and a redefinition of what may be termed the Indo-feminine in a global cultural context.

Bollywood: A Derivative Discourse

The best starting point for such a discussion is the highly contested terrain of 'Bollywood,' which has been copiously analyzed by Madhava Prasad and Vijay Mishra among others. According to Prasad in his article 'This thing called Bollywood,' 'Bollywood' has a commodious control specifically as it has an indeterminate ('ill-defined') purview, demonstrating a somewhat unbiased incorporation of all the existing models of the Bombay film industry, from the regressive, the popular to the ideological model. Commenting on the insertion of the term into the cultural discourse of the media, Prasad raises a very pertinent question as to whether Bollywood is a symptom of some other social and cultural processes and whether or not it points towards a social transformation that is indicated by a new genre that signifies the Bollywood presence in the global market. He goes on to comment:

> They have figured prominently in the emerging new culture of India, where consumer capitalism has finally succeeded in weaning the citizens away from a strongly entrenched culture of thrift towards a system of gratification more firmly in its (capitalism's) own long-term control. They have produced another variation of nationalist ideology of tradition and modernity, and most interestingly, they have relocated what we might call the seismic centre of Indian national identity somewhere in Anglo-America.[1]

Prasad's focus on the growing commercial power of the NRI in the Indian film industry is corroborated by statistical findings of the growing NRI market for the films, especially since the nineties. Two decisive strides in technology, the VCR and satellite TV have played a crucial role in the 'Bollywoodization' as these have proven to be two most important resources of entertainment for the Indian Diaspora. According to Pendakur and Subramaniyam, in 1991–92 the overseas video market generated more than 100 million rupees ($2.5million).[2] Since then, the video market has taken a down swing, and the film market has been on the rise. Cable and Satellite are the markers of the new changes and offers more flexibility in terms of availability and financial commitment. Vijay Mishra goes on to point out that TV ASIA and ATN are available in North America through the satellite channel Direct TV. In Canada ATN television devotes a considerable number of hours to news and entertainment from Doordarshan India.[3] While both Prasad and Mishra diagnose the diasporic or NRI intervention as the catalyst in the transformation of the semantic marker, both handle the cultural implications of the insertion in somewhat unproblematic ways. Prakash enumerates the NRI appears to be a totalitarian essence, ignoring the schism within the group along the historico-cultural divide. Mishra, who clearly differentiates the two forms of diasporas – old and new – identifies NRIs as 'the diaspora of late capital':

> The new is the complex and often internally fissured communities of Indians primarily in the United States, Canada, Britain, and Australia who have had unbroken contact with the homeland. For many the space occupied by the new diaspora – the space of the West – is also the desired space of wealth and luxury – that get endorsed, in a displaced form, by Indian cinema itself.[4]

Mishra goes on to point out that whereas in the former, race was a pre-given term for ethnic classificaton, the privileged few, questions of race and ethnicity are related to questions of justice, self-empowerment, representation, equal opportunity and so on. Yet, even as Mishra points out the concepts that are introduced into the diasporic desire that offer commercial incentive to the film industry, he forgets to mention, in absence of an established term, the 'second-generation citizen migrants,' for whom Bollywood is the most readily available mode for establishing cultural contact with a homeland-that–has-never been. If 'Bollywood' is a signifying operation of the diasporic imaginary, the ambiguity, the contradiction, the double subjectivity and double consciousness[5] discernible in the Hindi films of the nineties calls for a further revisiting of these categories to incorporate the 'structures of feeling' of this *third* category, which, while tries to keep a tentative hold on the twice removed Indian-ness, interrogates its very assumptions, calling for a drastic reconfiguration of cultural stereotypes, together with the choice of narratives in the cultural reproduction of the celluloid nation-state.[6]

Further, in the transglobal context, 'western' life, is very much a part of Indian culture, of urban Indianness, and with it comes numerous 'universal cultural trends': nightclubs, pizza, and baseball caps; reggae music and rap; Stephen King novels, Chicken Soup for the Souls, TV soap operas and, of course, the 'techies.' Indians today are less apt to reject the benefits of a materialist world, and the 'anti-colonialism of the earlier part of the century has given way to a nationalism that is not uncomfortable with the aggressive westernization of everyday life.'[7] And along with economic liberalization, a new burgeoning middle-class, technological advancements, CNN satellite transmissions and MTV in Indian living rooms, there is the arrival of shifting social relationships and attitudes. In 'Sex Appeal and Cultural Liberty: A Feminist Inquiry into MTV India,' the authors, Cullity and Younger does an ethnographic study of MTV India and states:

> The original intention behind our case study of MTV India was to look at television images that might register to the viewer as 'Western' and examine how they function in an indian context. Our research, however, revealed that MTV India programming had been largely indigenized or 'Indianized' so that MTV could stay afloat in the robust Indian television market. Furthermore, findings pointed to the emergence of a new form of cultural nationalism, seen in the 'indigenization' of the global media.[8]

This indigenization started in 1995, when MTV dissociated from Star and decided to revolutionize marketing strategy in the face of a fast disappearing audience, to 'Indianize' the programmes in order to remain on air. One of the means adopted among others was replacement of western music videos by Hindi film clips, popular song and dance numbers taken from hit films that could make for independent videos. Following this transformation, two-third of MTV'S music became Hindi music, with western music videos pushed over to the non-prime slots.

'Bollywood', like MTV India, is emblematic of the shifting paradigms of culture that neither ignores, nor accepts wholeheartedly the East-West divide of earlier post-global optique. The semantic symbiosis that is inherent in the term is reflective of the new reality of the trans-capital world. According to Sheila Nair:

> Inarguably, many of the 'advancements' and possessions that have come to symbolize modernization are peripheral to the average filmgoer's world. The fantastical 'stages' of Bombay – generic, lavishly grand offices and homes, stripped of social context – upon which most stories unfold, are not integrated into the lives of the film characters, perhaps the same way the filmgoer is not integrated into the (affluent urban) world of the movies, with its swimming pools, race cars, company ownerships and honeymoon trips to Switzerland. But, today, 'television and advertising have brought the good life in reach. Moreover, the whole world and what it has to offer in material terms is pouring into [Indian] consciousness' (Jain 57). Materialism can no longer be scornfully attributed to the West its consequences are now very much Indian as well: its vices and pleasures, and the resulting envy, greed and aggression. Subsequently, there is the flux and reinterpretation of one's relationship to the West: the West functioning both as an emblem of modernization, and concurrently as a caveat against a crude, materialist parasite on Indian tradition. Within this strained dichotomy, the relationship to the West is marked by (1) the process of becoming 'westernized' (perhaps the term modernized is more acceptable); and (2) the West as signifying the Other (that which represents the non-Indian, a lack of Indianness.[9]

An aspect of this new 'dichotomy,' as Nayar puts it, is the dependence of the films from the nineties on Hollywood plots since the 1990s. *Anjam* (Consequence, 1994) is partial reconstitution of *Awakenings*; *Darr* (Fear, 1993) – to which this article will soon return, is close to *Dead Calm*; *Sadak* (The Road, 1991) a desperate takeoff from *Lethal Weapon*, *Cyborg* and *Taxi Driver*; *Hum Rahi Pyar Ke* (On the Path of Love, 1993) is *Houseboat* with the houseboat gone missing.

What, however, is more interesting in the emergent dichotomy is a transforming attitude towards female sexuality, that increasingly, since the nineties, attempt to redefine the limits of feminine desire and question the traditional assumptions about its allure. It is a transformation that fits in with the changing attitudes of a significant section of the audience, who are women in their late teens and twenties, completely immersed in the culture of jeans and spaghetti straps and reinterpreting physical exposure as enabling, rather than commodifying. Mishra's comments on the questions of justice, self-empowerment, representation, and equal opportunity are now directed in some of these films at exploring what it may mean in terms of feminine desire and significantly, the cultural markers of the traditional Westernized Vamp (cigarette-smoking, asset-flaunting, and leg spreading) are now quite often shifted to the heroine, whose claim to purity (translated earlier in terms of 'no premarital sex') is quite often suspect. Such explorations lead to significant interrogation of the traditional dichotomy between the 'pure (read heroine)' and the impure (read vamp). Whereas in the Hindi films till the eighties, the latter category is the repository of the anxiety about female sexuality and its portrayal as aberrant and socially destabilizing (read 'West'), the former is a transparent receptacle of a mythical, pure Indianness and Indian womanhood. The nineties inaugurates the New Woman, who in these new films is not only seen in western outfits formerly reserved for vamps, but who also throws herself at the scopophilic gaze even as she openly celebrates her own body with a *jouissance*, without surrendering her claim to the special status as the heroine. The symptomatic demonstration of desire, of course, almost never crosses the permissible limits of representation.

'You Can Leave Your Hat On': Wife, Not Whore

Of films released in the nineties, one Western 'product' does appear as a direct import, which, though not directly incorporated into the world of the actual film becomes a significant marker of the hybridization of female desire.

> Baby, take off your coat, real slow.
> Baby, take off your shoes. I'll help you take off your shoes.
> Baby, take off your dress. Yes, yes, yes.
>
> You can leave your hat on.
> You can leave your hat on.
> You can leave your hat on.
>
> Go over there, turn on the light. No, all the lights.
> Come back here, stand on the chair. Ooh, baby, that's right!
> Raise your arms in the air, now shake 'em.
>
> You give me reason to live.
> You give me reason to live.

You give me reason to live.
You can leave your hat on!

Suspicious minds are talking. That's right, they'll tear us apart.
They don't believe in this love of ours.
They don't know what love is.
They don't know what love is.
I know what love is.
You can leave your hat on.
You can

Kim Basinger performs a striptease in front of her popcorn-licking lover in Adrian Lyne's *9½ Weeks* (1986). The male voice of the singer and the erotic masterfulness that the lyric expresses, together with Kim's deliberate and explicit gestures, create a two-fold fantasy in which the out of breath male voyeurism within the diagetic gaze represents the explosive moment outside the frame. Yash Chopra's *Darr* recreates the same clip with a telling difference. In *Darr* Sunny Deol, as a husband cavorting in Switzerland with his newlywed wife, 'accidentally' chances upon a television broadcast of Kim Basinger's writhing performance in a negligee. The young, attractive wife turns off the television, but not before the audience has been sufficiently and voyeuristically permitted to watch, and instead of censuring him, she puts on a less contagious version of the dance (to an English song and *not* out of a negligee, but a male western outfit). Her very action creates a moment of semantic shift in which the unbridled sexuality of Kim Basinger's performance helps the virtuous wife realize a sudden desire to be similarly expressive, thus divesting the (western) female sexuality of its earlier dissolute implications. (Interestingly, this very same clip is seen in *Yeh Dillagi* (Bollywood's 1994 adaptation of *Sabrina*), where a brother replaces his sibling's business tape with a cassette of the strip tease, and we watch as the unsuspecting brother tries to grope his way out of showing it to some colleagues (our voyeurism somewhat watered down by the 'trick' played on him and, subsequently, the audience). However, what may be taken as the unambiguous representation of male voyeurism in *9 ½ Weeks* is rendered much more complex in *Darr*, in the Indianized implantation of the female gaze through the wife who discovers her own sexual fantasies through Kim, and appears to be no less moved by Kim's rhythmic gyration. She translates her pleasure through her subsequent action. As an instinctive response to this newly opened up erotic vista, she begins to strip flirtatiously, but never beyond the levels of decency, and the sexual play is strategically interrupted by a phone call from the family. What is important to remember is this is not a scene extraneous to the central plot of the film through a dance and song sequence (through which, in the Hindi films till the eighties, the erotic is virtually always shifted to the limits of the main narrative). Juhi's un-wifely performance is part of the storyline, as the audience soon realizes, and not a temporary getaway from it.

Darr was advertised as 'a violent love story.' It is difficult to say whether both the violence and the love can be imputed to the obsessed lover or whether his fragile captive has a share in it. Juhi Chawla plays a young woman stalked by an infatuated young man, who threatens her life if she dares to marry her boyfriend, then follows her and her macho (army-officer) husband on their honeymoon to Switzerland (Switzerland is simply a locale confined to a series of backdrops and pictorial settings). The obsession is all engulfing, and Juhi Chawla is a captive to his erotic and emotional frenzy from start to finish. The choice of cast is extremely significant. The infatuated lover is played by Shahrukh Khan, (also known as 'King Khan' in recent Bollywood vocabulary), one of the most popular male stars in India. Nayar points out that:

> It was the Chawla-Khan musical numbers set amidst the snowy Alps that largely garnered the public's attention, and made their way into film ads – despite the fact that Chawla is oblivious to Khan for the duration of the film. Khan's physical advances may be but mental fabrications, but songs in Bollywood can function as temporary gateways into a character's fantasies, whether shared by the love interest or not. So when we enter Khan's song, his fantasy, Chawla is completely at his disposal – passionate, responsive and smitten, and squirming seductively after him.'[10]

Khan is the lost, deprived man incapable of possessing the woman he desires, an obsessed young person thrust overboard by his passions, embodying the sexual anxiety of his (and his audience's) time. He is frustration sparked by anonymity. One might even speculate that he is acting out the role of the male viewer, attracted to and titillated by the movie actress persona. Sorely unattainable, Chawla comes to be both desired and despised by her perpetrator. Her proximity is too much to bear, and eventually provokes his violent attacks. The fatal attraction of desire (Shahrukh Khan) gets a stronger momentum in the film and Juhi's momentary surrender to Kim's erotically stimulating number becomes a strong though fleeting symbol for the dark, (reprehensible) desire that Juhi tries to conceal and harness behind the veneer of a virtuous wife to a virile and responsible, but much less appealing Sunny Deol.

In *Darr*, Juhi Chawla embodies the hybridity in the articulation of female desire. Although her sexuality outside the musical performances does not disrupt the sweet docility that she comes to embody as the wife of a socially responsible man, so far as the audience is concerned, her erotic buoyancy in those very performances with her dark and dangerous lover far outshines the propriety with which she conducts herself elsewhere, in the rest of the film. Interestingly, contrary to the situation of the woman in *Dead Calm*, there is no consummation of desire. Die it must. And whereas in *Dead Calm*, marriage is not the focus of the script (the visit by the crazed lover comes on a boating trip the couple is taking in order to get over the death their child in a car accident), *Darr* symbolically institutes marriage as the counterpoint to raging sexuality and localizes its significance in Deol, a benign but viable hunk, and a much less *desirable* option to his adversary: 'King' Khan.

What may this *mean* to the urban, middle-class female spectator of *Darr*? In 'Afterthoughts on 'Visual Pleasure and Narrative Cinema,'' Laura Mulvey analyzes the concept of character function in Vladimir Propp's *Morphology of the Folk-tale*;[11] Mulvey investigates the Western and comments on the function of 'Woman' as a narrative signifier of sexual difference as personification of 'active' (masculinity) and 'passive' (femininity) elements in the story. She analyzes *Duel in the Sun* as follows:

> In a Western working within these conventions, the function 'marriage' sublimates the erotic into a final, closing social ritual. This ritual is of course, sex-specific, and the main rationale for any female presence in the strand of the genre. The neat *narrative* function restates the propensity for 'woman' to signify 'the erotic' already familiar from the *visual* representation. [...] Now I want to discuss the way in which introducing a woman as central to the story shifts its meanings, producing another kind of narrative discourse. *Duel in the Sun* provides the opportunity for this. While the film remains visibly a 'Western', the generic space seems to shift. The landscape of the action, although present, is not the dramatic core of the film's story; rather, it is the interior drama of a girl caught between two conflicting desires. The conflicting desires, first of all, correspond closely with Freud's argument about female sexuality...that is: an oscillation between 'passive' femininity and regressive 'masculinity'. Thus, the symbolic equation, woman equals sexuality, still persists, but now rather than being an image or a narrative function, the equation opens out a narrative area previously suppressed or repressed.[12]

Tying up Freudian psychoanalysis with Propp's analysis of Folk-tales, Mulvey states that in the film the heroine is no longer the signifier of sexuality (function being 'marriage'). The strong female presence causes the story to be actually *about* sexuality and strives to go beyond the ritualistic closure symbolized in 'marriage:'

> It is as though the narrational lens had zoomed in and opened up the neat function of [...] 'what next?' and to focus on the figure of the princess,

waiting in the wings for her one moment of importance, to ask 'what does *she* want?' Here we find the generic terrain of melodrama in its woman-oriented strand. The second question ('what does she want?') takes on a greater significance when the hero function is split... where the heroine's choice puts the seal of married grace on the upholder of the Law.[13]

Although Darr's *status* as a heroine-oriented film is debatable, as the presence of two very celebrated male stars determines the cinematic experience, in a striking parallelism of narrative structure, the representational attributes of the two male characters, played by Deol and Khan, derive their oppositional meaning *from* Juhi Chawla and represent two different sides of her penchant. *Darr* thus becomes a statement on the woman's sexual identity, between alternative paths of development and Juhi's tryst is finally compromised by her symbolical surrender, from the point of the narrative, to the socialized identity of the feminine self.

If Mulvey's analysis is to be taken as a convenient point of departure, the female viewer of *Darr* will possibly be placed *more* with the villain than the hero and while, together with the heroine, she may ultimately acquiesce to the eroticism and cultural convention surrounding her 'look', in a transgressive move, she may well find furtive, surreptitious pleasure, given the logic of the cast, with/in the 'active' Khan, and, she *would* dance with Juhi to 'You can leave your hat on!'

Although parts of Mulvey's observations on the female spectator are extremely valuable, it leaves a telling gap in understanding the shifting economy of feminine desire in the present times, a point that is extremely important in the context of this article. The Freudian-Lacanian optique, on which Mulvey's study is based, freezes the set of binaries (active/passive, male/female, subject/ object, looking/looked-at) as an irreducible essence and disempowers the female spectator of assuming control of her own fantasies as actively erotic, sexually-charged creatures. In other words, the 'regressive masculinity' and 'passive femininity' recognize sexuality as *only* a male impulse, to which a woman can only claim unconscious trans- sexual voyeuristic entry. It is a dubious perspective in our times as women are experimenting with the erotic, and the experiential transformation gives them the impudence to contemplate a new aesthetic possibility of viewing; while the masculinist tools may not be dismantled, it may very well be disrupted by the insertion of a *different* perception of the female erotic not accommodated by the Freud-Lacanian theoretical slant. Viewed from this new aesthetics of voyeuristic pleasure, Juhi's interruption and simultaneous insertion into Deol's gaze is fraught with meaning. What the female viewer may see in Juhi's attempted strip tease is an attempt to arrest or disrupt the male gaze by divesting it of its clandestine pleasure, duplicating the scene in real life, depriving her wonderful half of the secret pleasure of seeing another woman in the nude, and thereby, drawing him out of his scopophilic fantasies surrounding the savory nudity of Kim Bassinger, even as she expresses her own dark desires, albeit in a half-playful performance.

One must also be cautious about overarticulating the exclusive visual experience in Hindi Films. Relegating the cinematic experience strictly to the visual level is giving the lie to a fundamental commercial principle that the Bollywood films have derived and accentuated from the preceding tradition; it is the representation of the erotic through the visual *and* the musical where the latter accentuates, gives additional meanings to the possibilities of staging the aesthetic excess (female body) through dance *and* song sequence. Songs in commercial Indian (Hindi) film, function as metanarratives, allowing the spectators to create meaning within the larger, narrative space. Consequently, they may provide, for the discerning audience, interesting insight into an otherwise melodramatic narrative. At the level of the 'real world,' the popularity of a song from a film often determines the failure or success of the film, depending on its mass appeal. The economic success is largely indebted to the 'catchiness' of the tune. Neepa Majumdar's discerning work on the connections between stardom and song sequences is worth mentioning here. She argues for a connection between the star system in Bollywood and the 'song picturizations' that take place on-screen. According to Majumdar, the very definition of the term 'song picturization' renders meaning to the image 'in the terms set out by the song'.

Majumdar points out that much before the Bollywood era, because of its emphasis upon song, Hindi cinema had always relied on the use of playback singers to dub actor's voices, and in the 1940s attempted 'voice casting, or the use of a singing voice that matched both the speaking voice and personality of the actor.' Later, and continuing to the present day, 'Hindi cinema dropped the practice of voice casting and created a new model of stardom in which both the on-screen actor and the playback singer achieve stardom with a split between visual and aural stardom. While the onscreen star may be cast according to principles like those of Soviet or Hollywood cinema, the playback singer, cast as only a voice, and equal to or greater in stardom than the onscreen actor'[14] In 'song picturization', then, resided the aural *and* the visual pleasure that gave Hindi cinema its unique nature. The split between the singing voice and the performing body on-screen became the desired norm by the 1950s. Song-and-dance sequences, which had already been part of the formulaic device for Hindi cinema, became one of the key transmitters of Indian culture even before the introduction of the MTV, since the music industry and the consumption of music through radio broadcasting relied a great deal upon films to package music as commodity. The 'extra-textual' insertion of the playback singer adds to the 'non-filmic investments that are integral to its [the film's] popularity and reception, the multiple positions from which its performance is conducted'[15] Therefore, a 'more complex knowledge is conveyed around the musical performance.'[16] Thus, cinema constitutes songs, along with other 'para-narratives,' as 'narrational instances of its own authority.'[17] At the same time, however, as Vijay Mishra states in his discussion on songs within the film, 'the song sequences (often also dream sequences) do permit excesses of phantasy which are more problematic elsewhere in the film, for they allow the continuities of time and space to be disregarded.'[18] Thus, Hindi film songs may be said to operate both within and outside the diagetic frame. The particular dialectic that exists between the two spaces anticipates a revision of the function of pleasure and its connection to the songs, and the corroborative visual counterpart.[19]

Tu Cheez Bari Hai Mast Mast : What the Public is Wanting!

In *Midnight's Children*, Saleem gives a very succulent summary of 'Hindi film' in his narrative. 'Lurid,' 'melodrama piling upon melodrama,' with 'too much incident,' a stereotypical Hindi film is described vividly in the rantings of Pia, the actress wife of Hanif, the failed director:

> ...[P]ut in dances, or exotic locations! Make your villains villainous, why not, make heroes like men...put in a little comedy routine, a little dance for your Piya to do, and tragedy and drama also; that is what the public is wanting!

The very description comes back in a slightly altered version in Narindar Dhami's *Bollywood Babes*:

> The one thing that everyone thinks they know about the Bollywood films is that they are outrageous, melodramatic over the top and unrealistic compared to Hollywood movies ... Bollywood films are just different. The heroes are usually good guys, the heroines are usually good girls, everyone loves their mums and baddies get killed or arrested at the end, after various *songs have been sung and dances danced*.[20]

The two excerpts trace the history of Hindi films to the Hollywood era within the fictional mode; while Piya underscores the importance of dance, Amber, the narrator in Dhami's novel, points out to the interactive function of song and dance in a Bollywood film drawing attention to the fact (an extremely important one) that pleasure in the context of Bollywood films is both visual *and* aural.

In 'Picturizing American Cinema: Hindi Film Songs and the Last Days of Genre,' Corey Creekmur condemns the colonizing tendency among scholars to compare the entire range of Bollywood films with the Hollywood musical. He points out that a song in a Bollywood film (as in trans-historic Hindi films in a generic way) is 'picturized,' which suggests that a song is served by the image and not the other way around. He points out to a very important feature of the commercial marketing of Bollywood films:

> [S]ongs in Bollywood films are commonly dubbed by 'playback singers' such as famous sisters Asha Bhosle and Lata Mangeshkar or legendary male vocalist Mohammed Rafi leads to very different marketing situations in which songs from a given film are more important cultural artifacts and financial objects than the film itself. This leads to a blurring of the lines between songs recorded for a film and songs recorded for a 'regular' release.[21]

One may remind the readers in this context that almost no films exist without 5–7 song and dance numbers. Nightclubs and dance floors at parties provide a very convenient site for these performances. Crooning and wriggling becomes, quite often, an outlet of sexual display. The film to be analyzed in this context is the 1994 blockbuster *Mohra* (The Pawn). It is a standard Bombay *masala* featuring stars like Akshay Kumar (as Amar Saxena), Raveena Tandon (as Roma Singh), Sunil Shetty (as Vishal Agnihotri) and Naseeruddin Shah (as Mr Jindal). Vishal is put away in the jail where Roma's father is the Superintendent. Roma goes to visit her father's jail in order to write an article about it. There some prisoners try to rape her. Vishal rescues her from them. Roma finds out that Vishal is imprisoned for murder. On probing she finds that Vishal had been married and his wife's sister had been raped and killed by some boys in her college who were under the influence of drugs. Due to a corrupt prosecutor the boys went off the hook. Afterwards, they tried to rape Vishal's wife and so on and so forth. Roma, with the help of Mr Jindal, the blind owner of the paper she works for, arranges a second 'trial' for Vishal in which his case is reviewed and he is released. Mr Jindal convinces Vishal that he should exterminate the 'baddies' behind his wife and sister-in-law's deaths aka drug dealers. Amar Saxena is a police officer, who is also involved in busting the two main drug dealers of their city, the evocatively named Tyson and Gibran. Vishal goes on a rampage, exterminating their agents, but Amar gets on his trail, although, by the time he gets him, Vishal finishes them off, mostly. Jindal now instigates him to kill the Commissioner of Police who, according to Jindal's version, is corrupt. But Vishal realizes that this is a setup and confronts Jindal. It turns out that Jindal is not blind and he is actually an evil mastermind who wanted Tyson and Gibran to be destroyed so that he could become the undisputed king of crime. Jindal kidnaps Roma, (who, of course, is now engaged to Amar), and is about to run off with her when Amar and Vishal, get together on the mission, foil his plans in the expected way. What one remembers the film for this immensely forgettable narrative, but its two musical items highlighted a very interesting aspect of the Hindi film.

Mohra packed the theatres because of one of its songs: '*Tu cheez badi hai mast mast*' (roughly translated this means 'you are hot (intoxicating) stuff'). Months before the actual release of the film this song was at the top of the various top ten or top twenty countdowns which became an integral part of TV and radio programming in India in the 1990s. Indian viewers saw fragments of this song every week. A regular exposure to these fragments before they saw the film established Raveena Tandon (the actress, as distinct from Roma Singh, the character) as the point of reference for this film. She was seen cavorting on TV screens months before the relevance of this cavorting in the narrative scheme of the film was established for the people who saw it. This was a process existing outside the framework of the film but it went a long way in making two associations for the viewing audience. The first was that the character that Raveena Tandon is playing in *Mohra* (later they will discover that she is called Roma) is an *intoxicating thing* (*Mast cheez*). The second is that she, Raveena Tandon, is a *mohra* (literally pawn, or piece on the chessboard).

It is the security of this knowledge, according to Amitabha Bagchi, of the assertive male principle, gained before entering the theatre, which allows the audience (or at least the male component of the audience) to accept Roma's sexuality and even 'revel' in it:

> Divested of all politically unsettling possibilities Roma can relax into '.. [the] traditional exhibitionist role [in which] women are simultaneously looked at and displayed, with their appearances coded for strong visual and erotic impact so that they can be said to connote *to-be-looked-at-ness*.' (original emphasis.) This fragment of Laura Mulvey's analysis (from her essay 'Visual Pleasure and Narrative Cinema') is not the only relevant one in the context of the two song sequences that we are discussing (*Tip Tip*... and *Tu Cheez*...). In both these sequences the woman serves as an erotic object for Amar Saxena on screen and the male audience in the theatre, which is expected to identify with him.[22]

At the most obvious level the song has a nominal diagetic purpose. *Tu Cheez*... is the moth-eaten Hindi film device for penetrating the villain's stronghold by means of song and dance. This is a song that bears marginal relation to the plot and is inserted into the movie a few weeks after its initial release to induce repeat viewing. *Mohra* has another insert which is called *Main cheez badi hoon mast mast*

(I am a very intoxicating stuff). Both the song sequences we have talked about are choreographed with movements, which simulate sexual intercourse. The first level of meaning is the explicit reassertion of the voyeuristic principle. The subtlest way of doing this is via body language. In *Tu Cheez...*, Akshay Kumar and the accompanying male dancers dance steps which are organized around pelvic push forward whereas Raveena Tandon and the female dancers tend to twist around. The sexual position being implied is the male dominant one with the man doing the job and the woman as the receptacle who has to be seen as enjoying what is being done to her.

However, the songs demand more careful analysis because they have more involved agendas. The spectacle is only one of the layers of meaning that the song sequence is made to bear. The other and more important layer is the text of the lyric that underscores the erotic performance of Raveena Tandon. While Bagchi's Mulvean reading of the inserts highlights the overt meaning of the performance, especially for the male audience, he leaves open the crucial question of female response (not the trans-gender Mulvean, but the feminine optique suggested in this article in the context of *Darr*). However, it is in the context of the female viewer that the significance of the two lyrics in the form of a dialogue becomes vital. Although the analysis of the two lyrics offers a veritable feast for the discerning critics, this article will confine itself to the analysis of the first stanzas.

Tu Cheez Badi Hai Mast Mast Tu Cheez Badi Hai Mast
Nahin Tujhko Koi Hosh Hosh Uspar Joban Ka Josh Josh
Nahin Tera Koi Dosh Dosh Madhosh Hai Tu Har Vakt Vakt
Tu Cheez Badi Hai Mast Mast...
Aashiq Hai Tera Naam Naam Dil Lena Tera Kaam Kaam
Meri Baahen Mat Thaam Thaam Badnaam Hai Tu Madamast Mast
Tu Cheez Badi Hai Mast Mast...

(You are hot stuff/ you are crazy and intoxicating evey moment/ (Baby) you are hot/Your name is love/you are a thief of hearts/.../you are intoxicating/Hot stuff.)

The song's counterpoint is the feminized rendition of the same sentiment with a subtle but telling shift to the first person narrative that challenges the ideological import of the earlier song.

Main Cheez Badi Hu Mast Mast...
Main Cheez Badi Hu Mast Mast Main Cheez Badi Hu Mast
Nahin Mujhko Koi Hosh Hosh - 2 Uspar Joban Ka Josh Josh
Nahin Mera - 2 Koi Dosh Dosh Madhosh Hu Main Har Vakt Vakt
Main Cheez Badi Hu Mast Mast Main Cheez Badi Hu Mast

(I am hot stuff/ I am crazy and intoxicating evey moment/ I am hot/ / I am intoxicating/ Hot stuff)

The shift to the first person, while the words are kept in place, turns around the meaning of the song. The implicit reckoning with female passivity (You are hot stuff) is countered by an ironic discursive shift in which self-denigration inaugurates through transcription, a new, complex articulation of female desire. The self-denigration (I am hot stuff) is also a telling moment of feminine self-assertion.[23]

The juxtaposition of the nearly identical songs-but-not-quite may have an interesting significance for a section of female viewers. While in reflecting back the gaze Raveena is definitely fulfilling and vindicating the fantasies of the male viewers twice over, she also introduces female desire or female eroticism unafraid by the excesses that emerge from a project so deeply entrenched in a male view of a woman. The insert 'I am hot stuff' may be seen as mockery, a mode of punishment for the metaphorized male desire, without altogether shunning the pleasure given to the male viewer. The transposition by *Main* (I am) of *Tu* mocks the male desire by transforming its smut (both at the site of the song and the dance) by turning it into a confident, liberating gesture. It turns female sexuality into an assertive principle by erasing the Self/Other divide at the heart of voyeuristic pleasure. Thus the very act of self-denigration is turned into an act of self-assertion and the gyrating body of Raveena acquires a groundbreaking significance. As she reveals her own fantasies of sexual desire they become, through identification, the fantasies of many women viewers; her musical wriggling takes her up and delivers her from being expressed only through masculinist rhetoric and its audio-visual representation. She takes her own gestural and rhetorical stance, drawing her argument out to the most ridiculous extreme, making fun of herself and the male) audience at one and the same time. Feeling her power enough to forget her traditional, socialized self, Raveena emerges as a woman who practices a form of *active* seduction through comedy.

While Raveena Tandon's sexual aggression is ultimately contained by her ultimate status as Amar's wife, she leaves a lasting impression on the audience with the explosive performance in the song and dance sequence despite what Bagchi calls 'her coy and submissive behavior [...] in tune with the expectations generated by the way in which she holds out her *mangalsutra*.'[24]

The Model for the 2000s: *Aitraaz* (Objection, 2004)

In the world of women you either play by their rules or...[25]

In contrast to the restrictions placed on the heroine of the nineties, the films of the next decade generate strategic rhetorical means for upper/middle-class women for asserting their presence in the local/global scenario. While the earlier model teetering precariously on the margins of 'Home' and 'World', the films of the nineties inaugurates the woman of the world, who veers away from the domestic sphere and do not necessarily position themselves around heroes and realize their feminine goal in maternity. Further, this new role is beingprojected on the celluloid by a new breed of women, whose only claim to fame is not their halter tops. In an interview to Bob Garfield regarding the Shilpa Shetty-Richard Gere controversy on WNYC Radio, Tejaswini Ganthi comments on the representational status of Bollywood heroines:

> [T]he dominant moral values about chastity and controlled sexuality, that is problematic in terms of limiting women's choices and perspectives. But at the same time, there's the flip side of these films, which is that all of the women involved in the production of the films are some of the most independent and autonomous and liberated women in India, and they serve as some type of role model for young women in terms of seeing women as career women in one respect.[26]

Thus sexually provocating outfits of these women no longer signify pornographic contract. Rather, they go on to give a certain metaphorical meaning to the new *worldly* women who are not bound by normative definitions of what it means to be an *Indian* (sexually submissive) female. Although the male pleasure is still certainly the principal criterion, the open flaunting of sexual liberty undoubtedly determines a shift in women's perception of their own sexuality beyond the sphere of the virtuous and the domestic.[27] Parallely, a trend noticed in the Bollywood films of the twenties is a significant change in the visual techniques adopted in the representation of the female body. In terms of the economy of the female body in the celluloid market, films do acknowledge commodification, and privilege male impulse; yet, for the female viewer, certain techniques definitely signify demystification of the female body and female sexual identity at the heart of such commodification. This subversive trait is apparent in camera angles that reduce women to shapes and outlines. Some devices for achieving this effect are panning over the body, looking down onto a woman's breasts and fragmenting body parts, or inserting the lens, precariously, between her legs. According to Cullity and Younger:

> In the early nineties, the controversial hit film song 'What's beneath the blouse' was on of the first camera shots that lingered on the female artist's breasts. In just a few years, the camera has grown used to lingering quite a bit more. In the last decade, Hindi films have become much more sexually explicit, exposing more of the body. While the links have to be explicitly established, there is a general sense that the traditionally sublimated eroticism of Bollywood films has given away,

especially in musical sequences, to a frankness derived in part from their dual status as music videos.[28]

The change in the visual representation and the 'frankness' contributes to a significant deaestheticization of the female body and translates/transcribes itself in terms of fragmented female body parts and articulates femininity *sans* metaphoricity, *sans* pretence. What is missing from such frames is, ironically the woman herself, who gives herself to be looked at, provided the look is anonymous and furtive. In the maze of body parts without a face, there is, so to speak, no pleasure from pleasure of others watching her. The images being consumed are not looking at the voyeur. Because they have no eyes, there *is* no woman![29] The proliferation of such images in films (and video clips) creates for a new mode of visual awareness in which the definition of desire shifts to a neutral space that can be claimed by the new female Subject.

A Tropic Digression: *Disclosure* (1994)

Tom Sanders (Michael Douglas) runs into trouble with a treacherous supervisor. Douglas plays an executive at DigiCom, a leading computer software firm. DigiCom is about to launch a new virtual reality-based data storage system that is expected to revolutionize the industry, and Bob Garvin (Donald Sutherland), the owner of the company, on his way to negotiate a merger that could inject USD 100 million into the firm. However, while Tom is expecting a promotion, he discovers the position has been given instead to a new person, Meredith Johnson (Demi Moore), with whom Tom had affair years ago, before he was married. After her first day of work, Meredith invites Tom up to her office and makes a concerted attempt to seduce him; while Tom doesn't fight off her advances with zest at first, eventually he decides things have gone too far and leaves in a huff. The next morning, Meredith charges Tom with sexual harassment, and he realizes this was merely a power gambit to get him out of DigiCom for good; Tom, determined to fight, files a counter-suit, which threatens the merger, as bad publicity could very well botch the final amalgamation.

Halfway through *Aitraaz*, a Bollywood take on Barry Levinson's *Disclosure* Sonia (Priyanka Chopra) tries to ensnare Raj (Akshay Khanna). Once upon a time, they were lovers. But when Sonia, a pushy model, prefers abortion to motherhood, Raj drops her. But that was once upon a time. Now, she is his boss and uses her privileged status to rekindle the passionate affair. Under the pretext of a staged appointment at her house, Sonia starts to undress him, whispering, 'Show me you are an animal.' When he refuses and walks away, she screams: 'I'm not asking you to leave your wife. I just want a physical relationship. If I don't have an objection, why should you?'[30]

The choice of the subject and a locale that is not-quite-Indian, and a female character that openly prepares the audience for a shift in the definition of sexual morality advertise the changed cultural scenario India as reflected in the current set up of the Bombay film industry. The film, which may be taken as the third trope for the purpose of analysis, has to be understood against the backdrop of cultural and ideological parameters that have redefined the limits of the permissible. Sex is no longer dirty, and actresses, more than actors, are now more than willing to negotiate with the changing definition of the body and the moral implications of what they may do with it.

The Show Begins

As the camera zooms in on the title scroll, the introduction of the two actresses, Priya/wife (Karina Kapoor) and Sonia Roy/ lover (Priyanka Chopra), the erogenous zones of the two female bodies are shown as part of a collage, in which the lips pf Karina Kapoor and the lower torso of Priyanka Chopra constitute, within the frame, a code of female desire to be deciphered by the audience. The very fact that the wife and the seductress come together as disjunctured, yet continuous discourse on female body, the oppositional discourse on the good and the bad woman, endemic in Hindi films, is already destabilized in the title scroll; however, the story must go on.

Take One

The introduction of the narrative takes on, initially, the form of a kitsch, in which the film mocks the improbable and often unrealistic situations in Hindi films in which the hero meets his heart's desire.[31] The engineer (Akhshay Khanna) and the barrister (Annu Kapoor), looking for a housemaid and a legal assistant respectively, end up getting the wrong person. In a rehashed version of mistaken identity, the legal assistant (Karina Kapoor) ends up making tea and the maid refuses to work on legal matters and volunteers to help with the cooking and the cleaning! However, the film whose title *Aitraaz* (Objection), could be read at many levels puts a hasty conclusion to its own kitschiness to return to more important matters at hand, but not before the engineer gets to marry the legal assistant turned maid, in a 'closing social ritual.'[32]

The Show Begins, Again

A song and dance sequence on a sea beach follows in which Karina Kapoor, in her legitimized status, performs an erotic number within the same cinematic frame with other unidentified, scantily clad women, who bring back the celebration of the female body into the film with a narcissistic edge.³³ As these women wear their faces like masks, the emotional content of their performance is significantly undermined, the camera focusing entirely on the self-adulating, gyrating bodies of the performers/spectators that divests the pretty wife of the privilege of grabbing the camera even as she remains a part of the fetishized spectacle that is quite *openly* inviting to the voyeuristic impulse of the audience.³⁴ *The wife* is thus shifted to the margins of the spectacle that prepares the audience for greater things to come as she announces her pregnancy at the end of the scene and retreats for a while to the sanctity of domestic bliss.

Freitag's Triangle, or Mrs Sonia Roy

    Teri chaahton ke jal se -Bana hai, dil mein sanam
    Kuwaan kuwaan pyaar ka
    I wanna make love to you
    Gawaara mujhko nahin
    Aitraaz yaar ka
    Rock me baby, take me baby
    Kiss me baby, push me baby
    Rock me baby, take me baby
    Push me baby, rock me baby

(Your water of desire has made a well of passion in this heart, Love…)

Alternating between a female and a male song sequence this song acts as a trope for the usurpation of the erotic by the woman. She is female sexual energy and the desire is hers.

As the frame introduces Priyanka Chopra, a *male* dancer and a *male* voice announce the overarching theme of the film:

    Ho…ho…ho…ho…bas aaj hulchul ho jaaye
    Jab laher laher se takraaye
    Dariya mein jo toofaan aaye
    Talaatum woh kehlaaye

(It is a stalemate. When waves clash, cyclone it is)

Noticeably, Priyanka is *not* on the podium, dancing to the number at the initial stage. She is the diagetic audience gazing down, savoring the swaying male bodies with a mischievous smile. The shift in the privileged female status can hardly be overlooked in this initial shot. Although she does participate in the song and dance number at a later stage, her initial foray into the frame as a viewer and not a performer sets the mood for the film.

Likewise, the discourse on the seductress (Priyanka Chopra) in the narrative starts a deliberate semantic confusion that deliberately obfuscates the traditional moral concerns widespread in films from both the post-independence and the Bollywood era. Mrs Sonia Roy (Priyanka) is clearly not the morally repugnant vamp, who tries to jeopardize the marital life of the hero. Her moves are guided by her desire for the man she loves and her insatiate sexuality that must look for release in a man not her husband. As she is introduced to the audience, the camera celebrates her presence on the screen as an erotic symbol by insertion of the male gaze within the visual framework, as her new male colleagues marvel at her 'sexiness.' Yet, this gaze is disempowered as soon as it is established. In a dance number that clearly installs her as the Subject; she assumes agency of her own sexuality and, in a reversal of stereotypes, celebrates it, clearly disrupting the waiting to be 'pleasured' stance[35] as every moment of her erotic dance undermines the dominant male desire. It is clear that Sonia dances for her own pleasure. As a matter of fact, so far as the visual experience and the narrative mode of the film is concerned, the theory that there is no way out of femininity – except through the romance of the rebellious stance against patriarchy, or a periodic masculinity followed by a repression, is partially challenged, if not completely demolished. As part of this process of renaming female desire, the traditional demarcating line between the vamp and the heroine in Hindi films of the pre-globalization era is clearly erased.

It is common knowledge now that in a traditional Hindi Film the 'perfect lady...[who] represents the correct road' is differentiated from the vamp who on the other hand represents the incorrect stance of the transgressive female. Till the eighties, the vamp operated in the world of nightclubs and bars, was usually a gangster/villain's maul in bizarre western outfits, performing dances approximating the condition of the sexual act. As Rosie Thomas points out:

> Since it first emerged in the context of colonial India's fight for independence, Indian cinema, for a number of reasons, has been concerned with constructing a notion of Indian cultural and national identity. This has involved drawing on concepts such a 'tradition'. But a chaste and pristine India has also been constructed by opposing it to a decadent and exotic 'other', the licentious and immoral 'West' with the films' villains invariably sporting a clutter of signifiers of 'Westernization': whiskey bottles, bikini-clad escorts, or foreign limousines.[36]

The ideological implications of this binarism were sustained and reinforced in the vamp who became the sole guarantor of voyeuristic gratification of an audience, whose contradictory moral impulse was satisfied by the presence of a pristine wife/heroine who became the principal, if not the sole signifier of Indian woman-ness. Once her moral depravity and her 'sex appeal' had served their purpose, the vamp was ejected from the film in a narrative gesture that implied punishment for her threatening sexuality.[37]

The narrative and the visual in *Aitraaz* implement all the semantic markers of the vamp from the pre-globalization cinematic tradition and problematize its ideological implication. Mrs Sonia Roy, one of the Managing Directors of Car Talk, is no maul, nor is she the promiscuous female threatening social structures, although unlike Priya, she is always in provocative western outfits,[38] she remains a signifier swaying unsteadily on the borders of the legitimate and the transgressive, questioning and submitting to the demands of both. While the camera invites the audience quite unequivocally to shift its gaze from the indigenous Priya (wife) to the 'western' Sonia (seductress), the narrative demonstrates no intention of marginalizing her as a signifier of anxiety about her assertive sexual longing. Her primacy in the narrative is clearly established as she assumes control, not only of the employees of the firm and her decrepit husband, but also of the man whom she desires without shame. The symbolic defeat of the male principle is enacted out in the courtroom as Raj, the defendant, presses counter charges of sexual misdemeanor against Mrs. Sonia Roy, thus bequeathing the woman with the agency of the act. What is more interesting is that, in the court scene, as the wife, who also happens to be the defense counsel, draws the attention of the jury to the repressed sexual urges of the perpetrator and defines it as sexual deprivation, *not* depravity. There is consequently no question of punishment. As the visual narrative comes to a close, the camera zooms in on the lonely seductress, propped limply in an armchair in an empty room, minus desire, minus remorse.

The Final Take

A journalist stands facing the camera and announces to the diagetic audience that Mrs Sonia Roy has committed suicide by throwing herself off her high-rise apartment balcony due to shame and guilt.

Back To Bollywood

The somewhat abrupt and forced finale leaves the audience, wondering about the possible moral purport of such an ending and what it may mean in the context of female desire. It is perhaps in this ambivalent significance that the transformative location of the recent Bollywood films is to be located. According to Madhava Prasad:

> It is hardly necessary to list them, so widely recognized are these films, which, like teachers in Bangalore schools, are known by their initials. They have figured prominently in the emerging new culture of India,

where consumer capitalism has finally succeeded in weaning the citizens away from a strongly entrenched culture of thrift towards a system of gratification more firmly in its (capitalism's) own long-term control. They have produced yet another variation of the nationalist ideology of tradition and modernity, and, most interestingly, they have relocated what we might call the seismic centre of Indian national identity somewhere in Anglo-America.[39]

Many Bollywood films, true to their derivative taxonomy, have implemented methods of dealing with audiences with diverse cultural expectations, although the terms of their articulation have been not been unidimensional. Hollywood has catered to the need of a diverse audience since the establishment of the studios, organizing the films around genres, with its special 'system of orientations, expectations and conventions that circulate between industry, text and subject.'[40] It has helped the industry to envisage audience expectations and tailor the subject according to its ruling.[41] Yet, for Bollywood, the organization had to be implemented according to the complex demands of two distinctive systems of cultural representation. The symbiotic relationship as reflected in the films, is fraught with ideological dilemma, as it must fashion narrative strategies to address the unique Indian-ness that is the product of the MTV era. According to the complexity of the demand, western semantic markers must commingle with Indian substitutes to reflect the hybridized desires of the very mixed (inter) national audience. To quote Madhava Prasad, 'The desire for Bollywood is thus a desire for the reproduction of the difference that it represents on a world platform, which the industry itself, in its current reflexive moment, is responding to.'[42]

With an expanding market for *different* Bollywood films in the diasporic and the national market, the representation of the 'nation' and the 'national' functions in these films as a nostalgic 'pure' symbol of Indian-ness is emptied out of its initial significance. The 'seismic centre' of this audiovisual nation is largely located in sites where the meaning generated becomes a sign of the cultural continuities and discontinuities of the established systems of representations. These imaginary national and gender identities projected in these films are thus a product of what may be termed transglobal desire which, at the same time, must also destabilize a homogeneous definition of nation and woman by destabilizing established definitions.

In Appadurai's words, 'India thus operates as a complex sign in the Bollywood films as a 'synchronic warehouse of cultural scenarios.'[43] The register on which this complex sign operates has some interesting consequences in the definition of femininity and female desire. It dismantles the traditional binarisms such as: mind/body, virtue/vice, purity/corruption, passive/ active, love/seduction, wife/ whore, and the list may yet remain inexhaustible. In a global Imaginary where sex does not belong to the realm of the untouchable, the hybrid cultural condition of a number of recent Bollywood films install nubile women spinning to 'I want to make love to you' as the subject, instead of pushing them to the margins of the plot. Yet, the privileged, though understated half of the fast disappearing binarism (virtue, purity, wife etc), in this case, the sari-clad, sindoor-stained wife (Priya), though considered largely redundant to the narrative, lingers as part of a tropic configuration that must continue to assert 'tradition' as a somewhat unstable essence and crucial to a nostalgic understanding of an imaginary/imagined national identity. While Sonia Roy – the main attraction of the film – commits suicide, Priya Malhotra, an immensely forgettable spectacle, in a struggle of contesting representations, emerges victorious and returns home with her prodigal husband.

Chapter Five

GLOBALIZATION AND THE CULTURAL IMAGINARY: CONSTRUCTIONS OF SUBJECTIVITY, FREEDOM & ENJOYMENT IN POPULAR INDIAN CINEMA[1]

Gautam Basu Thakur

This paper seeks to problematize the construction of desire, subjectivity, and enjoyment in three recent Indian (Bollywood) films in relation to the spread of globalization in the subcontinent. Hegemonic expansion of globalization requires and is dependent on ideologically defining new sensibilities and cultures of living within a globalized universe. The fact that popular culture is complicit with this process is also well known. In what follows, I adumbrate this function and agency by focusing on the way this agenda is carried out within the domain of popular cinema in India. I argue that, Bollywood participates in the ideological construction of a globalized cultural subjectivity through the construction and privileging of a new ethics of globalized living; an ethics which is in opposition to established pre-global notions of cultural subjectivity. In considering the ideological dynamics of Bollywood as a discursive site for engaging with pre-globalized cultural mores, and for the production and dissemination of a new cultural ethics, I look at how the conflict between cultural discourses of pre- and present condition of globalization are staged, charted, and delineated for the purposes of reconstituting and popularizing socio-cultural and subjective sensibilities conducive to globalized living.

Jacques Lacan, in *Seminar* XVII (2007), defines discourse as 'social link' founded on language. This definition is particularly useful in studying how Bollywood forges connections between what may be called a pre-globalized cultural consciousness and what are represented as the ethics of living within universal social conditions of globalization. Since central to my argument would be the discussion on how popular cinema in India attempts to establish connections with the globalized 'First' world for defining an ethics of living within global community, Lacan's definition of discourse as 'social link' would be appropriate in guiding us towards understanding how Indian popular cinema functions to realign and reconstitute cultural conditions, consciousness, and contexts to meet the demands of universalizing globalization as a homogenous cultural condition. I elaborate this function by drawing attention to the 'forging', or suturing of particular and peculiar historical-cultural contexts with a globalized (read western) cultural consciousness, attempted by Bollywood for constructing a new ethical consciousness via a redrawing Indian cultural history and imaginary. More particularly, this paper looks at how Bollywood re-envisions history, global politics, cultural consciousness, and social ethics by reclaiming anew India's relationship to these. The character of discourse as reformulating and connecting the specific with the universal, or what claims to be universal, relies strongly on fictive reconstructions of Indian history and India's role within contemporary global politics.

The three films under discussion, Mani Ratnam's *Guru* (2007), Nagesh Kukunoor's *Dor* (The Bond, 2006) and Naseeruddin Shah's *Yun Hota to Kya Hota* (What If, 2006), articulate, beyond their immediately perceptible plots and storylines, a desire to reconceptualize and represent the Indian socio-cultural polity and subjectivity in relation to new forms of homogenous globalized existence. Interestingly, this ideological project is not pursued with blatant and trenchant arrogance – globalized existence and cultural ethics are not outrightly predicated as good. Instead, these involve staging of conflict between what are established as redundant cultural morals of pre-global living and a new ethics of individualism, freedom, and enjoyment. Consequently, what organizes the ideological agency of these films is an agonistic structure, which conceptualizes the itinerary of progress and development towards the ultimate goal of becoming 'globalized', both as a subject and society, in form of a struggle to escape social, political, and historical limits – limits which threaten the nation's success. Simply put, the conceptualization of a new ethics of social and/or cultural living, that is palatable with the modes of a globalized state of existence, requires the delineation of an agonistic structure, an Other, vis-à-vis which the itinerary of progress can be postulated. Thus, the difference between the present and the past, a globalized state of being and a non-globalized state of existence, becomes mandatory for imagining the nation as an international player. The distinction between the self and the Other is not made on the basis of morals – good versus bad – but mediated at the level of desire: the new ethics produced through an agonistic delineation of logic privileges the individual over the common moral good; at times redefining the common good through the individual ethical stance of having the freedom to pursue independent desires.

I must explain here the terms 'ethical' and 'moral' as I use them, following Lacan. While an ethical subject can be said to be a subject who refuses to renounce his/her desire, a moral subject is one who sacrifices desire in consideration of the others (Lacan 1997). Slavoj Zizek, reading Lacan's formulation, accordingly, argues that while the normative subject position is one of a moral-unethical subject, someone like Antigone, whom Lacan refers in his discussion of ethics, can be understood in terms of and as an ethical-immoral subject. As Zizek explains, '[I]t is by no means accidental that Lacan evokes as the exemplary case of pure ethical attitude Antigone, a woman who 'didn't give up'; (...) Antigone is not guilty, although she does not trouble herself at all about the Good of the community (...)' (Zizek 1994: 69). However, in this reading of the radical ethical attitude is also implicated the anxiety of 'excess' which this act engenders. This anxiety, as Zizek puts it, is of a social collapse if everyone pursues his/her own ethical stance by not giving up their desires. Consequently, restraint stems from the anxiety of 'what if everyone pursues their individual desires' (ibid.). As Ellie Ragland correctly observes, '[E]thics can never become a universal politics (...) because culture is an agreed upon set of exchanges concerning (...) [others] who have no *natural* relation one to the other. Culture, indeed cannot exist except in the conflictive terms of this imagined rapport *which is not One*, whether the non-rapport results in overt conflict or whether it remains denied or repressed. [emphasis in the original] (Ragland 1995: 156). The moral law of common Good is thus founded around the insistence of this radical ethics; and the law of distributive justice is established in order to stem the anxiety of the erasure of common Good. I have relied on this explanation of the terms to identify the ethical subject as the one who remains true and invested in his/her own desire in complete ignorance of others; while the moral-unethical subject as one who sacrifices his/her desire for the collective.[2] The desire of the collective, the conflictive imaginary of culture as in Ragland's observation, is, however, as Freud had shown as early as his *Future of an Illusion* and *Civilization and Its Discontents*, essentially imaginary. In the following sections I will discuss and illustrate this theoretical vector in more critical detail.

Towards a New Ethical Position

In a promotional video produced by India's leading newspaper house *The Times of India* on occasion of the 60th anniversary of Indian independence, legendary Indian actor and first man of Indian cinema, Amitabh Bacchan described the current condition of globalized India in terms of a Manichean struggle. In the video, Bacchan states:

> 'There are *two* India's in this country. One India is straining at the leash; eager to spring forth and live up to all the adjectives that the world has been recently showering upon us. The other India is the leash. (...) One India lives in the optimism of our hearts. The other India lurks in the skepticism of our minds. One India wants; the other India hopes. One India leads; the other India follows' [emphasis added]. [3]

'History,' Bacchan adds, is being made at this very moment – 'it is turning a page' and India is poised at 'time's great precipice.' Now, the video asserts, is the 'time to fly' and not look down hesitatingly at the ravine below.

This 'other' India is more clearly defined in the Hindi version of the video featuring the famous poet/lyricist/filmmaker Gulzar. This 'other' India, the Hindi version clarifies, is the India of superstition, poverty and a 'general state of carelessness' [my translation]. It is interesting to note that, the 'other' India is represented in both narratives in terms of immobility and stagnation and, thereby, in contrast to the exuberant energetic moves of the 'new' India that is ready to take the skies. What constitutes the degenerative disposition of this 'other' India, as the Gulzar version spells out, is a state of apathy and carelessness. Towards what one may ask? Surely it is the social problems like superstition and poverty, which, as the video points out, are the restraining factors hindering the full fledged growth of a 'new' India. It appears then that, what both videos emphasize is the historical moment, the temporal juncture at which the Indian nation state is poised, as that which must not be ignored or carelessly handled. This, one may note without hesitation, is a vision of history tempered with revolutionary fervor – a vision of history as a constitutive process, whereby a 'new' India can be forged. A 'new' India that has reached a threshold where the tide of historical, social, political and global forces have brought it – and, correspondingly, a moment for the emergence of the 'new' Indian social subject who must be a free individual but not apathetic to the cause of national construction. And it is this construction of a new Indian subjectivity that parallels and complements the reconstitution of the nation state at the global level. For what is being implied in the videos is a certain dynamism and agency required for constructing a new subjectivity. The role of Indian media is therefore not merely limited to the representation of social history, but entails the delineation of a new ethical identity, thereby participating actively in the organization of history. How else can the purpose of these videos be understood? These do not simply observe a certain historical situation but demands our participation in this moment of socio-subjective rebuilding. In fact, the website devoted to the videos asserts this agenda categorically:

'A two-pronged action plan marks *The Times of India*'s christening of 2007 as the 'Year of India' and the ensuing six-week long 'India Poised' campaign. Sweeping aside the euphoria and headiness surrounding Brand India, T[imes] O[f] I[ndia] will bring you a critical assessment of India's readiness for any serious claim to international fame. Along with our television partner, *Times Now*, we will pry open areas of public governance, infrastructure, health, business and economy, environment, social sector and culture, among others, to sort the stars from the non-performers. We will seek answers why, and *draw a roadmap with lucid action points*' [my emphasis].[4]

It is at this level that the Manichean struggle dissolves and the *agon*, qualified through the necessity of introducing a logical program of sifting 'the stars from the non-performers', assumes the form of a necessary structural prop holding up, and helping redefine, the new subjective and national imaginary and itinerary. But this agonistic structure of the two Indias' are not functional in terms of opposition to each other, rather they have a complementary disposition – the necessary evil of superstition, poverty and carelessness demarcating the limits of the historical situation for critically assessing 'India's readiness for any serious claim to international fame;'[5] and for formulating the ultimate teleological derivatives and trajectory of a new Indian subjectivity. It is this positive relationship between the two 'unequal partners' that is to be kept in mind while studying the dynamics of the Indian nation state and its cultural imaginaries in the era of globalization. The historical, temperamental, and ideological shifts that are often cited by scholarly work of Indian media as characterizing the cinema of post-globalized India should be revised in order to expose the implicit complicity that is being regularly drawn upon to construct the imaginary of India. As Madhav Prasad points out: to treat binaries and thematic conflicts arising from them in films as a 'transparent representation of some real conflict (...) is to fall into an ideological trap. For the construction of 'tradition' is part of the work of modernity.'[6] In other words, globalized India does not rely so much on distancing itself from its Other as much as it relies on this Other to help distinguish it. Though, at an imaginary level, this Other must be understood in terms of difference, its reciprocal function towards the imagification of identity nevertheless reveals the symbolic relationship structuring the Other to the self. The globalized vision, thus, cannot attempt to completely erase the Other, since its repeated invocation, articulation, and reinvention functions as a necessary symbolic support for organizing an imagined globalized subjectivity, nationhood, and existence.

It is imperative that, instead of reading the conscious agonistic narratives as representing an irreversible conflictual deadlock, we address how the agonistic structure acts as the symbolic fulcrum for organizing desires of global living. For a breaking away from the 'other' India does not simply guarantee freedom that can be understood in moral terms, but also the enjoyment that this freedom offers within the globalized context. And this enjoyment is not merely the enjoyment of unbridled consumption or promises of a globalized life style; rather it should be understood in terms of the symbolic function of the *agon* that acts as the essential factor behind this enjoyment. In this sense the films illustrate the essential quality of enjoyment as structurally founded around a prohibition (constructing jouissance as jouis-sans or enjoyment in the lack of enjoyment) and its role within globalization as fantasy.[7] What is, consequently, equally important is the recasting of India's relationship with her past – a reinterpretation of history and past ideas of freedom. What assumes the central stage here is undoubtedly the doctrine of individualism that seeks to redefine the relation of the 'new' India with its past. In the films under discussion, I explain the rhetoric of 'progress' and 'advancement' that characterizes globalized India today as essentially enunciating a culture of enjoyment and the global (Indian) subject as an individual having a right to enjoy. It is a discourse of freedom to enjoy, a corresponding image of the individual who is unconstrained from his or her pursuit of enjoyment and, consequently, the promise of a life beyond the 'precipice' that will inaugurate, or so it appears, to borrow Todd McGowan's phrase, the 'End of *all* Dissatisfaction.'[8] The films represent 'breaking away' to enjoy (*Dor* and *Guru*) and connecting with a shared trauma to perversely appropriate the self within a larger geo-political situation in order to establish sectarian relations with certain (read major) players of global politics thus fostering a sense of enjoyment in terms of belonging (*Yun Hota to Kya Hota*).

Enjoyment as the New Ethics of Global Living

Nagesh Kukunoor's *Dor* (literally translated as 'Strings of Bond') is a story about two women – Zeenat and Meera. Zeenat is a fiercely independent Muslim girl from the north Indian state of Himachal Pradesh; while Meera is a demure Hindu girl from Rajasthan. They are both from and married into lower middle class families, and both their husbands go off to work in Saudi Arabia for a better future. Till this point in the film there is no connection between the two families. However, in circumstances that remain unresolved, Meera's husband, Shunkur, is killed after falling off from his apartment balcony. It is brought to light then to Zeenat that her husband, Amir, has been indicted in Shunkur's murder since they both shared an apartment. The Indian Foreign Office informs Zeenat's family that Saudi law has sentenced Amir to death and only a mercy petition signed by the victim's widow can assure Amir's release. Zeenat sets out in search for Meera with the hope of convincing her to sign the petition. Meanwhile, Meera's life as a widow in a traditional and orthodox Hindu family has been reduced to staying within the four walls and doing regular household chores. She misses her freedom and, most of all, dancing. But, when the two women finally meet, friendship grows between them, and Zeenat succeeds in convincing Meera that enjoying should have nothing to do with the death of the husband over which she (Meera) had no control. Their friendship brings out the missing part in each woman's personality – Zeenat realizes the helplessness of losing one's husband; while Meera begins to question her own restraint and socio-cultural confinement. Infused with Zeenat's inimitable individuality, Meera begins to question the customary prohibitions that had been imposed upon her following widowhood. But Zeenat finds herself confronted with an impossible conundrum. She cannot reveal to Meera her motivation for visiting Rajasthan without risking the loss of friendship. At the same time she is pressed by the fact that if she fails to disclose everything to Meera and procure her signature on the mercy petition quickly, the death sentence on Amir may be carried out. When Zeenat finally tells the truth about her visit Meera she is shocked, feels betrayed, and refuses to sign the *maafinama* (statement of forgiveness). Zeenat though initially hurt, eventually accepts this and decides to leave Rajasthan. Meera, however, on returning home discovers that her in-laws were planning to sell her off to a rich businessman for money. On protesting she is locked up but manages to escape, with assistance from her grandmother-in-law, and eventually joins Zeenat, who was on a train heading back home, to freedom.

The film focuses most on the growing relationship between the two women and on Meera's gradual realization that marriage is not the only defining relationship in a woman's life. Meera realizes that traditional classification of a woman's life into daughter, wife, and mother, represses any life the woman as an individual may have outside of these roles. And it is this individual, her desires and freedom to enjoy life, which is emphasized in the film. Though the film's critique of traditional values and mind frame is nothing new, its emphasis on 'freedom to enjoy' as resistance to this orthodox compartmentalization of a woman is completely original. 'Enjoyment,' it appears from the film, means being able to jive to popular music, wear fashionable clothes, and live a certain life of fantasy, the coordinates of which are provided by Zeenat (to Meera) clothed in rhetoric of individual freedom and human dignity. The free subject, the subject who breaks out of defunct cultural values, is thus essentially a subject who participates in the circulation of the globalized world markets. The fact that old cultural values cannot exist in contemporary society is emphasized throughout the film. This discourse is carried out through the staging of Zeenat as the representative of new mores of living to Meera's cloistered existence.

In context of the contemporary world, the critique of social customs assumes a very different perspective. Unlike earlier films like *Arth* (The Meaning, 1982) or *Mandi* (Market, 1983), where orthodox social customs were shown as a pervasive social malaise, Kukunoor's *Dor* shows Meera's family as an aberration, a lack in the modern social world that needs to stitched up through Meera's adoption of a position within the circulatory system of enjoyment. What governs the ideology of social critique in *Dor* is, thus, a necessary co-option of the values of the market which insists unbridled enjoyment and consumption over a reclusive existence. What is not developed enough, however, is a critique of the orthodox values as morally and logically unjustifiable. Instead, the critique is founded around bringing the subject out of prohibition and into circulation. Just as the mercy petition functions as a metaphoric representation of returning Amir to free society, of not holding back anguish and anger against a person who may or may not be responsible for a crime, similarly, Meera's eventual emancipation is in reality a breaking away from the anguish of loss and restraint. In fact, Meera's return to life and living as an individual is metaphorically tied up with her signing the mercy petition and forgiving Amir. It signifies the return of Meera to a life free from pent up emotions and grievances.

Zeenat's ideological role, however, is not limited to her ability of convincing Meera about the necessity of not withdrawing from life. Zeenat functions to fill the gap in Meera's life that had been opened up by the death of her husband. She embodies and idealizes through her rhetoric of freedom and dignity a fantasy of liberated living, which allows Meera to question the prohibitive existence she was suffering following Shunkar's death. Yet, the ethical positions of these two subjects are differently implicated in their respective desires. As audiences we are aware from the begining that Zeenat's agency in Meera's life, or as Meera sees it till the point she is asked to sign the mercy petition, is organized around Zeenat's own desire to release Amir from the Saudi prison. Yet, we are never inclined to assess her negatively even though we are acutely conscious of Zeenat's ulterior motive in befriending Meera. Zeenat's desire to 'save' Amir does not color her liberatory function as hypocritical, instead the desire to 'return' Amir into circulation and guide Meera back into a life of enjoyment, hence (again) circulation, establishes her subject-position in relation to Meera and the audiences as rigorously ensconced in the cosmology of global living (of which the viewers are also a part). For the audiences the hidden motif of Zeenat's befriending Meera does not constitute a moral-ethical scruple. It appears that both her ethical position, as one who wants to save her husband (a traditional imaginary of the Indian woman), and her symbolic role, in motivating Meera to free herself from the prejudiced customs of widowhood, map seamlessly onto each other effectively establishing the cultural fantasy of global living. This fantasy, though fissured by Zeenat's own complicity with the role of the committed wife who wants to rescue her husband at all costs, does not disturb audience response. Nor does it compromise the ethical emphasis on the 'freedom to enjoy' and follow one's desire as an individual in the film. In fact, what conditions a sympathetic audience reaction to Zeenat is her fierce individuality tied to her traditional commitment to the husband – the new woman whose globalized sensibilities have not eroded her emotional ties to the husband.

This is but one instance of an inherent contradiction structuring the film and revealing the confused nature of the desire of globalized India. It cannot afford a complete retraction from values of traditional feminine positions and, thereby, struggles to balance it alongside the rhetoric of liberated globalized India. This aspect is most clearly borne out by the manner in which Meera's subject position is redefined as lying outside the agency of the phallic jouissance (enjoyment). The prison-house of widowhood that suffocates her existence is essentially constructed around customs that enact prohibitions of enjoyment *qua* the absence of imaginary phallic jouissance that the death of the husband implies. Zeenat in explaining to Meera that enjoyment is possible outside and independent of the presence or absence of the husband, who let's say can be identified as traditionally structuring enjoyment in a woman's life, opens up for women a position outside of the fictive constructions of traditional notions of patriarchy. This patriarchal position is still further abused when we see Meera's father-in-law planning to 'sell' her off to an industrialist to buy off his own debts. Against this condition of prohibition, Zeenat and the grandmother-in-law (who finally helps Meera to escape from her 'prison') offers a vision of liberation which, on the one hand, resonates with a critique of patriarchal values, determining its degenerate character while, on the other, ascertains enjoyment as independent of sexual positions. This point is further established through the opening scene which shows Zeenat and Amir in virtually reversed positions of traditional (read essentialist) roles of the Man and Woman. Nonetheless, the paradox returns when we analyze Zeenat's ethical position as a subject of desire constructed around the phallic equation – she wants to sustain her subject position in relation to the phallic economy of desire vis-à-vis Amir. The paradox is further complicated if we realize that audience empathy with Zeenat lies solely because of this ethical position and it is only this that allows Zeenat to escape censure for hoodwinking Meera into, what at least for the widow girl appeared as, uninvested innocent friendship.

It is not difficult to identify the tension within Kukunoor's narrative as characteristic of a tension within the vision of globalized living itself. If globalization, and capitalism and democratic liberalism as its symbolic supports, following Zizek (1991) and Todd McGowan (2004), can be said to be founded around the construction of an individual and an ethics of enjoyment that the individual should pursue, we inevitably confront the question of how far that pursuit can be extended in terms of morals or common Good. That is to say, to what extent a subject can be allowed to pursue and fulfill his/her dreams and what are the moral responsibilities of which he/ she must be aware. In *Dor*, Zeenat's ethical position of following her own desire for her own enjoyment encapsulates this dilemma by positing the ethical question in terms of a moral question as well – is capital punishment acceptable in our liberal-democratic age. Saudi Arabia becomes the metaphoric site for flexing out this question – it is at once the site to realize one's dreams and ambitions, but it is also the site of law which stands in opposition to the ethics of globalized individualism. In speaking of this, the cinematic text speaks the very language of human rights activists, who critique US-Saudi Arabia political relationship while articulating inversely perhaps the question of whether 'locales' like Saudi Arabia (and the Middle East in general) should be allowed to even exist within a globalized world. I find drawing out of this latent thread not only significant in terms of showing how Indian cultural imaginary is circumscribed by 'First world' rhetoric of global progress (that situates the Middle East as an impediment in its path of realizing the dream of a global world), but more importantly how the radical visions of freedom and critique of orthodoxy in this particular film, i.e. its desire, is in reality a desire of the Other.

The crisis of Indian globalization is in its fantasy of becoming an independent economic force since its desires, aspirations, and fantasies are all wrought in the hearth of the 'western' parties. In this context, the recent comment by Prakash Karat the General-Secretary of the Communist Party of India (Marxist) that favoring of Nuclear power by some members of his Communist party does not imply support for the Indo-US Nuclear deal becomes what it really is: a joke.[9] If India wants to stay true to its desire for producing nuclear technology, it is merely fantastic on the part of the Left parties to even conceptualize a resistance against US involvement, since the desire and its realization is not in the hands of India in the very first place. In other words, though the Marxists are morally opposed to any involvement with the capitalist-imperialist US state, it nevertheless desires to possess nuclear power for the masses, which unfortunately cannot be realized without US intervention. Moreover, the desire for nuclear technology is as a fetish – it really won't solve our power crisis but still it promises to grant India the coveted adjective of being a 'developed state.' This desire for being 'developed,' being recognized as such, is a desire for recognition from the Other. I am not suggesting that benefits of nuclear energy for the masses are false. But what is presented as the moral duty of the nation is in fact geared at gaining 'western,' as well as global, appreciation and identity. The fiercely fantastic and imaginary nature of the issue can be easily and summarily understood from the comments made by India's leading industrialist Ratan Tata. In an interview with Karan Thapar, Tata explained that if the N-deal fails to take shape it would not only be a serious loss for India's development, but it would make Pakistan and China happier.[10] The deal thus carries with it a baggage more crucial than simply the development of India, the alleviation of its energy problem, or rural poverty: it acts to establish India as a party and ally of the elite western nations, namely the USA, thus giving it (India) the much needed fillip for silencing its political Others. It is this unashamed desire to belong which more than anything characterizes the ontological crisis of globalized India. And it essentially exposes a conflict between morals and ethics, which is being surreptitiously veiled in the rhetoric of national development.

Individuality & the Crisis of Moral-Ethical Being in Globalized India

In Mani Ratnam's 2007 film *Guru* the crisis between ethics and morals is revisited and a reconciliation between the two attempted. Set in 1951, *Guru* tells the story of an ambitious and fiercely individualistic villager who first moves to Turkey and then settles in Mumbai, to fulfill his dreams of becoming rich and successful. Once in Mumbai, Guru realizes that the business world is a closed community ruled by a handful of rich and influential people, who do not believe in sharing opportunities with new players. Despite barriers, he starts a company called 'Shakti Trading' and climbs the ladder of success at a furious pace. It is soon revealed that Guru's meteoric rise from a poor villager (who marries his best friend's sister for the dowry he 'needed' to set up his own business) to that of an industrialist was achieved not only through hard work or merit. For on his way to the top, Guru violated government laws and cheated the tax and revenue offices. More importantly, in marrying for money he abused traditional values and customs. We are, thus, again in familiar domain: a conflict between morals versus ethics. It is important to note that, while in films of the 1980s and 1990s such a crisis would have almost always ended in censuring of the morally unacceptable nature of the ventures, in *Guru* we are offered a very different proposition.[11] This is achieved by reformulating a synchronic yet critical relationship with the past and establishing the prohibitive laws of the country as not merely an obstacle to an individual's dream and aspirations, but also for the masses who though passive are benefited from what has been a concurrent fantasy of globalization as an economic phenomenon: the 'trickle down effect.'

Though there are a number of instances in the film which can be taken up for consideration, I will focus on only two: (1) the opening and ending scenes; and, (2) the scene where Guru is brought to court by the government to face charges of evading taxes and violating government trade sanctions. The opening shot shows an aged Guru saying: 'do not dream, dreams do not come true, my father used to say! But I dared to dream' [my translation]. What follows is a depiction of Guru's life and struggle for success through a series of flashbacks. But this opening shot and the ending scene, which returns the audience to the aged Guru sets the tone: dare to dream and transgress if you want to succeed in life. The traditional image of the father-son relationship is thus revised and the son is shown as being successful only through transgression.

This metaphor is carried further on in the film when Guru is shown violating and transgressing traditional bonds of husband-wife relations for realizing his dream. It is however the scene where he appears for the court hearing that his position is resituated within an ideology that attempts to justify Guru's transgressions against government laws. In this scene an ailing Guru is shown facing a panel of judges. As the camera focuses on Guru we hear the voice of a judge who, in a distinctive anglicized accent, asks Guru in English if he is aware of the charges he is facing. Guru responds by saying that he is a common man and does not understand the language of the elite. The judge replies, this time in Hindi, that he knows his mother tongue as well as English and asks the same question in Hindi. The camera shifts focus and the actor playing the role of the judge is revealed. Roshan Seth as the judge is undoubtedly a face most identifiable in the Indian/Bollywood imagination as that of an actor who has played the role of India's first Prime Minister, Jawaharlal Nehru, innumerable times, from Attenborough's *Gandhi* to Shyam Benegal's *The Discovery of India* and more recently in *The Last Days of the Raj*. He is without a doubt the quintessential 'face' of Nehru on Indian celluloid. Following this we have Guru defending himself by comparing his transgressions against government trade sanctions by comparing them with Gandhi's disobedience of British rule. Calling himself a son of the soil, Guru announces with dramatic élan, and in midst of all round applause from those gathered at the court, that he did whatever he thought would benefit the masses and the nation. The court after a long deliberation unanimously decides to drop all charges against Guru.

This anticlimactic scene in the film presents the rhetoric of freedom and individuality as the necessary echelons for achieving the goal, namely the betterment of masses and the country. The scene is also interesting for two other reasons. First, in constructing a digetic space where Guru compares his actions with Gandhi and the Indian nationalist movement, and in representing the Law that prohibits and sanctions with a voice, face, and disposition most characteristically resembling that of Nehru, the film resituates Guru's transgression against the history of Nehruvian socialism, i.e., against a historical phase in which Indian markets were comparatively closed to foreign investments and free trade. Guru's defense of his 'violations' is a discourse on free trade which proclaims an individual as free to pursue his dreams and trade without constricting laws or state paternalism, or, as the opening scene depicts, the father. While the father is represented as stuck in one place the son travels round the world chasing his dream and succeeds in leaving behind his humble origins and establishing himself as an industrialist. This equation of success with movement leads us back to the 'India Poised' videos, forcing us to recognize the subversion of futile state policies as critique of the old symbolic space and older Master Signifiers structuring that space. The analogous comparison with Gandhi attributes to this discourse a highly emotional justification and logic of disobeying all forms of rigid social laws that jeopardize the emancipation of the masses. It also functions to act as the new symbolic support vis-à-vis which the new symbolic order with Guru as its representative gains validity. The liberation of the nation and its people thus lies in freedom of trade. Government and state sanctions against free trade in effect become an organized bureaucratic subjection of the masses, who desire to move ahead in life and who, as the film puts it very clearly through Guru's defense speech in the court room, demands their rights to enjoy their lives as they want. In this particular case it is the enjoyment of the profits earned by Guru's ventures. What as a consequence is brushed under the carpet are the allegations of trade violation and tax evasion. Guru's ethical act of following his dream and desire reconstitutes the moral framework in alignment with the trickle down theory and, consequently, identifies pre-globalization state policies as anti-democratic.

What is represented in both the films is a demand for a society with complete absence of prohibition and a culture of enjoyment – a culture and subjectivity not restrained by either tradition or State, social customs or commercial regulations. Here I return to the point that, recent Bollywood films discourse and popularize freedom as essentially a freedom to enjoy. Critics studying the phenomenon of globalization in 'western societies,' especially the United States, have been arguing that what characterizes this phase of capitalist development is, to quote Slavoj Zizek, the 'prohibition of prohibition,' and, to quote Todd McGowan (2004), aligned with a 'command to enjoy' and pursue enjoyment. Both McGowan and Zizek, and others like Salecl, Dolar, Zupancic, Juliet Flower MacCannell, have been studying globalization through its manifestation at the level of material discourses and its agency in terms of Lacanian psychoanalytic discourse. Their works have repeatedly emphasized how a tectonic shift has transformed a Weberian capitalist culture into a culture of enjoyment. As McGowan writes, 'today, in the midst of a full-fledged consumer culture, we are surrounded everywhere by the demand that we maximize our enjoyment, this represents a significant departure from the way in which society has traditionally been organized.'[12] The problem stems from this shift in the ideology of global capital that attempts to shape contemporary societies not in terms of a prohibition of private enjoyment but instead commands enjoyment whereby 'private enjoyment becomes of paramount importance (...) and even acquires the status of a duty.'[13] The ethical pursuit of desire/enjoyment that was earlier the 'preserve of a few 'heroes''[14] who like Antigone were figures of tragic proportions, has today in the era of globalization become a duty for the ordinary people. It is most interesting to see how this culture of enjoyment maps onto and lends itself to a study of the representation and discourse of popular films in India today. While studies on the nature of transition from a feudal-moral set up to a middle-class capitalist ideology in Indian cinema has been brilliantly pursued by scholars like Madhav Prasad (1998), Jyotika Virdi (2003), and Sumita S Chakravarty (1993), I believe it is imperative that we recognize the more recent ideological shifts within capitalism and the cultural context/s these stimulate consequently in Indian film.[15]

The Desire to Belong, the Anxiety of Belonging

Naseruddin Shah's first directorial venture, *Yun Hota to Kya Hota* (2007) [literally translated, 'What If This Happened'], displays the real agency governing the fantasy of globalization by representing the desire to belong with the 'First' world. The film is made up of four different stories about four different families whose members travel towards the US on very different reasons. Their lives come together only through a historical event which binds them together as victims and audiences of the event. The characters share, experience, and suffer the same fate – they all stand affected in various ways by the September 11 attacks. Though the death of peoples of diverse nationalities in the September 11 attacks, especially on the World Trade Center, is a fact, what this film reproduces is the desire to belong on the side of the victims and construct September 11 not only as part of American history but also Indian and/or global. The deaths of the Indian characters in the attacks expose a perverse desire to share the trauma that befell Americans and reconstitute the position of the Indian nation state in alignment with this attack, which has been termed as an assault on every free, liberal, democratic nation. In representing the trauma as transnational, the film reveals the urgency to step onto a historical platform that would define it (the Indian nation) as having experienced the same trauma and thus as belonging to that select group of nations who stand in opposition to and in threat of being terrorized, for their liberal democratic models, by fundamentalist terrorist groups. What we have here in effect is a brilliant illustration, again, of the Lacanian maxim: desire is the desire of the Other.[16]

The desire to belong through the sharing of a common trauma is nonetheless fantastic as the title of the film itself suggests. However, it is important, to note, that the individual stories in the film are not only overshadowed by the 9/11 events, but the entire narrative direction from the very beginning is geared towards this fateful end. The characters and their lives function merely to add depth to our sympathies, to drive home the impression of how common people died in these attacks, and, most importantly, that these attacks were not something displaced and distanced geographically and politically. Instead, these attacks are envisioned, following the rhetoric of the American State which has since engaged in a war against terrorism, as being in opposition to freedom and liberty; and against peoples and nations who believe in these ideals. As audiences we are not only cautioned of how the 9/11 attacks are transhistorical and transnational, but also how it affects our own existences which are under constant threat from the terrorists who oppose liberty, freedom, and civic society.

One viewer, in her review of the film, expresses surprise at the name of the film.[17] She asks whether the film would not have made more sense if it was titled 'Yun Naa Hota To Kya Hota' or 'What If This Had Not Happened'. It is easy to identify her point: what could possibly drive anyone to associate one's self with a tragedy like the 9/11? But what it directs us towards is the perverse desire and anxiety that drives the film in the first place. The film's desire as representing the desire of the cultural imaginary also exposes its ethical position, which in the context of the other two films can be declared as the stance that attempts to reconcile itself with a moral framework through the rhetoric of greater good. If the four families who suffer on the day of the attacks enable the film to enunciate the cultural desire to belong, it also articulates this ethical position as embedded in a moral vision of all round good. The fantasy to belong with the victims of the 9/11 attacks demonstrates the construction of a national imaginary against the attackers.

This film returns us to the consideration of how globalized Indian cinema is working towards imagining new ethical positions and balancing them alongside the rhetoric of moral good. One is thus hardly surprised to discover this same rhetoric being employed by the ruling Marxist government of Bengal in their 'land grabbing' ventures. Defending 'industrialization', the Chief Minister of Bengal stated:

'Thousands of young people are waiting for their jobs. We cannot absorb them in agriculture. Another angle is that the second generation of farmers who has undergone educations, join schools colleges, they don't want to go back to agriculture. They want jobs in factories in business. The change is inevitable.'[18]

In the same interview, he further explained that the farmers whose lands are being taken over by the government will ultimately acquiesce to the change once they experience the 'new life' since, '[t]hat is happening all over the world'.[19]

While it may appear that the character of globalized India is confused it might also simply be the pathology of globalization itself – globalization needs to be reconsidered perhaps as facilitating and enabling apparently oppositional values, positions, and rhetoric to coexist and even appropriated for enlivening the ethics of progress and advancement. It is no surprise thus that the Marxist Chief Minister of Bengal, a state where the Marxists are in power since the mid seventies, can claim:

'I can't implement socialism. Socialism is impracticable. What I am doing here is just capitalism. *I am trying to use capitalism in the interest of the workers and the common people*' [my emphasis].[20]

What is crucial here to note is how capitalism itself becomes a means for achieving general (proletariat) welfare; and the capitalist ethics a tool for accomplishing greater moral good. I keep referring to the political situation of Bengal since it displays most candidly the transformative paradigm of globalized living that I have tried to locate in the films. Also, the Marxist negotiations (Karat's comments on Nuclear Deal and the Chief Minister's statements on industrialization) with capitalist discourse and globalization illustrate most poignantly the revised ethical-moral principles of globalized India today.

Conclusion: Towards a Freudian Hypothesis

The films studied in this paper represent revisionary discourses that are being reproduced at the socio-political level in order to affiliate the nation state in relation to global politics and the flow of global capital. But this reconstitution of the symbolic order in tune with the new ethics of global living necessarily entails the erasure of the old Master Signifiers that had held the old symbolic order in place. At the same time, the new symbolic order can only come into existence through the reconceptualization and /or invention of new Master Signifier/s to take the place of the old. Following Zizek's reading of Lacan, the Master-Signifier can be explained as 'that element which brings about the closure of an ideological field by way of designating the Supreme Good.'[21] The hole that the revisionary/revolutionary process creates in the place of the old Master Signifier is most apparent in the court room scene in *Guru*, but only through the agency of the reconstitution of a new Signifier – the alliance that is set up between Gandhian civil disobedience and Guru's own transgressions. The new Master Signifier is fabricated through a revisionary reading and interpretation of history. In *Dor* similarly what comes to occupy the position of the Signifier is 'enjoyment'; while in *Yun Hota To Kya Hota* it is the event of 9/11 or the 9/11 as an 'event'. These Master Signifiers reconstitute the (new) globalized symbolic order and exposit the function and field of the new ethics of global living. The moment of this (re)constitution is also the moment of alienation of the subject in relation to a limit that the Master Signifier consecrates at the instant of its edification. The revisionary signifiers that occupy the place of the hole, which emerges in the process of resymbolization, while moving from an old symbolic order to a new one, also institutes the limits of subjectivity by delineating precise symbolic-imaginary relations with these signifiers. These signifiers (9/11; enjoyment; Gandhian disobedience) ratify the very existence of the symbolic order and exemplify the structural impasse that their transgression, avoidance, or erasure would variously inaugurate. The possibilities of enjoyment, individualism, and belonging that these signifiers stage through their respective roles in organizing the new globalized symbolic order are, therefore, tangible only in terms of an absence, which is rendered present by their presences. The ethics of globalized living is therefore to be understood not in terms of a complete efflorescence of possibilities and potentials, but in relation to what is veiled in the process. The Master Signifiers in the films, as a result, emerge as captioning points (*point du capiton*), arresting the symbolic order from dissolving into nonsense, and as symptoms of an absentia that drives the arrangement in the first place. The enjoyment of these Master Signifiers is thus, paradoxically, an enjoyment of the absence or what the absence signifies, namely the Freudian death-drive. In other words the symptom as a coded message should be understood in terms of what in later Lacan is called the *sinthome* or a 'letter [signifier] permeated with enjoyment.'[22] The desire of a globalized world existence may at a conscious level be surely identified and critiqued for its excesses and ideological machinations, but at the psychological level it unravels its self as a symptomatic manifestation of repetition-compulsion or death-drive. Or, in Freud's words, the very life spirit of civilization – a conflict between ethics and morals, the individual and the common.

Chapter Six

RANG DE BASANTI: THE SOLVENT BROWN AND OTHER IMPERIAL COLORS

Manisha Basu

A little less than half-way into Rakesh Om Prakash Mehra's *Rang de Basanti* (Paint it Saffron, 2006), four young men – DJ (Daljit), Karan, Sukhi, and Aslam – are almost accidentally plucked out of their urbane, metropolitan, indeed remarkably privileged Delhi university environment to play the roles of the illustrious revolutionary quartet of Bhagat Singh (1907–1931), Chandrasekhar Azad (1906–1931), Hari Sivaram Rajguru (1908–1931) and Ashfaqullah Khan (1900–1927).[1] As the young students begin to prepare for what is to be an amateur documentary on the lives of these martyrs to the cause of national autonomy, the visual diagram of their own contemporary lives comes into contact with the 'quaint' lives and times of Singh, Azad, Khan and Rajguru – boys who were themselves no more than twenty-three or twenty-four when their paths intersected in the most volatile of fashions through the manner in which they chose to die. While Karan, DJ, Sukhi, and Aslam awkwardly grapple with the effort to approximate the roles of men who seem remote from them, in their lives, in their deaths and in their passions, what we view on screen in the first half of *Rang de Basanti* is the hesitant and stuttering encounter between two distinct visual worlds, estranged from one another by what appears to be an insurmountable chasm.

The encounter between these two distinct image-worlds is cinematically orchestrated through the figure of a young British filmmaker named Sue Mckinley. It is she who is the disinterested documenting eye, and thus a suitable conduit for historicizing a context that may not be devoid of history as it was once thought to be, but is nonetheless guilty of forgetting its past. Chancing upon her grandfather's old diary, complete with guilt-ridden, grisly tales of the time he spent as an officer of the Crown in India, Sue is drawn to an especially vivid account of the hanging of three young Indians, boys not older than twenty three or twenty four, yet defiant and unwavering in their stand against the atrocities of empire. Particularly moved by his narration of the revolutionary lives and times of these passionate martyrs, and especially surprised at the fact that no one is willing to fund a cinema based on such touching tales, Sue decides that it will henceforth be her vocation to tell the story not of the 'Gandhis' of the world as many have done, but in fact of other revolutionaries who 'do not sell.' With rather a high strung air, strengthened no doubt by the cloying guilt of her grandfather's colonial pen, Sue takes it upon herself to make an amateur documentary on these largely unsung heroes of the Indian freedom movement. She leaves London for Delhi armed with just an amateur camera, linguistic/cultural skills endowed her by Hindi night classes, and large dollops of moral indignation.

Once in India, Sue finds herself plumb in the middle of two fairly familiar, though contrasting images of a nation caught between attempts to erase capitalist-imperial histories of unevenness and efforts to write itself into the undifferentiated continuum of a globally shared neo-liberal present.[2] Sue thus alights at the Delhi airport to an impossible flurry of 'third-world' hustle and is the single white speck in a seething density of indigenous peoples and bodies. Smothered by the pressing attentions of swarms of taxi drivers and *coolies* shoving and pushing their way to help the *memsahib* with her luggage, Sue is canny enough to emerge unscathed from the onslaught of natives looking to make a quick kill from the foreign tourist. At the same time however, the young filmmaker is swept away, far from the heat and dust of such a decidedly third-world context. Closeted in a plush global-metropolitan sector of the city, Sue joins the ranks of young university students who loll in wide open verdant spaces, their lives disengaged in an apparently absolute sense from the sights, sounds, and smells of 'that other India.' This second is the broad context in which a young student named Sonia introduces Sue to her friends DJ, Karan, Sukhi and Aslam. More specifically however, the filmmaker meets the four protagonists in a peculiarly cinematic space, apparently a bohemian get-away for students, set against the backdrop of a glittering sky line, but itself dimly lit, surrounded by a placid body of water, and thus cloistered from the steamier aspects of the third-world metropolis. As a radical 'elsewhere' to the frenzied clamor and swooping mobs of the 'native' scene outside the airport, this is a languidly buoyant setting, peppered only intermittently with the sprightly movements of young, frolicsome, cosmopolitan bodies, some drinking, some painting wall graffiti, some swaying to music, and still others whiling away their lives in the very luxury of ennui.[3]

This is not to say however that such luxuriant ennui is enabled only outside the city limits. Instead, *Rang de Basanti* complements such luxuriance through a dizzying momentum of decidedly global-metropolitan MTV-style images which are the signatures that visually consolidate the lives of the protagonists. Paced as they are, these images signify an acutely desirable, if utterly inhuman speed whereby cinematic time congeals into the rigid contours of accelerated, yet at the same time firmly arrested tableaus of lifestyle. Such tableaus of lifestyle re-imagine, overwrite and transcode the contours of the city, for as convertible jeeps career wildly through the Delhi nightscape, destroyed jeans and colored headscarves satiate the screen in a flush of colors, and distorted city lights dissolve into a kaleidoscope of neon, the metropolis is emptied of all markers of asymmetrical underdevelopment. The sequences in which the four boys along with Sonia and Sue drive into the city are concerted through a series of friezes, one swiftly overlaying another through disjunctive editorial splices, and rhythmically intercut with the most desirous snatches of the aptly named song sequence 'Masti ki Paathsala' As the lives of the young students are called into being in a pulsing parallel to this staccato interplay of bodies, gestures, sounds and textures, the city emerges alongside as a veritable playground for the mobilities of this cosmopolitan *beau monde*.

Comfortable in the metropolitan globalism of such a visual universe, Sue recognizes, almost in a flash, within just a few days of being with her new found friends that she need look no further in her search for the revolutionary quartet of Azad, Singh, Khan and Rajguru – for '[she] saw the men like they'd leapt out of the pages of [her] grandpa's diary (*Rang de Basanti*).' The epiphanic moment comes to the filmmaker in the very heart of a typically musical-rhythmic frame, with Karan at the wheel of his convertible jeep and Aslam, Sukhi and Sonia, on their legs gyrating to the beats of 'Paathsala' while at the same time cheering on DJ who zips and zooms alongside them, racing Karan's jeep on his motorbike. It is at this very instant that, Sue while intimately participating in the pace of the young students' lives, but still watching them as if from a distance, sees DJ's urbane body literally mutating, dissolving, if you will, into the arid, sepia tones of the archaic body of Chandrasekhar Azad. Surprised as she is that the men 'leap' out to her as if straight from her grandfather's diary, Sue makes up her mind instantaneously. Karan is to play Bhagat Singh, DJ will be Chandrasekhar Azad, Sukhi will ideally fit Rajguru, Aslam of course given his Islamic roots, will essay the role of Ashfaqullah Khan and even Sonia, she believes, will slip with sovereign ease into the role of Durga Bhabi.[4] Sue's recognition of her characters clearly has to do with the affective pressure of image-worlds which have the ability to reterritorialize and transcode the sordid conditions of a third-world metropolis. But in diegetic terms, the filmmaker's decision is presented as a flashing occasion of insight, an intuitive moment of perceptive acumen (rather than a syllogistic rationale) which becomes the first contact zone for an encounter between the quaint world of pre-independence revolutionary martyrs and the remarkably trendy *savoir faire* of young, MTV generation coca-cola swigging students.

The initially gauche traffic between these apparently disparate image-worlds is expressed in the film largely through comic incongruity, and in particular through interludes involving Aamir Khan who essays the role of Daljit/Chandrasekhar Azad. In so far as his preparations for the role are concerned, Daljit is in many ways already close to the role he is to play, for he is the principal figuration of visual and aural energy in the group just as Azad, even though an almost exact contemporary of Bhagat Singh's, was widely considered to be the latter's mentor and a guiding force of the militant revolution. As he himself reveals later in the film, it has actually been over five years since DJ completed his degree from Delhi University – so he is in fact older, maybe even wiser, than any of the others – but he chooses to continue living his life as if he were still a student. Sheltered away from the big bad world outside, this he believes, is the only place where he can claim to be 'somebody' rather than just one anonymous face amongst many. Ironically overwritten by the megastar face of Aamir Khan, Daljit is at his best in precisely such a university setting, and he goes out of his way to ensure that by no conceivable means is he relegated to a place of silent anonymity. For it is after all he who takes winsome potshots at the student leaders of the Hindu Right, it is he who protects the token religious minority figure of Aslam from their barbed comments, he who bribes the police to stay away from internal brawls between student factions, and again he who takes the young filmmaker Sue decidedly under his wing, cultivating a relationship with her that in the final analysis proves responsible for the group coming together to act in her film.

Visually conceived much like the rest of the group through signatures of an MTV-generation life-style like destroyed jeans, motorbike gloves, and bright bandanas, Daljit is rendered remarkable by his use of the 'Punjabi vernacular' which at once sets him apart both from his friends and other students at the university, and from his own urban-metropolitan place in the narrative. Presumably then, his boisterous, robust and strongly rhythmic vernacularization of the united 'Hindi' of post-independence India should make it even more difficult for Daljit to have access to the world of Chandrasekhar Azad, for the script that Sue hands him is written in precisely that homogenous national tongue, undistinguished by the thumping consonants and vigorous meter of the vernacular Punjabi, a tongue more mild, and more assonant than that which DJ speaks.[5] Yet, surprisingly enough, and despite a rather long national history of violent struggles between linguistic regionalisms, this unique parlance resides very comfortably, and at the same time very consciously – indeed with something of an undertone of comic affection, rather than any strain of antagonism – alongside the standardized Hindi of North India.

Before DJ's tribulations vis-à-vis his script can come into being on screen as problems of enunciation, they are absorbed into an intriguing tableau of comic vignettes in which we see Khan rehearsing his script alone, away from the inseparable group of four. These singular rehearsals – given that Daljit's effort to approximate the quaint and seemingly archaic idiom of Chandrasekhar Azad and his comrades becomes increasingly intertwined with the banality of his everyday life – materialize in the most ludicrous of settings and indeed, this is in large part what contributes to its comic effect. For instance, while he is spending time away from campus, at his clearly rustic family home, DJ speaks his lines – for want of a better audience – before a cow outside his mother's cow shed. Staring back at the boy with her limpid, if vacant eyes, the poor creature chews thoughtfully, and one is sure philosophically, at her cud while the aspiring actor merrily rotes on from the sheet of paper in front of him, carefully explaining to this proverbially peaceful beast, the insurrectionists' intricate plan for the famed Kakori train robbery of 1925 – a violent episode through which Khan, Singh and Azad had assailed and raided the carriages of the British railways. In other words, instead of expressing itself in a manner immediately identifiable with his own person, Daljit's bewilderment, his difficulty at confronting the obsolescence of a semantic and syntactic world lost to his contemporary sense of being is transferred and displaced onto the supreme incomprehension of a beast with no imaginable access to the historical products of human language.

In telling his mother's unsuspecting beast of the plan for the robbery, Daljit brims over with a linguistic verve and resourcefulness that overwhelms realistic representation in the interests of language itself, for the actor clearly diverges from the grimness of the script to capriciously rattle off about how the insurrectionists might raid the train at Kakori while they gorge themselves on Kakori kebabs. Compelled as he is by the lusty cadence of the Punjabi vernacular as well as perhaps by a more recognizable universe of identifications than violent upheavals of the state treasury and gun toting Imperial sepoys, DJ alliteratively links 'Kakori' to 'Kakori kebabs' rather than to the train robbery of 1925. The comedy generated in the rhythmic alignment between 'Kakori' and 'kebabs' and the infectious musicality with which that phrase is plunged, quite unsuitably, into the semantic environment of revolutionary practice and its dynamics, are both signatures of DJ's initial labors and his irresistible impulse to deploy the stout tempo of a local dialect to tame those very animosities. Indeed, the same pattern surfaces yet again, just a few seconds later, when Khan plays with the word 'bomb' as he announces to the his mother's unsuspecting beast that the Indian revolutionaries planned to buy bombs and other ammunitions with the money they were to raid from the government treasury on the train to Kakori. Clearly unfamiliar with the historical burden borne by the word 'bomb' in the context of the militant freedom movement, DJ repeats the word a few times, lingering over it, massaging and mulling it for an especially hard consonance, giving it an audibly Punjabi musicality, wringing this terrible weapon of destruction for an entirely rhythmic comedy, and thereby familiarizing it to his own syntax of being from which it had once seemed so far removed.

The comic appeal of Daljit's rehearsals, stem as we have seen, from the incongruity between what appear to be implacable opposites – the obsolescence of the militant freedom movement on the one hand, and the novelty of India's entry into the undifferentiated continuum of a globally shared neo-liberal present on the other.[6] The non-coincidence is thus between the anti-colonial urge of nationalist liberation struggles and the chronological tempo of postcolonial teleology, signaling as it does an attempt to move beyond the specific conditions of colonialism and third world movements for autonomy. The post-independence Indian Republic was always caught in this tension between the chronological terms of postcoloniality, and postcoloniality as the political-cultural thematization of issues arising in the aftermath of the colonial encounter.[7] The resulting battles between tradition and modernity, nation and empire, east and west, and self and other were however soon to be rendered even more complex with India's emerging prominence in the global information revolution, its spectacular drive toward complete economic liberalization, and its emerging status as a subaltern military power central to US imperial interests in Asia. The rush to smoothen a lived experience of colonial unevenness through neo-liberal tenets of state like economism, militarization, and technologization decidedly moved the discourse of postcolonialism in one direction rather than another. This is why for instance DJ, Sukhi, Aslam and Karan can recode and reterritorialize the third-world context that they inhabit, inducting it into one uninterrupted chimera of supranational terminals for the mobilities of globally shared metropolitan desires.

Shades of Past and Sheets of Present

Yet what could be the relationship between this newly reterritorialized space and the remarkably dense clutter of its history, the wayward strands of anti-colonial, post-colonial, and neo-imperial urges that in a quickly changing context like the Indian one race ahead and slump back in an unreliable syncopation? How do the urban hubs of the Global South, cleansed as they increasingly are of the histories of colonial unevenness, once again mobilize a distinct articulation of the past? What identities do they deploy in these articulations and in the name of what political visions and goals? Released in theatres worldwide on January 26, 2006 (quite determinedly a Republic day affair in India) Mehra's film slickly negotiates precisely such questions, bringing the past to bear on the present, but in doing so, erasing all the messy business of history, and making past and present transparently meet each other on a single plane of normalized regularities. The film begins with an austere epigram that unabashedly calls for sacrificial blood, and for the martyrdom of a generation of youth in the name of the nation:

> Abbhi jis ka khoon na khawla, khoon nahin woh pani hain, jo desh ke kam na aayen woh bekar jawani hain. (The blood that does not boil even at this, even now, that blood is not blood but watery cowardice, that youth which is of no use to the nation is not youth but sheer profligacy.) (Epigram from *Rang de Basanti*)

The hypnotic lure of these lines of course counts on the commonsense of a naturalized desire to serve 'one's country' rather than recklessly lay one's life to waste. It also inextricably links the discourses of economics and politics such that to relinquish life at the temple of the nation is to practice husbandry, while to live life in the void of the national cause is to be profligate, squandering, and wanton. Yet without the valence and glamour invested in them through the distinct, indeed distinguishing voiceover of Aamir Khan, the budding thespian cum superstar of commercial Hindi cinema, even these otherwise seductive lines would have seemed mere platitudes, ritualistically monumentalized (in Nietzschean terms) in one version or another, in film after Bombay film.

In particular, being just fresh from the title role in *The Rising: Ballad of Mangal Pandey* (2005) a tale of epic sweep based on the life and times of the heroes of the sepoy insurrection of 1857, Khan had already proved that he could dabble in screen patriotism, for *The Rising* ends with Mangal Pandey defiantly walking to the gallows, his head held high in service of what members of the Hindu Mahasabha were to go on to designate the nation's first war of independence.[8] This spectacularly lofty role in *The Rising* apart, rumor was already rife at the time of the release of *Rang de Basanti* that Khan was to play martyr to a different cause in his forthcoming film *Fanaa*, an intriguing title denoting the key element in Sufi thought, where *fanaa* means 'the annihilation of the self,' indeed, of all that is contingent, through a frenzied approximation of the immutable attributes of God. Thus, even though *Mangal Pandey* did not entirely live up to the star's blockbuster standards, and *Fanaa* was still in the making, Khan seemed to have wholeheartedly given himself to the world of historical/biographical films, films of empire, and patriotic films, his increasingly conscious sacrificial screen persona thus becoming a further testimonial of authority to the call for martyrdom he issues at the beginning of *Rang de Basanti*.[9]

Khan speaks the epigram at the beginning of *Rang de Basanti* in the cadenced measure of the *ghazal*, that most classical of Urdu poetic genres which also came to be singled out, following the suppression of the insurrections of 1857, as the genre par excellence of Muslim decline and decadence. As Aamir Mufti shows in 'Towards a Lyric History of India,' with the collapse of the tottering social structure that had been the basis of the Urdu literary culture of the *ashraf*, or 'noble' elites in northern India, 'reform' became the slogan of what he calls the *reluctant embourgoisement* among these social groupings. In such a climate, the *ghazal* came to be considered decorative, subjective, and impervious to nature, incapable of the sober intellectual effort and didactic purpose called for in the 'new' world. In *Rang de Basanti* however, the ghazal-like rhythm of Khan's voiceover cleanses itself of this complex historicity, and instead, merges almost imperceptibly into the rousing pitch of a Sanskrit mantra. The notes of the mantra follow upon the caressing strain of the epigram and as they rise to their climax, the first image of the film – a figure behind bars, tinged in arid tones, and ritually washing himself as he pours holy water over his near-naked body – appears on screen. As the camera pans with an almost malignant silence across the gloomy outer surfaces of prison cells, moving away from the iconic figure of the holy Hindu, the lofty music of the mantra gradually fades away, and the doors of one of the cells creaks open to reveal another young Indian prisoner. Remarkably collected and poised despite his situation, the man is reading the works of Lenin.

At this juncture, the camera rests on the works of Lenin as something of an end-point, for beginning with the gentle, yet alluring assonance of classical Urdu poetics, transcoded by the resonant and almost hypnotic measure of a divine Sanskrit, and finally, overwritten yet again by the unwavering defiance of Lenin's 'Letter to the Tula Comrades,' the sequence clearly constitutes itself as a regularization of such coincident points, held together by the words of James Mckinley's Diary. Given that these words will become an enduring refrain to the larger design of *Rang de Basanti*, the Diary is consolidated as the frontispiece of the sequence, for in a dimly lit, perhaps deliberately Orientalist frame, as the young officer of the Raj audibly scratches away in his leather-bound journal, complete with gilt-inscribed initials on the cover, we both see and hear the lines he has penned:

'I always believed there were two kinds of men in this world: men who go to their deaths screaming and men who go to their deaths in silence. Then I met the third kind...' Sometimes in my dreams I can still see them making that long last walk. They never faltered. They never so much as broke their stride. But above all else I remember his eyes...how they looked at me. Clear, defiant, never wavering.

From Mckinley's Diary which begins proceedings in *Rang de Basanti*

The shift in the consciousness of the protagonists of the film – from an entirely buoyant youthfulness whose appeal lies precisely in its unthinking spontaneity, to a frugal wisdom in service of the bleeding mother land – was fast becoming a co-ordinate for the two long decades that the star Aamir Khan had by this time already spent in the Bombay film industry. Starting off as the boyish, youthfully impetuous face of the late eighties, Khan was moving slowly, but surely towards what could perhaps be called a socially conscious cinema, having charted along the way comedies of conjugality (*Hum Hain Rahi Pyar Ke aka We are Travelers on the Path of Love*: 1993), rebellious on the waterfront type personas (*Ghulam*: 1998) and more recently, the lives and times of new-age professionals calling into being a society no longer yoked to the binarized poles of tradition and modernity (*Dil Chahta Hai* aka *Do Your Thing*: 2001). If indeed Khan was to die on screen (which at the beginning of this scene, viewers do not yet know) then *Rang de Basanti* would bring his evolving star persona to a climax. But more importantly, it would mark a new cinematic situation in which *Dil Chahta Hai* met *Mangal Pandey*, the MTV generation youthfulness of the former becoming one with the historically specific martyrdom of the latter.

The opening sequence of the film however ends not with the death of the Khan character, but with the hanging of Bhagat Singh played by the actor Siddharth. As the black mask of death is placed over his head, and Mckinley ritually announces the time, his pocket watch burdened by this act of imperial atrocity, slips to the ground from his hands. In a match cut, time literally leaps forward – the flash forward indicated by the change from the sepia hues of an archaic world to the naturalistic color transparency of the present – transporting the narrative to the life of the young filmmaker Sue Mckinley who sets off for India in search of the contemporary faces of pre-independence revolutionaries. Despite formalistically comprehending their 'touching' martyrdom however, Sue does not actually understand that determined to forfeit themselves to the cause of autonomy from empire, life could be made meaningful for Bhagat Singh, Chandrasekhar Azad, Hari Sivaram Rajguru and Ashfaqullah Khan only in the way that it came to its end. As such, death was not a threat to life, but paradoxically, the fullest, indeed most abundant occasion of life, an occasion to be encountered as a loving, tender, even perhaps rapturous liaison. Indeed, it was bewildered by such a relation to death, that James Mckinely had written of coming upon a new and 'third kind of condemned man,' – a man who neither screamed, nor was silent, but instead met his end with clear defiance, never wavering, never breaking his stride. In the course of her quest then, what Sue McKinley is thus searching for is not merely the contemporary faces of antiquated freedom fighters, but rather, this unknown, arcane, and unresolved notion of death.

Bhagat Singh, Chandrasekhar Azad, Hari Sivaram Rajguru and Ashfaqullah Khan were sentenced to death and hanged in the tempestuous early decades of the twentieth century when the Indian struggle for autonomy reached its final and most bloody peak. Singh and Rajguru along with fellow revolutionary Sukhdev (who does not feature as a principal figure in *Rang de Basanti*) walked to the gallows in 1931, condemned for their involvement in the murder of J P Saunders, a deputy superintendent of the British Police. Azad, a master of disguise who foiled repeated attempts at capture, finally shot himself to escape arrest in 1931 and Ashfaqullah Khan was given the death sentence and hanged for his part in the Kakori train robbery, in December 1927.[10] Given that the episode at Kakori had touched the lives of all four men, the centre piece of Sue's documentary is to be the spectacular train robbery itself and she is surprised that her new found friends are not even acquainted with what grandfather McKinley's diary had called an episode of such great significance that 'nothing was the same after that.' Sue's high-strung indignation at her friends' ignorance of history is similar to her surprise when she finds that no one is willing to fund a cinema based on the tales of unknown revolutionaries like Bhagat Singh and Chandrasekhar Azad. Yet clearly, such indignation is possible only because DJ, Karan, Sukhi and Aslam (and even Sue herself) are too young, and too novel, their minds too much of a tabula rasa, to bear traces of the historiographic restorations undertaken and programmatically developed by the post-independence Indian state.

Much as the imperial British had to induct the 'history-less' subcontinent into a grand movement of the world-historical Spirit, Sue has to assume the role of an objective historical intelligence. As such, she is the one figure in the course of the film who is always in control of all recording devices, be it the movie camera, or her grandfather's diary – explaining to DJ, Aslam, Sukhi and Karan that in order to essay their roles, they must be able to think historically, and actually put themselves in the place of the revolutionaries so as to feel and act as Singh, Azad, Rajguru and Khan once did.[11] The boys seem to finally understand such historicity in the title song sequence of the film which culminates rather flamboyantly in the actors clothing themselves for their performances in period costumes hurriedly cast on over rugged jeans and casual t-shirts. Synchronically intercut with the episodes of Daljit's comic rehearsing, the song and dance number 'Rang de Basanti' begins by plunging the young university students headlong into the bacchanalian spirit of a country carnival, complete with the clammy bodies of bucolic wrestling feuds, the heat and dust of fiercely contested horse races, and the lustful gyrations of Punjabi peasants heartily celebrating the close of the local harvest season. Such distinctly local shades notwithstanding however, the lyrics of 'Rang de Basanti,' embrace a pan-Indian patriotism based on a shared notion of the motherland, visually orchestrated in this case through a dazzling array of long and top angle shots which recast the local, rustic landscape as a perfectly unified national tableau of fused ways of being. Panoramically orchestrating a veritable ensemble of unique textures, sounds, rhythms, and gestures, this extended song sequence moves quickly from the bodies of markedly urban-metropolitan youth licentiously invading the countryside – their furious automobiles powering across a bare landscape – to the thumping sounds of Bhangra illicitly mating with the standardized Hindi of DJ's script, and finally, includes in its sweep even the quaint pastimes of the rustic bumpkin as they become prey to the anthropological eye of the homogeneous pan-Indian camera.

In the course of Sue's developing intimacy with the boys and Sonia, her camera had been established as the principal instrument for transmitting and circulating increasingly hastened flows of aspiration between the metropolitan center and its asymmetrically related national peripheries. Leading the boys to their fated roles, this song sequence consolidates such currents on another register, irretrievably merging into a museum of national togetherness the urban figures of the young students with the totemic bodies of a bucolic Punjabi folk. The blending of such heterogeneous regionalisms into the confined boundaries of the nation becomes a cinematic metaphor for the way in which Daljit fuses together the two incongruent image-worlds he has been struggling with, to finally master the role of the revolutionary martyr, Azad. As the concluding strains of the catchy Bhangra score fade away in the background, DJ is seen as Chandrasekhar Azad, before what appears to be a large theatre screen playing black and white footage of imperial atrocities against the native Indian population. Mediated by the eye of Sue's naturalistic camera, and against a background saturated with alternating images of police brutality followed by news clips reporting 'casualties,' Daljit holds himself ramrod straight, his arms crossed under his bust, and with a statesman-like air, much like the archaic Azad himself might have. Yet, even as he performs his lines, the iconic images and newsprint that had so far served as backdrop, move almost surreptitiously to overwrite and transcode his venerable statesman-like body. Rendered at once strangely luminescent as well as darkly grim by the obsolescence of the images and words that inscribe his person, DJ now appears as a sepulchral figure, neither of the contemporary world that he has until now inhabited nor of the archaic world of early twentieth century revolutionaries; in short, at once radically novel and profoundly obsolete.

Who's Afraid of Radio in India

It is precisely as such a figure, that is, mediated in different ways by the technology of the cinema that Daljit is able to speak his lines to perfection – and this time with no hint of the hard, if lovable consonants of a distinct Punjabi accent, no bewildered audience to call into being an absurd situation, and therefore, no moments of faltering comedy. The cinematic frame, or more broadly the technology of the cinema thus emerges as that interface or that instrument of representation that can propose to dissolve difficulties such as DJ's, bringing into being a neutralized meeting ground for the two unique expressive worlds which have been called upon to converse with one another. Once the diegetic space of *Rang de Basanti* has arranged such a neutral zone of contact for the two incongruent image-worlds, the filming for Sue's documentary – the film within the film, as it were – takes on an accelerated pace. This speed expresses itself principally through a series of almost geometrically matched editorial seams whereby the banal, everyday episodes in the lives of DJ, Karan, Sukhi, and Aslam begin to merge increasingly frenetically with Sue's passionate documentation of occasions in the lives of the early twentieth century insurrectionists.

Immediately after the carnival of national togetherness, DJ and Aslam for instance are seen riding on what appears to be an old-world maintenance car for railroad engines, crunching audibly into large rustic hunks of rustic cane, and sweepingly viewing the vague mass of the country around them. The others in the group are also in this banal scene, playfully balancing themselves on the tracks and lightheartedly frolicking with each other, just before a train steams down the railroad. Even as the engine is powering across the screen however, overwhelming viewers in a remarkably tight close-up, it suddenly mutates, through a lap dissolve, into quaint tones of a rusty brown. The railway cars of today become the besieged carriages of the Kakori robbery of 1925 and the young people who minutes ago comfortably inhabited the present, are transported in full period-costume to their assigned revolutionary roles.

Yet, Sue's camera does not rest for too long on the hurly burly of Kakori and therefore on the ardor of the heroes of the occasion, for according to her grandfather's Diary, the robbery as well the fierce upheavals that came upon it, were after all only a fit response to the violence that General Dyer had unleashed in Jallianwala Bagh.[12] Indeed, it was the sheer malignancy of this imperial act that in Mckinley's own words, forced 'an essentially peaceful people to take up arms.' Sue's lens is thus urged by a stifling colonial guilt to plummet deeper into the past than even Kakori, and true to the spirit of McKinely's Diary, it lingers almost amorously over the terrifying incidence of terror at Jallianwala Bagh. Recycling a string of visual clichés, Sue's camera sensationalizes innocent men being viciously gunned down, human bodies rioting to set themselves free, women and children throwing themselves into the depths of a well to save their honor and orphans screaming in baffled horror. Despite the fact that the revolutionary heroes of McKinley's tale have no place in Sue's filmic resurrection of Dyer's atrocities, it is through the sweeping vista of Kakori and Jallianwala Bagh as one unit that her documentation in fact comes full circle. For while Jallianwala Bagh is on the one hand the causal link to the guilt of Sue's imperial lens, it is on the other, a visual passage for Bhagat Singh's decision to leave his home and family and join the revolutionary forces headed by Chandrasekhar Azad.

The points of contact between the lives of the students and the filming of Sue's documentary continue to develop unabated in this fashion until they are temporarily interrupted by the appearance of Sonia's fiancé, Lt. Ajay Rathod. Ajay is the soul of the young MTV generation, the duty-bound national patriot, who functions as the melodramatic fulcrum whereby a new age transnational youth meets a sentimentalized version of its own history. Having infused the film with an explicitly articulated and highly moralistic, if naïve, air of national duty, Lt. Rathod dies tragically as the MIG aircraft he is flying crashes into the countryside. In keeping with what we know of Ajay's person, news reports tell his family and friends that Lt. Rathod was an exceptionally brave man who rather than jumping from the aircraft he was piloting and allowing it to crash into the densely populated part of Ambala city, steered it to the vague expanse of the countryside, thus giving his life to save thousands of city dwellers. The paraphernalia of the melodrama gathers momentum from here on for after the saccharine state ceremony of the virtuous Lieutenant's cremation, the trope of martyrdom which had always been the principal strain in Sue's documentation of the past, begins to bear down rather heavily on the landscape of the present. When Ajay's mother – herself the widow of a martyred officer of the Indian army – and friends hear media buzz of the growing scandal around findings about the compromised quality of MIG aircraft, they organize a candlelight vigil in memory of Lieutenant Rathod, who is now constituted as an unblemished soul caught in the crossfire between sacrifice for the sake of a corrupt state and martyrdom in the name of a nurturing nation.[13]

Seeing the danger of such a binary, the Minister for Defense – who has already made a public address shielding the quality of the MIG liners and instead holding 'inexperienced' pilots like Lt. Rathod responsible for the accident – orders that the peaceful memorial be broken through the sheer violence of paramilitary forces. The scene that follows these orders is many ways the focal point of the melodrama for as a large mass of human bodies, suddenly struck by terror, jostle with each other to escape this unexpected show of force, the camera endures in slow motion over the brutality, as if seductively caressing the element of surprise in the shedding of peaceful blood, and resting with particular attention on the violence against very young children, irreproachable older citizens, and finally even the blameless figure of

Ajay's mother, who is struck on the head and goes into a coma. As the visual parallels between the carnage sanctioned by a corrupt postcolonial state and Sue's documentation of the imperial horror at Jallianwala Bagh become more and more clear, the figure of the Minister of State for Defense appears on screen in the aging brown tones of pre-independence times. Transported from the present landscape of MIG airliners, untarnished air force personnel, and protesting students, this scapegoat of the present political scenario is irretrievably inducted into an earlier visual diagram, from within the folds of which he orders his men to fire at Ajay Rathod, just as General Dyer had imperially authorized that innocent men, women, and children be gunned down without mercy and in the name of a secure imperial state.

Ajay's death and its aftermath thus appear at this point to be not only a means whereby young coca-cola swigging youth are awarded soul and sentimentally made aware of their relation to a patriotic past. Rather, it is only after the episodes elaborating the life and times of Lt. Rathod that the geometrically aligned congruencies between obsolescence and contemporaneity take on a different and even somewhat sinister aspect, one not merely being mediated by the other, but inextricably intertwining and becoming one with the other. In other words, no longer does the naturalistic color transparency of the present have to mutate into the browned shades of the past in order for the former to approximate the latter. No longer do the figures actually have to dissolve into one another, and no longer do the actors actually have to rehearse their performances and costume themselves in full period garb, for an anachronistic idiom to become synonymous with the idiom of novelty. Rather, at this stage in the film, the archaic visual diagrams called into being by Sue's documentary script snugly fit the present political occasion the young people find themselves in, so much so that one not merely represents the other, but in fact *is* the other, even without the arbitration of the filmmaker or her documentary apparatus. For instance, in a landscape outside the city, dotted with ruins, yet recast through aerial shots as a panorama of perpetual presents, the boys debate what they are to do about the evil Minister of State for Defence.

As they mull the question, DJ suddenly announces, just as Chandrasekhar Azad had almost a century before him: *humein aisa kucch karna chaiye jo use jad se hilade* ('we should do something explosive, something that will shake them at their very roots'). In her incarnation as Durga Bhabi, Sonia, who has been transformed from a jaunty young student into the silent counterpart to her fiancé's martyrdom, answers: *Mardalo* ('kill him'). Inhabiting the ruinous remains of chronological time, DJ and Sonia find themselves almost inadvertently responding to the crisis as in fact Chandrasekhar Azad and Durga Bhabi had, for the lines they speak have taken flight from Sue's script and become coincident with the emergent occasion of the present. Indeed, it is from this point in the film that the filmmaker and her camera gradually begin to disappear from the narratological terms of the script, even to the extent that they no longer bears witness to any events, whether the assassination of the Defence Minister, or the final encounter between the state and the new insurgents. In such a condition of perfect convergence, past and present can comfortably coexist, even without the arbitration of the documentary instrument precisely because time as a contingent medium of rupture and as the instigation to strife has been increasingly rendered obscure and finally even erased. In such a condition of harmonious simultaneities, Daljit can be one with Chandrasekhar Azad just as Karan can indistinguishably inhabit the same persona as Bhagat Singh. Similarly, the Minister for Defense of a post-independence Indian state can be coincident with the figure of the imperial General Dyer, Lenin's 'Letter to the Tula Comrades' can have the same transformative effect as Sue McKinley's indignant address to her young friends, and obsolescence can be identical to novelty, without any gaps, fissures, or pauses of temporality as distance or difference.

As the contemporary lives of the young people plunge wildly into the archaic pages of James Mckinely's historical document, the plan to assassinate the Defence Minister is hatched swiftly and even executed, at least in so far as screen assassinations are concerned, with precious little fuss. Not surprisingly, given the frenetic pace at which congruencies between past and present come to a head, the boys' murderous act of protest against the MIG aircraft scandal is immediately rendered afloat in a discourse of cross-border terrorism much like the killing of J.P. Saunders had been condemned as a mutinous act against the British State. In the aftermath of the killing of Saunders, Bhagat Singh had argued that were the revolutionaries to give themselves to the British police, the subsequent juridical process would pit their own insurgent rhetoric against the rhetoric of mutiny proposed by the imperial state. In other words, the hope was that since in this way language of government would be compelled to converse with the language of revolutionary protest, the idiom of the martyr would force its way into the existing legislative discourse and making itself part of the current economy of legalisms, perhaps mobilize dissent on a spectacular mass scale. In his avatar as Bhagat Singh, Karan thus argues in a similar vein that to draw attention to dissent as a viable politico-juridical category, the young men must be able to make a public display of their murderous act and its intentions. They must be able to bring about an exchange between the warring tongues of a corrupt state and its dissenting citizens, they must attempt to call into being a neutral contact zone for the two, they must, in short, be able to *speak to the state*.

The boys thus decide to forcibly capture one of the studios at the All India Radio Station from where they will make their public declaration. As they stride in, one after the other in a single row, they are no longer DJ, Karan, Sukhi and Aslam, but rather even without being in costume, even without being shaded in the sepia hues of the past, Singh, Azad, Khan, and Rajguru. In their by now completely transformed avatars as historic revolutionaries of the independence movement, the boys chose the medium of radio rather than live television as the technological mode best suited to a national address. This choice is, as we shall see, an important one in view of the cinematic encounter that *Rang de* Basanti proposes between an obsolete image-world of the past, and the radically novel visual diagram of the present. In 1991, three months after CNN's historic live broadcast of the First Gulf War, urban Indian homes were for the first time exposed to satellite television when programming from the communication satellite Asiasat – 1 infiltrated the confines of national programming by way of a messy network of quasi-legal cable operators. As the operators herded themselves into ramshackle entrepreneurial establishments that voraciously bred more and more of their own kind, and the success of the Star TV network prompted a large proliferation of commercial channels, this still 'disorganized sector' began to challenge the widespread and monopolistic tentacles of state-run television. In 1993, in an effort to clamp down on a mediatized space increasingly slipping away from its control, the lower house of Indian parliament floated a disciplinary Bill that it believed would tame the errant *cablewallahs*. The Bill was draconian in its declaration that wayward operators be held criminally liable if programs broadcast over satellite channels were deemed objectionable by a government official of the rank prescribed. Not surprisingly, cable operators, now increasingly in demand, threatened protest, and the 1993 bill had to be tempered before it saw legislative light of day as The Cable Television Networks (Regulation) Act, 1995.

At the same time however, just as national interests were in this way being forced to retreat before the insurmountable domination of transnational capital, Parliament was further rapped on the knuckles by the historic Supreme Court judgment of 1995. The judgment expressly declared airwaves to be public property and not the monopoly of the Indian Government, and thus made it clear that alongside the national economy, legislative traditions of discipline too were rather conspicuously under duress. Yet, in this frantic bustle around the cable network, radio in India had been increasingly left out in the cold and even though in 1993, All India Radio Stations had begun to allocate meagre time slots for Frequency Modulation, it was not until 1999 that government finally announced a new FM policy and with a great deal of flourish invited private commercial broadcasters to apply to Parliament for licenses. In this first phase of privatization there was on the one hand a vigorous discussion around further opening up FM stations to foreign direct investment, such that they could finally be unchained from the oppressive clutches of state license fees. On the other hand, given that the medium was still conceived principally as a portal for beguiling and 'false' entertainment rather than as a cultural-pedagogical tool for the wisdom of the state, private FM channels in India are still sternly restricted by the austerity of law, which did not authorize them for instance, to broadcast 'legitimate' news. Indeed, when completely in synchronicity with their revolutionary roles as Chandrasekhar Azad, Bhagat Singh, Hari Sivaram Rajguru and Ashfaqullah Khan, the four protagonists march into the imposing structure of the All India Radio station in the national capital, they tap, even if unintentionally so, into precisely these schizoid resources of the medium.

As a platform for insurgency, radio bears discoverable traces of 'outmoded' revolutionary practices that proved remarkably effective during early twentieth century nationalist liberation struggles. At the same time, having arrived too late in India, only after the fact of satellite television, radio is paradoxically obsolete in relation to the novelty of a contemporary state, friendly to liberalization, and therefore quickly erasing and indeed killing its own quasi-socialist past. To be sure, in the conversation between the Ministry of Defense and the dissenting college students, it is the FM radio broadcast – hijacked as it is by the young revolutionaries – that shedding its frivolous, youthful, and capricious notes, takes on a sagacious, grave, and sober aspect. In contrast, the rhetoric of the state, traditionally the voice of disciplined restraint, emerges as impetuously murderous, unbridled, lawless, and needing to be tamed. Yet, in assuming this aspect of a somber and aged interlocutor that must play its part in harnessing the adolescent violence of a state that has commissioned the indiscriminate killing of its own youthful citizens, radio is also something of an impersonator. For, as we know, in the context of an emergent discourse of FM airwaves being released from the burdensome yoke of state monopoly, the second phase of FM privatization waiting in the wings, and suddenly a flurry of private stations glutting the market with their novel offerings, radio is in fact the centerpiece of contemporary trading circuits in South Asia. It is thus radically youthful in the ambivalent milieu of the present Indian media space. In that sense, it is also, as satellite television was in its early years, ungovernable and full of commercial abandon, and thus the figural truant which needs to be reined in by an increasingly impotent Parliament, threatened by its own declining stranglehold over the austerity of national airwaves.

The visual design of the final, bloody scene of *Rang de Basanti* comes to rest in this fitful face of radio as a medium, foregrounding through the schizoid aspect of the medium hidden, pitiless, intimacies between obsolescence and novelty, and calling into being a milieu which can comfortably accommodate seemingly unlawful familiarities.[14] Indeed, the very power and arrogance of *Rang de Basanti* lies in the energy with which it is able to bring such apparently dichotomous schisms into a festive flush of coincidence, making state and commerce, colonial and neo-colonial urges, and nation and empire reside on a single undifferentiated continuum of regularities. This is why the new nationalism that the film proposes does not attempt to either dialectically resolve or radically undo the long historical contentions between tradition and modernity, east and west, or self and other. Instead, bringing them into a transparent coincidence with one another, it threatens to undermine 'otherness' as the intellectual energy spawned of the gaps between these polarizations, as well as 'difference' as the rebellious pressure that had once energized anti-imperial struggles across the globe. The environment of language and images that *Rang de Basanti* conjures is one in which imperial adolescence and colonial venerability are not conceptually divided between unique national/imperial powers. Rather in this rhetorical-visual condition, it is India which is both the deeply historical land, sunken in a past replete with illustrious figures like Bhagat Singh and Chandrasekhar Azad, and again India herself, which is the unstoppable and newly emerging imperial power that relies on the global-metropolitan *savoir-faire* of boys like DJ, Karan, Sukhi, and Aslam. As the rebellious figures of yesteryear, these boys can as we have seen, martyr themselves in the name of the nation, while at the same time, in their incarnation as the newly awakened generation of an emergent global power, they can adventure into the world, wave upon wave, and with appetites insatiably renewing for global resources that are continually wasting away.

Chapter Seven

BETWEEN *YAARS*: THE QUEERING OF *DOSTI* IN CONTEMPORARY BOLLYWOOD FILMS

Dinah Holtzman

The Hindi/Urdu word *dosti* encompasses greater intensity and devotion than the comparable English term, 'friendship.' Bollywood's treatments of *dosti* entail physical intimacy and a moral code not necessarily shared in friendships between men in the West. Ruth Vanita elaborates, 'The continuum between romantic friendship and love is a slippery space where affection slides into or is coded as erotic without being overtly depicted as sexual.'[1] She draws parallels to Hollywood buddy films and remarks that Bollywood representations of *dosti* are also influenced by 'older Indian traditions of same sex love.'[2] Cinematic *dosti* is a fusion of Hindu mythology, Muslim *ghazals*, Sanskrit and Parsi theatre, Hollywood cinema and music video.[3] India's economic liberalization in the mid 1990s led to the introduction of satellite television on the subcontinent and a subsequent increase in imported Western pop culture. The shift from *dosti* as normative homosocial relationship towards the current trend of comic acknowledgement of the homoerotic undertones of *dosti* is tied to the recent influx of Hollywood film and American television in which homosexuality is a popular theme. Post-2000 depictions of *dosti* via its coupling with gay jokes is reflective of national concerns about how economic liberalization, the burgeoning middle class, Western style consumer capitalism and diasporic populations impact Indian national and diasporic values, culture and traditions.

An examination of Bollywood *dosti* films from the 1970s through 2004 demonstrates how the newly queered homoerotic *dosti* points to a possible national move away from a hegemonic heteronormativity that enforces marriage and reproduction. Although this shift does not represent a sea change in conceptions of masculinity and sexuality it reveals ambivalence about the future of indigenous traditions like homosocial *dosti* amid an increasingly globalized nation. Newly 'queer,' *dosti* is the result of changing perceptions of gender and sexuality (on the subcontinent and in the diaspora) as well as of widespread national, cultural anxiety and ambivalence about India's integration into a global economy dominated by Western popular culture. Popular Western texts promote culturally specific ideologies that may be perceived as both alien and undesirable in other nations thus challenging indigenous value systems.

    A comparative reading of three *dosti* themed films – *Sholay* (Flames, 1975), *Kal Ho Naa Ho* (Tomorrow May Not Come, 2003), and *Masti* (Mischief, 2004) – illustrates shifting audience and cultural perceptions of *dosti*. *Sholay* is often described as a 'Curry Western,' suggesting that it is merely an Indianized version of Hollywood and Italian 'Spaghetti Westerns.'[4] However, Bollywood indigenization of various genres of Western cinema offers a fascinating window into the cultural and ideological differences that permeate Bollywood, Hollywood and various European cinemas. Though Bollywood frequently borrows Hollywood plots, the characterizations and moral lessons are transformed to reflect Indian culture. Observing the changes made via the translation process pinpoints the arenas in which Western ideology is made more palatable to majority Hindu subcontinental and diasporic audiences. *Masti* is loosely based on an American independent film *Whipped* (2000).[5] Rewritten elements in the Bollywood version demonstrate how Western sexual values are transformed to appeal to audiences interpellated into Indian sexual ideologies; ideologies deeply imbricated in Hindu codes.

    Sholay (Flames) centers on two outlaws intensely committed to one another and their joint pursuit of a nomadic criminal lifestyle. *Kal Ho Naa Ho* is the story of a love triangle between two men and the woman they love. The dying Aman devotes himself to uniting his friend and his love interest in marriage before his death. *Kal Ho Naa Ho* is a contradictory paean to thwarted romantic love that ultimately reifies arranged marriage. However, the conclusion suggests Rohit and Naina's marriage includes three people, one of whom has died, but who lives on through their union. Aman's death, like Jai's in *Sholay*, is necessary for normative monogamous heterosexuality to thrive. *Masti* is the story of three male college buddies who reunite after marriage, bemoan the misery of marital life and agree to seek out excitement through extramarital affairs. The preservation of marital fidelity in *Masti* also results from a (fake) death. In all three films, the achievement of normative heterosexuality is intertwined with homosocial friendship, death, and homosexuality such that *dosti* appears to be a casualty of heteronormativity. While audiences may root for the fulfillment of normative heterosexual coupling, the conclusions suggest that same sex friendships complicate the institutionalization of monogamous marital heterosexuality.

    Although *dosti* is appropriate for early stages of life, it must be sublimated (often via death) to maintain and propagate the nation via heterosexual reproduction. Each film concludes with triumphant heterosexual coupling combined with a pervasive sense of grief over the loss of a *yaar*.[6] Mourning this loss is crucial to *dosti* films. In *Kal Ho Naa Ho* it is Rohit, not Naina, who last speaks with Aman before his death. In *Sholay*, Veeru, not the widow Radha, curses God for Jai's death to the sad strains of their earlier joyous duet, *Yeh Dosti*. Amar, Meet, and Prem remain friends in *Masti* though with the recognition that reconciliation with their wives means an inevitable end to youthful *masti*.

Sholay exemplifies cinematic *dosti* prior to economic liberalization while *Kal Ho Naa Ho* and *Masti* are illustrative of the newly queered cinematic *dosti*. Using Eve Sedgwick's notion of homosocial desire as the meeting point of homosociality and homosexuality as a model, a comparative reading of the films elucidates the ways in which Bollywood treatments of *dosti* have evolved.[7]

The proliferation of gay jokes in recent Bollywood films signals a departure from traditional conceptions of *dosti* towards an embrace of the conflicted love/hate approach to male homosociality and homosexuality currently popular in Western media. Contemporary Hollywood comedies dealing with male friendship such as *Dude, Where's My Car?* (2000), *Harold and Kumar Go to White Castle* (2004) and *Hot Fuzz* (2007) traffic in ironic acknowledgment of the homoeroticism of the buddy films.[8] These films deflect queerness through comic acknowledgement and disavowal of homoeroticism by the main characters. *Kal Ho Naa Ho* and *Masti* similarly acknowledge and deny the homoerotic dimensions of traditional *dosti* as represented in classic Bollywood buddy films like *Sholay*.

The newly queer(ed) *dosti* films feature comic subplots involving mistaken gayness. Misperception of the protagonists' homosexuality is the result of slapstick encounters in which the two friends are seen engaged in 'innocent,' non-sexual physical behaviors that resemble oral and anal sex.[9] What does it mean that scriptwriters assume Bollywood audiences find comic relief in gay jokes? Freud's theories of jokes provide a useful template for exploring the function of Bollywood gay jokes. In *Jokes and Their Relation to the Unconscious*, Freud affirms that jokes are an exposure of something 'concealed or hidden.'[10] Bollywood gay humor is an exposure of desire between *yaars*. Romantic/sexual attraction to a *yaar* may be deeply repressed in the unconscious but is nevertheless present, in some form, within the psyche. Gay innuendo enables a collective release of tension by simultaneously acknowledging and disavowing desire within same sex friendship.

Freud suggests that the purpose of the obscene joke is to '[C]ompel the person who is assailed to imagine the part of the body or the procedure in question and shows her that the assailant himself is imagining it. It cannot be doubted that the desire to see what is sexual exposed is the original motive of smut.'[11] The gay jokes force audiences to imagine the protagonists having sex via the characters who misperceive their relationship. But why are scriptwriters and film audiences interested in the exposure of gay sex (real or imagined) at this particular historical juncture?

Why Gay Jokes? Why Now?

A joke is successful only if the intended audience 'gets' it. Freud suggests that telling jokes is a social process, 'Every joke calls for a public of its own and laughing at the same jokes is evidence of a far reaching psychical conformity.'[12] The recent proliferation of gay jokes indicates that scriptwriters presume their audiences are familiar enough with homosexual sex acts to 'get' the joke/s and are therefore part of a 'far reaching psychical conformity' with regard to male homosexuality. Implicit in those assumptions is the notion that two ostensibly heterosexual men appearing to engage in homosexual sex are comic. What makes that particular scenario funny and to whom?

In *Masti*, mistaken homosexuality works as comic incongruity because the plot is premised on the desperation of sexually frustrated straight men. Ironically, the three friends are in search of the same thing (sex) and feel closer to one another than to their wives. The explicit slapstick gay innuendo disavows the protagonists' queerness while at the same time flirting with the obvious underlying question: why don't these horny men find sexual succor with one another? In *Kal Ho Naa Ho* the comic incongruity derives from the fact that Kantaben, Rohit's servant, believes the two men are in love with each other. The relationship between Aman and Rohit exemplifies Sedgwick's concept of homosocial desire and the queerly inflected rivalry of two men over the body of a woman: 'In any erotic rivalry, the bond that links the two rivals is as intense and potent as the bond that links of either of the rivals to the beloved …the choice of the beloved is determined in the first place, not by the qualities of the beloved, but by the beloved's already being the chosen of the person who has been chosen as a rival.'[13] In both films, heterosexuality is inseparable from the threat of homosexuality. Mistaken gayness is funny because it flirts with the strong undercurrent of homoerotic attraction underlying male bonding shenanigans. The friends' (over)investment in one another's sexual impulses may be a projection of their own sublimated desire for one another displaced onto the female body.

Masti's humor revolves around the suggestion that same sex sexual activity has fewer obstacles to overcome with regard to gender coded behaviors than heterosexual sex. Within India there are myriad cultural and religious prescriptions dictating appropriate interactions between men and women;

however, there are few rules governing conduct between same sex friends. If heterosexual men are thwarted by cultural prescriptions propagating the importance of Indian women's sexual modesty and are granted permission to dabble in taboo extramarital sex, homosexual sex with similarly frustrated men represents a solution to their frustration.

The humor of these gay jokes lies in the seeming incongruity of sexually unfulfilled men turning to each other for emotional and sexual satisfaction, though R Raj Rao posits that sex between men is prevalent in India: '[H]omosexuality thrives in covert yet recognized places in Indian culture...subtler forms of homosexuality are actually engendered under the auspices of normative patriarchal culture.'[14] For Rao, the comic incongruity lies in the fact that homosexual activity flourishes in a culture where heterosexual marriage and reproduction are considered social obligations.[15]

Bollywood gay jokes are comic because they suggest the 'preposterous' notion that ostensibly heterosexual male protagonists might voluntarily choose a life of *masti* (mischievous sexual activity) with a *yaar* despite expectations that Hindu men move from *brahmacharya* – adolescent years into *garhasthya* – the householder phase of Hindu life.[16] Choosing a life of *masti*, within Hindu prescriptions, is equivalent to remaining in adolescent stasis and shirking one's adult dharmic duties to marry and reproduce. Committing to a life with a male partner bears a strong resemblance to Western homosexuality. The gay jokes function as a form of release derived from the exposure of repressed desire of adult men to choose lives of perpetual *brahmacharya*. The unspoken possibility of homosexual relations in *Sholay* is made even more explicit in *Kal Ho Naa Ho* and *Masti*. Gay jokes appeal to male audiences by allowing them to vent fantasies of rejecting cultural prescriptions regarding heterosexual marriage and reproduction in favor of a perpetual youth of homosocial (and possibly homosexual) camaraderie. Importantly, much of the filmic nostalgia for *brahmacharya* and *masti* comes at the expense of women and marriage. In all three films, male protagonists must renounce their commitment to *brahmacharya* in favor of maturing into *grhastha*.

In all three films male *brahmacharya* is equated with pre-marital heterosexual promiscuity. Veeru, Rohit, and Meet are characterized as reformed cads who have opted out of promiscuous bachelorhood in favor of monogamous heterosexual marriage. However their alleged promiscuity is back story and sex outside of marriage is never actually physically represented in the films. In contrast, the gay jokes in *Kal Ho Naa Ho* and *Masti* imply explicit gay sex acts. Despite the ban on kissing and other overtly sexual behaviors in Bollywood films, audiences recognize simulations of oral and anal sex. Bollywood prudery regarding explicit representations of heterosexual sex is contradictory given the liberal approach to slapstick comedy redolent of homosexual acts. The fact that subcontinental audiences 'get' slapstick gay jokes demonstrates that homosexual sex is not entirely foreign to Indian culture.

Simulations of sex are a form of smut, which Freud defines as '[t]he intentional bringing into prominence of sexual facts and relations by speech.'[17] Freud insists that for a tendentious joke to succeed there must be three parties involved. Freud's discussion of the multiple relays involved in the telling of obscene jokes is resolutely gendered and heterosexual in motive, in part due to the time period in which he wrote *Jokes*. According to Freud, the three required joke telling participants are: the source of the joke (a man), the object of the joke (in Freud's formulation—a woman), and the receiver of the joke (also a man). The joke is act of aggression on the part of the joke teller directed against the object of the joke (the woman). The object of the joke is the joke teller's object of desire. The third party, the receiver of the joke, the other man, 'laugh[s] as though he were the spectator of an act of sexual aggression.'[18] Freud contends that the teller of the joke experiences pleasure from the exposure of his own repressed libido (directed at the woman/object) and that the other man, the receiver of the joke experiences 'the effortless satisfaction of his own libido.'[19] Freud ignores the possibility that the two male participants may be expressing their desire for one another via the woman/object. Although he discusses the transmission of obscene jokes in all male milieus, he suggests: '[i]f a man in a company of men enjoys telling or listening to smut, the original situation, which owing to social inhibitions cannot be realized, is at the same time imagined.'[20] In the absence of a female object, the joke succeeds only if one is fantasized into existence. However, in the absence of a woman, it is more likely that the 'real' object of his desire is the third party to whom he directs the joke. Consequently, the telling of obscene jokes in an all male milieu functions as a form of homoerotic flirtation thinly veiled by the presumably heterosexual content of the joke.

If we define Bollywood gay jokes as smut and attempt to use a Freudian model to explain how the relay of obscene jokes function between the characters within the filmic diegesis as well as between the film and its audience, we are left with a number of difficult questions. Who is the teller of the joke (both within and outside of the films)? Who is the object of the joke (both within and outside of the films)? Who is the receiver of the joke (within and outside of the films)? And what role does gender play in the telling and reception of the jokes?

Explicit gay innuendo is acceptable because the implied sex is not 'real.' Viewers may feel that there are no realistic circumstances in which the two protagonists might have sex with one another; this impossibility makes the mistaken gayness comic. However, the assumption that the protagonists are gay points to the fact that the 'sex' appears quite real(istic) to the characters who interpret their behavior as homosexual. That the protagonists are identified as gay suggests other characters sense something queer about both men and their relationship.[21] While the relationship between Veeru and Jai in *Sholay* has always appeared queer to me, a Western viewer, *Kal Ho Naa Ho* and *Masti* suggest that what was once considered strictly homosocial (*Sholay* in the 1970s) now appears queer in the twenty-first century. Mistaken gayness subplots illustrate the shifting relation of homosocial to homosexual bonds as well as changes in perceptions about masculinity and masculine friendship over the last thirty years. These changes are largely the result of India's economic liberalization and Bollywood's newfound appreciation of NRI audiences.

Scriptwriters' assumption of audience 'psychical conformity' regarding male homosexuality is attributable to a shared sense of nationalism and ideological topicality that transcends geography and resonates both on the subcontinent and in the diaspora. Bollywood gay jokes are directly correlated to a widespread desire within India to maintain a sense of national identity rooted in Hindu hegemony despite the nation's new status in the global economy.[22] India's embrace of transnational capitalism is accompanied by anxiety that the national economic shift may lead to changing cultural values. Jyoti Puri suggests that,

> Idioms of virility and strength, of 'colonial penetration,' of rape and plunder of one nation by another, and of beauty pageants and sexual respectability routinely sexualize our language of nationalisms. We use these sexualized idioms in order to imagine and give meaning to nationalisms…[N]ationalisms such as India and Korea, have been described with words such as 'chastity' and 'modesty'…the sexualization of nationalisms is no aberration but is the way we ascribe characteristics to nations and imagine nationalisms.[23]

India, a postcolonial nation, must deal with the legacy of colonialism and the ways in which nations are both gendered and sexualized via the discursive tropes of colonial ideology. Indigenous forms of homosocial bonding are in danger of re-interpretation by popular Western media. The queering of *dosti* can be construed as an effect of global Western neo-colonialism. In the West, male homosexuality is often equated with a lack of masculinity and/or behaviors thought to be 'feminine.' Positing *dosti* as 'queer' by Western standards implies that Indian masculinity and male-male friendships are feminine by contrast. The suggestion that *desi* masculinity is more feminine or lacking harkens back to the era of British colonialism when native 'effeminancy' was cited as justification for British 'benevolent' paternalism and the 'civilizing mission.'[24] Leela Gandhi suggests, '[T]he oft cited anti-colonialist/nationalist endeavor to self-reform in the image of the aggressor, by recuperating a 'lost' native masculinity can be said to herald the onset of a postcolonial heteronormativity—tragically collaborationist and fraught by the pressures of a newly internalized homophobia or fear of effeminacy.'[25]

However, the queering of *dosti* may be a positive development as it reflects increased openness to homosexuality though it may also be read as a form of homophobic reverse colonialism which identifies homosexuality as a Western phenomenon. Indeed, homosexuality is never a viable option in these films, at least not for the heterosexual heroes. That the homoerotic aspects of *dosti* have become fodder for comedy represents a departure from more fluid conceptions of masculinity and male sexuality such as the relationship between Veeru and Jai in *Sholay*.

Sholay

Sholay is commonly described as the quintessential 'angry young man' film, reflecting widespread feelings of cynicism during the contemporaneous national political climate of Indira Gandhi's Emergency.[26] Though *Sholay* is structured like a Hollywood Western, the visual codes of the Bollywood *masala* film are incorporated into the filmic diegesis. The film's melodrama, song and dance numbers, intense homosocial bonds and depictions of behaviors indicative of traditional *dosti* contribute to the tendency of Western viewers to interpret *Sholay* as gay camp. Contemporary Western readings of *Sholay* as camp are likely heavily influenced by the recent mainstreaming of queer readings of Hollywood Westerns provoked by the widespread popularity of *Brokeback Mountain*.[27] Classic Hollywood Westerns featuring heroes like John Wayne, the embodiment of a rugged individualist masculinity, are now widely read as gay camp. Something similar is happening with Bollywood films. The formerly implicit homoeroticism of *dosti* films, like that of Hollywood Westerns and buddy films, is now ironically acknowledged via gay jokes.

Sholay details the relationship between two professional outlaws, Veeru and Jai. Their friendship is the template for both traditional and newly queered *dosti* which frequently reference dialogue or song lyrics from *Sholay*. For the angry young man of the 1970s, *dosti* is an attractive alternative to marriage since his business life revolves around a homosocial network of gangsters. Because he comes from a fatherless home, elder crime bosses act as surrogate fathers and represent a more potent version of his own emasculated absent father. Whereas romance was the forte of the 1950s Bollywood chocolate box hero, for the angry young man, monogamous heterosexual commitment represents an emotional trap and inevitable emasculation. His fight against a corrupt society involves rejecting cultural conformity and traditional heterosexual relationships.

Inevitably, however, the hero recognizes the sinful wages of his anti-establishment lifestyle, gives up his criminality, and commits himself to a new life as a law-abiding husband and father. His change of heart is generally due to female influences – the 'bad' Westernized woman turned 'good' Hindu and his long-suffering devoutly religious mother. Fareeduddin Kazmi suggests,

> The latent aim of the narrative is to neutralize, absorb or displace any potential of genuinely deviant, subversive activity and project a totally different concept of the individual...overtly the film hero is depicted as one embodying the fiercely independent Promethean vision of the person. And yet the same hero is at every turn bogged down by fate. Our 'superman' is dominated and subservient to nature (fate), God (religion), mother and country.[28]

Despite the truth of Kazmi's characterization the appeal of the angry young man lies in his initial refusal to abide by convention. His inevitable renunciation of rebellious non-conformity redeems him as a hero and distances him from the villains he so closely resembles.

Jai and Veeru are prototypical angry young men as they embrace a life of crime and have no immediate family to act as moral guides. Their relocation to Thakur Singh's village provides them with a surrogate family and a renewed sense of morality. Their commitment to an individualist homosocial criminality must ultimately give way to their incorporation into a community as husbands and fathers. The intensity of their bond, prior to relocating to the Thakur's village, is obvious in the song sequence, *Yeh Dosti* (This Friendship).[29] The heroes celebrate their mutual devotion while riding a motorbike and sidecar across the country. The lyrics translate as:

> We vow to remain friends;
> We'd rather die than sever our friendship.
> Your distress I share
> Just as you share my joy.
> Our love is reciprocal.
> Though two in body
> We're one in soul—
> Never shall we be separated.
> We eat and drink together
> We'll live and die together.[30]

Their relationship is a marriage, complete with declarations of lifelong commitment.

During the duet, the sidecar comes detached, sending Veeru flying while Jai continues to steer. Although the scene is comic, the separation of the two via the broken motorbike foreshadows their ultimate separation at the conclusion of the film. Veeru magically reappears behind Jai on the motorbike, arms wrapped around his waist. Reunited, the friends leap up and down in joy.

The song *Yeh Dosti* appears immediately prior to their planned incarceration and subsequent escape from jail. The jail sequence is a comic episode involving a warden 'since the days of the British' who fancies himself a small scale Hitler. A fellow prisoner, coded as gay via his eye makeup and feminine hairstyle, befriends Veeru and Jai and helps them to escape. Intriguingly, the two protagonists never appear uncomfortable with the effeminate character's desire to befriend them although his solicitation suggests that he senses an element of queerness in the heroes' relationship. The 'sissy' prisoner also provides a foil for the heroes' machismo. Despite their physical intimacy and obvious love for one another, the film indicates that 'real' homosexuals are effeminate. If homosexuals can be easily identified by their make up and hairstyles, the macho protagonists are not homosexual. Defining who is and is not homosexual is largely determined by gender presentation.

Same Sex Sexuality in India

Although the word homosexuality is used within English speaking India, critics remark the concept does not translate widely. Ashok Row Kavi foregrounds some of the problems involved in transposing Western gay identity to an Indian context:

> The gay Anglo-American sexual fantasy/ideal of two men going off together to make a life for themselves does not exist in India. This idea, which became the cornerstone of much Western 'gay' thought is counter to Indian culture.[31]

Yeh Dosti is a paean to such a fantasy/ideal though it is ultimately compromised by Veeru's desire for heterosexual marriage. Only after Jai recognizes Veeru's movement towards *garhasthya* (post-puberty familial stage) does he too decide to marry, suggesting that for Jai, *garhasthya* is a consolation prize for a failed attempt at same sex marriage.

According to Indian public health literature, few men who have sex with men define themselves as homosexual, gay or bisexual since many do not speak English. For many men who have sex with men, self-identification involves terms like *kothi*, *panthi*, *giriya* or *jiggery dost* which refer to gendered behaviors and specific sexual acts rather than to communities united around shared political or ideological identities.[32] In this regard, sexual identity labels are inextricably intertwined with notions of normative gender roles. Men who exhibit visual signifiers of normative masculinity and are not sexually 'submissive' are presumably heterosexual. Many men do not identify themselves with any of these labels and consider the sex they have with other men *masti*, a natural part of pre-marital (if not post-marital) life for 'heterosexual' men.[33]

For the Western observer, it is tempting to ascribe homosexuality or bisexuality to men who engage in such behaviors.[34] However such a designation would be anathema to Indian conceptions of sexuality. Shivananda Khan suggests, 'The debate on sexualities, may even at times be perceived as a form of neo-colonialism whereby Western sexual ideologies have 'invaded' Indian discourses in sexuality and identity...whereby indigenous histories and cultures become invisible.'[35] For Khan, as for Ashok Row Kavi, the desire to categorize Indian sexuality according to Western sexological terminology is mired in neo-colonialist assumptions of universality.

Kal Ho Naa Ho and the Western Diaspora

Contemporary Bollywood cinema models gender roles, expressions of sexuality, patriotic nationalism, and consumerist lifestyles reflective of India's current geo-political status as a rising economic superpower. A number of recent films reveal changing attitudes towards Indians who have relocated in the West. In these films, representations of the nation's economic liberalization and newfound embrace of diasporic Indians display some of the tensions inherent in navigating globalization while maintaining a strong national identity grounded in the celebration and retention of cultural and religious (primarily Hindu) values and traditions. In the mid 1990s the ruling Bharatiya Janata Party (BJP) encouraged non-resident Indians to invest in the homeland and offered incentives such as the Overseas Citizenship of India Act, making it possible for diasporic Indians to live abroad while maintaining national, familial and economic ties to the subcontinent.[36]

One effect of national economic liberalization has been governmental championing of diasporic populations as an integral (though satellite) part of the nation and nationalist sentiment. Government courtship of NRI investment is motivated by a desire to continue to build the national infrastructure at a pace fast enough to keep up with national economic growth. In 1998, recognizing the popularity of Bollywood cinema and its role as a national ideological tool, the Bharatiya Janata Party officially recognized the commercial film sector as a business industry entitled to tax protections. In response to government recognition, Bollywood film producers began to craft features reflective of the Bharatiya Janata Party's Hinducentric political mandates and desire to woo NRI investors. Myriad post-1994 films feature NRI characters and are set in metropolitan diasporic cities such as New York and London.

The courtship and glamorization of NRIs via popular media poses a striking contrast to 1960s and 1970s Bollywood representations of NRIs. During that era, NRI characters were portrayed as national traitors, tainted by time spent in the West; their only hope for salvation lay in the hands of the patriotic protagonist who teach them the error of Western ways and convince them to return to the homeland.[37] Contemporary NRI characters are represented as traditional and nationalistic, often more so than their subcontinental counterparts.

Cinematic recognition of the potentially queer dimensions of *dosti* is closely connected to Bollywood's aggressive courtship of NRI audiences. Second generation NRIs are more likely to view representations of traditional *dosti* as homoerotic, since their understanding of gender and sexuality is formed outside the subcontinent. Diasporic audiences, savvy to the current hipness of all things gay in the West, may interpret physical displays of affection between men as queer precisely because that is the sort of reading encouraged through the lens of Western binaristic delineations of 'normative' heterosexual versus queer sexual behaviors. The introduction of gay jokes in contemporary Bollywood films suggests that Bollywood *dosti* is increasingly read as queer in ways that *Sholay* was not. *Kal Ho Naa Ho*, set in New York City, is a Bollywood film calculated to appeal to NRI audiences. The comic element of the film deals with the liminal space where homosociality and homoeroticism overlap—notably, not in India but in the Western diaspora.

As with many classic *dosti* films, *Kal Ho Naa Ho* revolves around the plot device of two friends in love with the same woman. The *dosti* love triangle exemplifies Eve Sedgwick's concept of homosocial desire and the queerly inflected rivalry of two men over the body of a woman. Although Aman and Rohit meet via Naina, there is a strong element of *dosti* in their relationship. Only when Aman appears does Rohit realize his feelings for Naina are more than platonic. Although Aman and Naina are in love, Aman essentially offers her to Rohit as a gift. He stubbornly adheres to his mission to see Rohit and Naina marry despite Naina lack of interest in Rohit. In the absence of a father figure for Naina, Aman hands her to Rohit during the wedding ceremony. Rather than moving from her father's home to that of her new husband, Naina is passed from her would be lover to his handpicked stand-in.

Cinematic *dosti* demands that one of the two friends concede the woman out of homosocial love in order to facilitate monogamous heterosexual union. In *Kal Ho Naa Ho*, Aman both gives up Naina and proceeds to die after his role as matchmaker is fulfilled. The gay jokes surface once Rohit's servant, Kantaben, becomes convinced that Aman and Rohit are a couple. Her mistaken assumption is meant to be farcical. However, her confusion acknowledges the repressed element of homoerotic desire often sublimated in homosocial relationships. Faced with Kantaben's visceral homophobia, neither protagonist suffers homosexual panic. Aman recognizes her reaction as homophobic and aggressively challenges her by pretending that Rohit is his lover. Aman's antics are represented not as an anti-homophobic intervention but as boyish pranks. In some diegetically inexplicable instances, he continues his queer theatrics though Kantaben is nowhere to be found, at one point agreeing to marry Rohit. Rohit is not bothered by his servant's assumption that he is gay or by Aman's delight in playing the part. He plays the 'straight man' to Aman's 'queer' comedian.

Rohit's father brings him to a strip club (the dancers are white women) for a confrontation about his sexuality. Neither father nor son appears distraught over his 'gayness.' His father is relieved that he is heterosexual, but there is no hysterical threat of familial ex-communication. Rohit does not violently disavow the possibility that he is gay. However, after his heterosexuality is confirmed father and son punch fists and speak in gruffer tones. That both men attempt to act more 'manly' after their conversation implies that the mere mention of homosexuality undermines their masculinity.

Although homosexuality functions as a joke in *Kal Ho Naa Ho*, there is a song and dance sequence that complicates the representation of homosexuality as exclusively comic. Rohit and Naina dance and sing their way through Manhattan, bonding with various couples including two white gay men. This carefully placed shot celebrates the existence of homosexuals in the metropolitan West. Inclusion of the gay couple shifts the film's initial treatment of male homosexuality as comic by celebrating white Western homosexuality, while simultaneously disavowing the queerness of the *desi* protagonists. The only other queer character is a guest at Rohit and Naina's engagement party. Like the jailbird of *Sholay*, the mystery party guest wears makeup, apparently a visual signifier of Indian male homosexuality. Kantaben, the homophobic servant, vents her hostility towards gays by violently shoving the effeminate man after he applauds Rohit and Aman's dance. Later during a particularly energetic song and dance sequence, Kantaben happily dances (hand in hand!!) with the same effeminate man she assaulted earlier. Perhaps her witnessing of Rohit and Naina's vows helped her to overcome her fear that Rohit is gay, therefore permitting her to befriend a non-familial gay man. Her acceptance of non-familial homosexuality resembles the overall message of the film: homosexuality is fine for white Westerners and perhaps for South Asians to whom one is not related.

The fact that Kantaben mistakenly assumes Aman and Rohit are lovers in New York City, reinforces the nativist idea propounded by right wing Hindu fundamentalist groups that *desi* homosexuality is catalyzed by time spent in the licentious West. In the West, homosexuality is associated with coming out narratives – public and familial self-identification as gay or bisexual. In India, individual sexuality is not commonly discussed with family members. The discussion between Rohit and his father is comic because of the incongruity of two Indian men attempting to enact a stereotypical Western coming out scenario. Prior to confirmation of Rohit's heterosexuality his father remarks, 'This is America. Anything is possible. Look at my fate, I asked for a daughter-in-law and I am blessed with a son-in-law.' His comment suggests that a gay son is something possible only in the West.

However, the relative calmness with which various characters react to mistaken gayness suggests that the revelation of Indian homosexuality within the metropolitan Western diaspora will not necessarily result in the inevitable dissolution of the traditional Indian family. That Rohit's father would not have disowned him if he were gay suggests the destruction wrecked on Naina's family by the patriarch's adulterous union and subsequent suicide is a far greater tragedy than having a gay son in the diaspora. While this is not a ringing endorsement of diasporic homosexuality, it offers significant possibilities for a wider range of sexual practices.

Masti

Masti is the first Bollywood film to point to the behaviors associated with *dosti* as borderline homoerotic on the subcontinent. As with the Hollywood buddy films mentioned earlier, the protagonists of *Masti* joke endlessly about homosexuality. However, the film ultimately demonstrates that effeminate men, *hijras* and transsexuals are the 'real' queers.[38] The heterosexual hijinks planned by the protagonists are formulated only after a drunken Amar begins to sing *Yeh Dosti* to his similarly inebriated friends, Prem and Meet. Amar's performance indicates their nostalgia for the carefree days of bachelordom and alleged heterosexual promiscuity – *brahmacharya*. The invocation of Veeru and Jai's musical paean to homosocial love also points to the ways in which traditional *dosti* has become queer(ed).

In an early scene, Dr. Kapadia, who suffers from homosexual panic and an intense curiosity about homosexual sex, witnesses the joyous and physically affectionate reunion of Amar and Prem. Although their physical display of affection is similar to that of Veeru and Jai in *Sholay*, Dr. Kapadia assumes the two are lovers. *Masti* differs from *Kal Ho Na Ho* in that Amar and Prem are mistaken for lovers in New Delhi, suggesting that behaviors associated with *dosti* are increasingly interpreted as 'queer' not only in the Western diaspora, but in metropolitan India as well. Just as Aman appears to revel in Kantaben's mistaken assumption, Amar and Prem deliberately encourage Dr. Kapadia's misinterpretation.

Masti also involves the exchange of a woman's body between male friends. However, in *Masti*, one woman is 'shared' by three men. *Masti* begins with the premise that heterosexual marriage is at best unsatisfying and at worst a veritable prison. Amar hallucinates being shackled and whipped by his wife who is clad in a Nazi uniform. Another fantasy sequence features Amar dressed in a woman's nightgown serving breakfast to his wife who is clad in a male business suit. Both his wife and mother in law frequently mock his lack of manly brawn. Meet's wife is pathologically obsessed with him and uses techniques for spousal control commonly associated with abusive husbands. For example, she 'forces' Meet to wear dowdy clothes and a nerdy hairstyle to insure that other women will not find him attractive. She also physically tracks his movements via cell phone. Prem's wife is a devout Hindu, perpetually praying and fasting for his well-being. Intriguingly, when Geeta cites the *Law of Manu* to him as a sign of her marital devotion, 'a woman's heaven lies at her husband's feet.' Prem responds 'It's a little bit higher.'[39] He suggests her heaven resides in his groin, but Geeta coyly misinterprets his statement to mean her heaven lies in his heart. Their relationship undermines idealized conceptions of the perfect traditional Hindu wife. Prem desires a wife who is sexual rather than submissive and adoring. Amar, Meet and Prem's attempts at adultery are motivated by the desire to regain some sense of masculine power and privilege. Reclaiming their masculinity is literally about exercising their phalluses.

During a reunion the three friends confess their marital woes and decide to seek out extra-marital affairs. None of them actually bed Monica, the woman they 'share.' Amar participates in extramarital sexual activity only to discover that he has made out with a transsexual man. Immediately after their kiss, Amar vomits and obsessively tries to clean his 'tainted' mouth. In *Masti*, homosexuality is alternately a punishment for potentially cheating husbands or a sight gag. Ultimately the men are made to see that they should appreciate their wives' loyalty instead of pursuing other sexual partners.

Prior to the revelation of the heroes' bad behavior all three couples are shown visiting temples. This interlude appears to inspire feelings of guilt and regret in the three men. Their presence in a Hindu religious space affects their collective change of heart against committing adultery, suggesting that the maintenance of monogamous marriage is morally correct because it is ordained by Hinduism. Ultimately, the film reaffirms the stereotypical role of the chaste, modest and devoted Hindu wife and teaches viewers that extramarital sex is not the answer to marital problems or a means to avoid emasculation. The gay joke subplot in *Masti* suggests the suppressed possibility that the real *masti* in the film is sexual activity between male friends. Though *masti* translates into English as both 'fun' and 'mischief,' according to *BenGAYliz Times* the word 'is often used to describe sexual tensions between young men.'[40] The film's title is a double entendre pointing to the possibility of sex between men.

Conclusion

The proliferation of gay jokes in recent Bollywood films reflect culturally variant perceptions of gendered and sexualized behaviors. Physical expressions of affection and friendship between men are perceived as non-sexual by Indians, but may be interpreted by Westerners as indicative of homosexuality. Homosexual panic has permeated many Western cultures to such a degree that any sort of physical demonstrativeness between men is reason to suspect homosexuality. This is not the case in India where it is quite common to see men holding hands. Although they may be lovers, neither can we assume that they are not lovers. On the subcontinent, boundaries between sexual and non-sexual physical behaviors between same-sex friends leave greater room for ambiguity than in Western cultures.

India has long absorbed foreign cultural practices. Bollywood cinema was born of western film technology combined with an indigenization of foreign film genres allowing for the maintenance of Hindu moral/cultural ideologies. Jawaharlal Nehru remarks in *The Discovery of India* that,

> Ancient India…was a world in itself, a culture and civilization which gave shape to all things. Foreign influences poured in and often influenced that culture and were absorbed. Disruptive tendencies gave rise immediately to an attempt to find a synthesis. Some kind of dream of unity has occupied the mind of India since the dawn of civilization. That unity was not conceived as something imposed from outside, a standardization of beliefs. It was something deeper, and within its fold, the widest tolerance of belief and custom was practiced and every variety acknowledged and even encouraged.[41]

For Nehru the ability to negotiate and absorb foreign influences is one of the nation's preeminent talents. Bollywood gay jokes may be just such an attempt to negotiate and potentially indigenize western forms of homosexuality. The national desire to emulate Western capitalism necessitates a confrontation with foreign cultural values and practices that may appear at odds with Hinduism.[42]

Within India, homosexuality until very recent times has been widely perceived as a Western phenomenon. Bollywood gay jokes acknowledge fears that Indians may adopt Western style homosexuality as a result of prolonged exposure to media reflective of Western cultural practices or time spent in the West. The jokes have been a reflection of the nation's attempts to navigate Western style capitalism without being ideologically colonized by Western culture and values. The recent films do not vilify homosexuals; however, they project ambivalence about the possibility that Indians may begin to identify with Western forms of queerness.

Homosexuality is an especially potent symbol of a 'non-traditional' lifestyle and is facile shorthand for the West and perceptions of Western 'disregard' for the sanctity of monogamous heterosexual marriage and reproduction e.g. high divorce rates, adultery, pre-marital sex and same-sex partnering. Gayness is a surefire indicator of traditional heteronormative values gone awry as well as a convenient trope for the national struggle to navigate Hindu tradition vs. secular modern capitalism.

The gay jokes also reveal anxieties that heterosexual marriage and reproduction may become compromised as national, cultural, and social priorities as the nation's economic growth continues unabated. The jokes are a counter-phobic response to the threat that increased exposure to Western capitalist culture may lead to an epidemic of non-heteronormative and non reproductive sexual behaviors among its citizens – particularly among men. The films discussed here affirm the existence of homosexuality both on the subcontinent and abroad. They go so far as to suggest that there are *desi* homosexuals; however, they are easily recognized as *hijras*, transgendered/ transsexual, or obviously effeminate. 'Real' Indian men, as represented via film hero stand-ins, can only be comically mistaken for homosexual. And while the comedy is rooted in incongruity, the explicit acting out of 'accidental' homoerotic behaviors only underscores the possibility of homosexuality while attempting to disavow it.

Each film ultimately reifies the importance of heterosexual marriage and reproduction over and above the *masti* of homosocial *dosti*. *Sholay* and *Masti* in particular demonstrate that homosocial *dosti* is the highlight of men's lives. The conclusions suggest that men's natural exuberance, playfulness and spirit will be crushed through monogamous marriage. The names of the protagonists in *Masti* translate as immortal/eternal (Amar), friend (Meet) and love (Prem). The combination of the characters' names function as a synopsis of the film's moral lesson: homosocial friendships should be cherished though not at the expense of one's marriage. The film foregrounds the cultural prescription that a man's destiny is to be a (sexually) faithful husband to an appropriately devoted and deferential Hindu wife. The *masti* of the trio is presented with a nudge and a wink as typical 'boys will be boys' and 'men behaving badly' fare. However, the triumph of heterosexual marriage in the films' conclusions does not necessarily negate any of the queerness of the *masti* that preceded it or the mourning of its loss. Muraleedharan T. suggests that, '[queer subtexts] may be dismissed by some as comic interludes or seen as disciplined by the heterosexist conclusions of the films. But the question I would like to raise is whether such conclusions – that is the eventual union of the male hero with a woman—necessarily undermine the queerness of such films?'[43] He goes on to cite Alexander Doty's strategies for privileging queer readings of mass culture:

> The queerness some readers or viewers may attribute to mass culture texts is not in any way less real than the straightness others would claim for these same texts. There is a queerness *of* and *in* straight culture. The so called hegemonic straight culture in India can be seen to have many queer traits, and examination of this 'queerness within the straight' can provide us with a better understanding of sexual subjectivities in this region.[44]

Although these comic gay subplots do not function as a straightforward celebration of *desi* queerness, they acknowledge that queerness exists in India and the diaspora. Moreover, these films affirm the 'queer' connotations of the homosocial continuum in patriarchal and homophobic societies both Indian and Western. The birth of the comic gay subplot suggests that Bollywood audiences are beginning to recognize queer possibilities in evolving cultural traditions.

Chapter Eight

IMAGINED SUBJECTS: LAW, GENDER AND CITIZENSHIP IN INDIAN CINEMA

Nandini Bhattacharya

'Integral to heteronormative commercial cinema's creation of desire...women offer a heuristic means to comprehend a film's labored production of a secular, modern society in relation to its internal differences'[1]

'[T]he people embed their present in the past'[2]

I would like to offer some reflections on imagining a violent history of nation-making in India's cinematic 'present.' How do structures of feeling, belief and conflict affect graphing and 'remembering' history in Indian cinema? What is the status of the legal, civic or violent 'event' – such as the Indian partition of 1947 or the communal riots of increasing frequency since the eighties – in films? What is Indian cinema's imaginary relationship with historiography, and what does it mean to represent an 'event' within available 'structures' of historic narrative in this cinema frequently described as 'national'?[3] In discussing the 'vexed problem of the relation between structure and event,'[4] and in calling "structure' – the symbolic relations of cultural order...an historical object,'[5] Marshall Sahlins invokes the essential structural backdrop of historical 'events,' wherein 'an event is not simply a phenomenal happening... An event becomes such as it is interpreted. Only as it is appropriated in and through the cultural scheme does it acquire an historical *significance*... The event is a relation between a happening and a structure (or structures)....'[6] What emerges in Sahlin's comment as an entwining of an 'anthropological' mode – the search for structure – and a 'historical' mode – the narration of an event – can be seen in Indian cinema as a perpetual disjunctive dialectic between discourses of the structure of national identity and discourses of eventful citizen-formation. In my larger project of which this essay is a part I focus longer on the yield of entwined anthropological and historical theories of memory for South Asian cinema. I argue that in Indian cinema's techniques of memory, 'structure' and 'event' are divergent imperatives; as a result, a liminal space emerges between the indexicality of violent social events and the iconicity of their representation as historic phenoemena. Within that liminality, the national subject emerges through legal, political and aesthetic representations, including issues of gender, social justice, and violence. In this essay, it is the liminality of gender that concerns me: I find it in the politico-civic narrative of women and the nation-state's others in Indian cinema of the fifties, and also in post-globalization Indian cinema.

The anthropological term liminality refers to identities that are experienced in boundaries and thresholds of cultures, that suture seemingly irreconcilable realms and interests, and that are always constructed performatively.[7] Covering the terrains of performance, ethnography and politics, then, liminality is an ideal prism through which Hindi cinema's projection of identities is refracted. Especially in the Indian context, the religious, the visual and the political cannot be meaningfully separated.[8] Cinematic and political commentary here lend equal support to Victor Turner's insight that 'public ritual dramatizes secular, political, and legal status relationships.'[9] In 1952, Baburao Patel, the irascible and inimitable editor of the popular film journal *FilmIndia* wrote: 'our power-crazy Gandhian Politicians ushered our freedom by dividing our land, by allowing the rape of thousands of women...and finally by appointing our enemies as trustees over our nation's granaries.'[10] Indian cinema's representational topoi of the 'secular national' and the 'citizenship' questions – these framed and liminal spaces rescued from cultural, graphic and political turmoil – have repeatedly touched upon the paired crises of territorial and sexual chaos. The need to stabilize conflicting memory caches of nation-making expressed itself in the apparently stable topos of history, and the inevitable subversions of that precision modulated historiography itself into volatile myths of heroism and dastardliness.[11] History came to be a matter, often, of imagining the state-sponsored present tense of a fragmented mythology of national independence.

Briefly, two cinematic epochs of revisionist historiography are found in the nineteen-fifties and the nineteen-nineties and after (to the latter I will refer as the post-nineties from here on). First, the bloody ethnocide of the Indian partition occurred in 1947: approximately two million people died, and perhaps six million people were displaced. Muslims in India escaped in numbers to the Islamic state of Pakistan; the Hindus of Pakistan similarly cross-migrated to India. British bureaucrat Cyril Radcliffe's arbitrarily and artificially drawn border became the topos of formless terror and mutilation of the nations and their subjects. In the fifties we witness the first cinematic and legislative era of re-membering this ethnocidal history, of reconfiguring the gender and ethnicity of citizenship. This reconfiguration and self-recovery was actualized through a law known as the Abducted Persons (Recovery and Restoration) Act (1949), which was passed by both the Indian and Pakistani governments after partition, and was intended to recover abducted and missing Hindu or Muslim persons (in effect, women and minor children) on both sides of the border.[12] On the Indian side, the act was meant to re-'patriate' the (violated) female Indian citizen and also, more controversially, such minor children as had been born to her, to their state of origin. It was state activism for enumerating and identifying the female citizen whose sexuality had been alienated from the nation-state; according to some, though, it was akin to state-sponsored terrorism upon women's sexuality because the women's consent was not a factor in the operations.[13] Parliamentary debate on the bill raged on questions about purity, legitimacy, continuity and normative citizenship – in brief, on proper identification of the citizen.[14] In the disputes and excesses of the Abducted Persons Act appeared instances of apparently 'structural' conflict between secular, democratic and 'modern' civic frameworks – the new 'Indian' spirit – and 'traditional' indigenous, 'pre-national' Hindu ones that equally denigrated women and Muslims. This conflict foreshadowed the constellated contradictions of citizenship adhering to the subsequent Hindu Code Bill debates, discussed below.[15]

Issues of legitimacy dominated the political representations of violation, and representations of abducted and the abductor proliferated trauma as well as uncertainty and ambiguity.[16] Violence was repeated on the bodies of women of one's own community as well as that of the 'other.' It was the simultaneous 'othering' and 'mirroring' of repeatable and repeated acts of violence that made meaning impossible. The absent 'voice' of women violated at Partition can be explained by Derrida's idea of the constitutive incommunicability of the 'event.' Derrida wrote of the 'speech event' as the decontextualized iteration of experience – iteration meaning both 'repetition' and 'otherness' as per the Greek root 'iter' – which thereby forever eludes context. The communicative act denaturalizes and makes unavailable – constitutively, according to Jacques Derrida's notion of the impossibility of communication – the 'iteration' of the singular event.[17] Partition narrative is the limit case of discourse because it is the case of the impossibility of the 'unique' signature of a communicative 'event.'

This trauma appears vividly emblematized in *Lahore* (1949), a film I will discuss further on.[18] Later, 'social' and familial dramas with a nationalistic impetus – such as *New Delhi* (1956), *Mr. And Mrs. 55* (1955), and *Kathputli* (*The Puppet*, 1957) – added filters and supplements that incompletely mediated the inevitable familialization of political and sexual crises. In the late fifties, the epic genre made a significant if temporary comeback in Mehboob Khan's *Mother India* (1957), and myth reigned supreme as a gesture of reaching out through an imagined history to an illusory coherence and consensus that had eluded the bureaucratic, taxonomical grasp over the nation and its citizens.

In the post-nineties, in tandem with renewed ethnic violence, gender oppression,[19] and state-sponsored anti-minority sentiment,[20] cinema erupted with imagery of recuperation of the unidentified or 'lost' female citizen/other, whose sexuality becomes the psychic border between India and Pakistan, fratricidal foes. In *Gadar: Ek Prem Katha* (*Gadar: a Love Story*, 2001) and *Veer Zaara* (*Veer and Zaara*, 2004), the itinerant, defamilialized female citizen – a Muslim in Hindu-dominated India in both instances – became a cipher for the liminality of citizenship.

Citizenship, Secularism, and the Nation-State

The term 'secular' was inserted in 1976 in the Indian constitution to mitigate developing 'communal strains.'[21] The new nation-state in the fifties faced the problem of reconciling the dyarchy of universalist secular values and indigenous and plural traditions with the concept of the body politic.[22] Harold G. Coward provocatively reminds us that the Constitutional 'this-worldly' guarantee of equality in some senses directly contravenes the enshrined majority Hindu principle of 'natural inequality' based on a theology of the 'impure body,' such as of women and untouchables, in Indian Yoga and Mimamsa philosophy.[23] In 1951, the momentous Hindu Code Bill was introduced in Parliament by the reigning Congress government;[24] this bill sought radical changes in customary Hindu personal law regarding marriage, succession, adoption, guardianship and maintenance in an attempt to 'modernize' colonial law codified by the British on the basis of pundit- and patriarch-derived interpretations of religious texts.[25] In particular, Hindus saw these changes as empowering Hindu women against their menfolk, while they saw minorities (meaning mostly Muslims) as not facing interference in their equally 'traditional' personal laws.[26] The Hindu Code Bill was seen by Hindus as evidence of minoritization of the numerical majority, themselves. Muslims on the other hand opposed the establishment of a Uniform Civil Code – a universal code of private law for all Indian citizens regardless of ethnic identification – enjoined upon future legislators by the original drafters of the constitution,[27] arguing that this would assault their rights as minorities.[28] Once again, lines drawn between gender and citizenship presaged war.

These topoi of fractured and contested political representations resurfaced – along with renewed demand for a Uniform Civil Code – with the Shah Bano case in 1986, wherein a Muslim woman's right to maintenance after divorce was first granted under the provisions of the Indian Criminal Procedure code and then withdrawn and reassessed in terms of Islamic Shariat law as a result of resistance and pressure from Muslim religious patriarchy and governmental pusillanimity regarding minority women's rights.[29] This case in turn led to renewed Hindu nationalist outcry about 'minority appeasement' and eventually to more cataclysmic political violence against Muslims in India. Cinema mirrored these representations and identifications in both the fifties and the post-nineties because of simultaneous 'structural' and 'eventful' imperatives at work in discourse on the national subject.

The Past, the Present, and Hinduness: 'Epics' and 'Socials' of the Fifties

I begin with a survey of a relatively unknown film in which the question of gendered citizenship is mediated and filtered through the narrative of the refractory family romance. Traces of the interrogation of citizenship and gender frameworks are apparent in this romance. Amiya Chakrabarty's *Kathputli* (The Puppet, 1957), like its contemporary *Mother India*, was released a few years after the passage of the Hindu Code Bill (1955–56). *Kathputli* is the story of a street waif rescued from obscurity and an abusive marriage to a disabled and dishonest man by a theatrical impresario. The theme song '*Bol re kathputli dori kaun sang bandhi/ sach batla tu nachey kiske liye*' ('Tell, O puppet, with whom you've tied the knot/ Tell truthfully for whom you dance'; my translation) sweeps into montage the fate of the professional actress as gloss on the fate of the devoted Hindu wife and woman. Marriage and motherhood for the latter are definitive, prescriptive destinies. Escape from those destinies is elusive even when other forms of liberation are tantalizing possibilities. As the heroine's theatrical career takes off, her husband feels emasculated and her marriage falls apart; the jealous husband decamps with their child, whose recovery forms part of the story. The depiction of marital rupture through the debatable rapture of female empowerment and self-identification via newly acquired rights of citizenship in modern India appears – through the repetition of the song, for instance – as the life of the new woman as well as performer. This opens for interrogation the entire national and governmental 'performance' of new rites of secular and modern citizenship for and by women.

Made around the same time as *Kathputli*, Mehboob Khan's *Mother India* (1957) is the national/popular cinematic 'epic' *par excellence* that deepens the import of excavating 'tradition' in conjuncture with secular 'modernity.' Since both the terms tradition and modernity as invoked in *Mother India* notate the cultural politics of decolonization,[30] *Mother India*'s concatenated representation of the major themes of the Nehruvian era – development and modernity, village India and the incommensurability of women's sexuality, etc. – made it a cult film of the fifties. The village girl Radha is married to Shamu in a prototypical village in a pre-modern Indian landscape, and realizes that her mother-in-law has mortgaged their land to the extortionist village moneylender Sukhilala to pay for the festivities. At this moment, a close-up of Radha's face, her head turned to her right picking up her mother-in-law's muttering, shows her beginning to remove her bridal jewelry, symbols of both her personal fortune and her familial status.[31] From this shearing the camera cuts to a spinning mortar at which Radha is shown grinding wheat; her labour for the family has begun. The connection between land, woman and family well-being thus firmly established, the film moves through Radha's happy marriage and hard work with her husband, the birth of children, the downturn in their fortunes due to drought, the husband's farm accident and loss of his arms, his abandonment of the family, Radha's struggles against poverty and the moneylender who tries to violate her in return for feeding her family, her surviving sons' polarization into good and bad sorts, the delinquencies of her younger and best loved son Birju, and Radha's eventual sacrifice for the collectivity – the village a stand-in here for the nation-state – by shooting Birju to death when he turns bandit, kills the moneylender, and abducts his daughter.

The cyclical melodramatic ordeal of the heroic Mother is precisely that of restoring the sacred to the familial wherein traditional authority – in the form of parents, elders, or husbands – has failed. I am thinking here of Ravi Vasudevan's influential application of Peter Brooks' troping of melodrama – as the recovery of the sacred in the familial space – to this cinematic context, and the evisceration or disembodiment of this Sacred in the context of social crisis.[32] Mother India's psychic cosmos is grasped well via Vasudevan's reading of the reprise of social reality and the realization of the sacred as parents or household gods in the melodramatic: 'melodrama...penetrates to repressed features of the psychic life and into...family dramas'.[33] When Radha shoots her own son, she is doing so for a greater good than her own mother love and family; she is saving the honor of the village/nation, which inheres indiscriminately in its women.

Yet she has to enact this cataclysmic and self-destructive violence because familial and traditional authorities have failed in a moment of crisis that figures the larger crisis of women at risk in postcolonial India. Earlier, the abandoned Radha goes to beg food from Sukhilala for her children. In the crucial scene of impending rape by Sukhilala, the almost vanquished Radha or 'Mother India,' played by the legendary star of the era, Nargis – mudcaked, and therefore quintessentially Mother Earth – turns from her molester to the household deities before whom Sukhilala dares her violation, and questions their power or existence. The sequence that ensues is a shot reverse shot direct address between Radha and Sukhilala's household goddess Lakshmi, the Hindu goddess of wealth, with Lala hovering somewhere off-centre. Sukhilala puts a gold chain around Radha and calls her his 'Lakshmi;' the irony of this under the circumstances will be obvious.[34] As Sukhilala begins to lead her away, Radha throws her mangalsutra – symbol of Hindu wifehood – at the goddess, laughs bitterly, and addresses the deity and the camera, saying 'Devi, did you not feel shame in coming in my shape? If you've appeared as me, then, then you should feel no shame in my dishonor' (my translation). The goddess appears to be silent witness to sacrilege.

This is one of the most troubling bits of dialogue in this film. Radha seems to be saying here that she intends to hold the goddess responsible for the loss of her honor. Addressing the sacred construction of womanhood in the profane world of women's devaluation, the hunted and haunted Radha here turns rebel against a gender-violent society where women are used and then abandoned. The reverse shot shows Lakshmi resplendent, still, a mere doll in Sukhilala's house. Suddenly the camera switches from medium to extreme close-up. Radha's mudcaked face with the huge rolling whites of her eyes – the face of the brown indigene – glowers in bitter anguish at the camera and makes the following address through clenched teeth, 'Don't laugh. Don't laugh. You may bear the world's weight, goddess, but you would not have been able to shoulder the burdens of maternal love' (my translation). Obviously sutured with the gods, the spectator hears the maternal manifesto as a parallel discourse of the fallen woman's self-vindication, her defiance of social and sexual morality. Here are echoes of the discourse surrounding the Abducted Persons Act. Some 'abducted' women, we learn from recent feminist scholarship, resisted repatriation and rehabilitation, and refused their automatic relegation to victimhood or infamy. What should have been abjection turns into rebellion, momentarily. The reverse shot shows the same silent goddess. Radha continues in extreme close-up, saying, 'Become a mother, and your feet will stray too.'

Sukhilala now steps in to remove the enshrined goddess but Radha suddenly wrestles the little shrine from Sukhilala's hands. The 180 degree line of the camera is now crossed so that Radha and the goddess are on one side of it and Sukhilala on the other side, where Radha previously stood. Radha says now to Sukhilala, 'the goddess will not go anywhere. The goddess has given you wealth and brought me before/in front of you as the indigent. I will tell the goddess that it is easy to point the way but hard to walk it; to watch the public farce is easy, but to become the public farce is very, very hard.' The bitter story of inequality is being told as the story of exploitation of poor women, but not, I would emphasize, without an echo of the story of the violated female citizen. Radha is now also in an identificatory mode, clutching the shrine to herself, pathos replacing rage, and Sukhilala cordoned off to the other side of the central axis of vision. Thus, Radha/Nargis is allowed to recover her faith just in time, and to reclaim the goddess. Now the moment of counter-cultural non-traditionalist dis-identification, of rebellion in the female citizen, passes. In the scuffle with Sukhilala over the shrine, Radha's *mangalsutra* (symbol of her married status) drops back on her miraculously. As faith is restored via the sign of the conjugal and the familial,[35] the tyranny of the economic and the class nexus of modernity are obliterated, the would-be-rapist is struck down and the Mother returns to her children. A scene of reconstructive dredging of the flooded fields follows, and the village population returns and reconstitutes as the pre-partition territorial map of India.

However, this melodramatic portrayal of a plenary topos of restitution – as the restitution of sacred and traditional authority – is utterly catachrestic, because once faith is lost, the loss must return as remainder in the future crisis of the heroic mother's struggle against her son.[36] Mishra and others have argued that the film's resolution clearly privileges the 'non-violent,' law-abiding Dharmik tradition in Radha's heroic elimination of the rebel agitator Birju; this is to overlook the catachrestic function of the scene of the mother's rape (a national preoccupation at partition, as we have seen), and its return in the abduction of the moneylender's daughter, which signifies the irreducibility of memories of betrayal and abandonment. Radha's original moment of recognition, that the gods are about to fail her and her honor, returns via Birju's rebellion to haunt the bright future of Nehruvian village India with its dams, cranes, tractors, jeeps, trucks, farm machinery, and pylons.

Christian Metz identified spectatorship as a form of self-identification, as the 'imaginary signifier,' and spectatorship and citizenship are both concerned with forms of 'self-identification': the Indian state in the 1950s was ardently engaged in both.[37] Thus Rajadhyaksha's motif of spectator 'identification,'[38] encompassing and exceeding self-identification to enclose 'social' identification,[39] leads to a third political and historically weighted space of 'identifying' citizens, namely the dual political narrative of the Indian state readjudicating women's 'lost and found' citizenship claims as well as women's legal rights after Partition (1949–53) and with the drafting and passage of the Hindu Code Bill (ca. 1951–56).[40] These three manifestations of the uneasy pursuit of the ideal citizen/spectator emerge from *Mother India*, the quintessential cine-text of the female citizen/subject: mother, sexual object, one of the masses and yet the figurehead of the familial and communal that must be forever reprised through re-imagining a lost sacred and authenticity within the Nehruvian visual frame of development. Structural narratives about the reprising of tradition through the very materiality of the modern thus continue to depict gendered contours. In other words, gender is the ground for the figuration of new nationalisms.

In this sense, the film engages the question about spectatorship that was burning in the 1950s: who was the citizen for whom films were to be made in the new nation? Identifying the film's 'cultural syncretism'[41] is the beginning of a response. The presumably unconscious posing of history as anthropology – the depiction of social reality according to anthropological structural insights as opposed to historicist analyses of 'eventfulness' such as murder of one's child –

onto the film's body was best visualized in a most 'technical' and 'excessive' melodramatic moment, when the call of the Mother who has almost lost her all (except of course her 'honor') restores the sacred community; the migrating villagers return at her song to fall back into a formation that spectralizes and spectacularizes the map of (pre-partition) India in 1957. The villagers' enacting of 'India' answers questions about spectatorship, citizenship and national integration in one perfectly contrived moment and movement, but, as I have already suggested, cannot obliterate the trace realization of the permanent troubling of the eternal sacred in the context of identitarian rape (read as rape of mothers), and national fragmentation.

If partition and abduction are partially hailed historical 'events' in the quasi-anthropological pre-symbolic of *Mother India*, they had been directly addressed as historical events in *Lahore* (1949) directed by M L Anand. This film reorganizes the structural bases of memory as pure historical event. *Lahore* is a relatively obscure film about a woman victim of partition and abduction. The star, however, is an already well-known Nargis, who plays the abducted Punjabi Hindu girl Leelo whom her old lover Chaman rescues after abduction. Nargis had by this time acted already for Mehboob Khan, her director in the future *Mother India*, in the film *Taqdeer* (1944), and it was well known that she was the daughter of an influential Muslim courtesan by a Hindu father. The film tells the story of Leelo left behind in Lahore during the chaos of the partition; there she is abducted and immured by a Muslim man. *Lahore* is the unstudied ur-text of Nargis the Muslim star, and the pre-figuration of the threatened Hindu woman in *Mother India*, yet finds no mention at all in the critical filmographies of Nargis, *Mother India*, etc.[42] This silence is remarkable; indeed, I would suggest that the scene of attempted rape in *Mother India* is replete with associations of Nargis's role as the abducted Leelo in *Lahore* and her life story up to that point in ways that transform a reading of that scene. *Mother India* read as the post-figuration of *Lahore* makes explicit the importance of understanding that when the status of the woman is that of the helpless victim rescued by others, only an 'event' orchestrated by the state can be understood to have occurred, whereas in Mother India the woman's self-help literally reconstitutes the nation as a visible 'structure' of piety and geo-piety. Such logic also helps clarify the edification of Nargis' star text between 1949 and 1957, from sexual prey to Mother India.

The spectator of *Lahore* views the routing of gender and chastity through the 'contaminated' body of the Muslim actress, Nargis. Her personal scandal weaves through the diegetic trauma of crossing the border of partition; the film itself could not cross the border, since it had been banned in Pakistan.[43] Nargis the courtesan's daughter, playing the Hindu woman mythologized into 'abduction victim' embodies the border within the nation, so to speak. By this time, Nargis' star-text was inflected with many layers of stories of abduction and betrayal: her mother had allegedly made her available to act in films for her friend Mehboob Khan, as well as 'sold' her to a wealthy Muslim prince as courtesan.[44] Nargis plays the abducted Leelo with a despair and deathliness that cannot but evoke something of her own life as we know it from Thomas's and Roy's accounts.

Rajadhyaksha's potent allegorization of the identificatory energy of the newly nationalized state towards its citizens and the suturing of this identificatory process with cinematic hailing of the citizen spectator is instructive, but it too makes no mention of this specific juridico-political project of recuperating abducted women in the fifties, and the cinematic narrative popular in the post-nineties, that of describing and enumerating the 'lost,' 'violated' or 'abducted' citizen, usually a woman. It is this other process of 'identification' in cinema's liminal mediation of civil society and state that I am fleshing out. This prosopopoeic enterprise makes unsurprising the return of every analytical turn about the cinema's base to questions of nationalist/state identifications and/or interpellations of citizens and spectators.

From these two films that openly or covertly address the female citizen liminalized in the late forties and fifties, one might turn to the paradigmatic genre of the Indian cinema of the fifties: the 'social.' In the complicated and progressive 'social' of the fifties, purely private existences, identities and cultural norms became ambiguated in the interests of a wider secular modernity. Ravi Vasudevan defines the 'social' thus: 'In the Bombay cinema of the 1950s the 'social' film...was the genre which the industry understood to address the issues of modern life.'[45] Vasudevan, however, keeps the family in focus as one level or layer of that wider 'social' space: 'it is not through a play of individual subjectivities that we are being asked to register the space of the social code, but as a structural field with definite points of authority and notions of convention,' represented by the 'tableau' mise-en-scène.[46] The fifties cinema mediated – in both the juridical and aesthetic senses of that term – this suturing between individual, state and family, differentially and incompletely, not unlike the state itself, as witnessed in the botched demographic project of the Abducted Persons Act. Cohering around the icon of the vulnerable or violated gendered body, the moral/familial keeps reprising as the politico-legal conundrum as well as the cinematic mise-en-scène of the time.

A 'social' film that might be usefully compared with the political epic form of *Mother India* for its reprise of the familial in this regard is *Mr. And Mrs. 55* (1956),[47] a hymeneal romance engaged in the reinvestment of tradition as truer modernity. It depicts the difficult choice of an ideal life partner in a modern world of fluid, indeterminate identities. The heroine Anita faces the double dilemma of a paternal injunction to marry before she is twenty-one or forfeit her deceased father's fortune, and a matriarchal injunction from her feminist aunt to divorce her husband of convenience so she can maintain her independent 'feminist' identity. Naturally, divorce is conceivable only by the provisions of the new Hindu Code Law, and the film's intent, as Jyotika Virdi has eloquently shown, is to undercut this legal genealogy and genesis of modernity.[48] Anita is unable to follow the 'modern' script, however. She divorces the man hustled up by her aunt (Preetam, aptly named the Loved One) after marriage, but seeing the example of other modest Indian women and wives she defies her aunt's 'feminist modernity' to reunite with Preetam. The marriage choice in '1955' is complicated for Anita for two reasons. The first is the Hindu Code Bill, and the second the undeniable indeterminacy of the new male citizen, the denizen of India's new modernity, by turns rogue and nobility; he matches with his moral and social slipperiness her own sliding between the scales of the new normativity of gender rights (the right to divorce, primarily, seen as a western plague) and traditional narratives of feminine normativity. The film achieves, however, a 'traditionalist' and heteronormative resolution, and in this way acts as a moderating cinematic mediation of burning questions about gendered citizenship agitating pubic discourses of law, religion and national belonging. The anonymous *Filmfare* reviewer wrote in 1955: 'the film unfolds a page from life itself, throwing the spotlight on evils of today which strike at the roots of our civilization and culture.'[49]

As the effort to craft a code for reforming and modernizing the personal laws of Hindus – namely, the Hindu Code Bill – proceeded, cinematic metadiscourse had warmed up to the opportunity, as two cartoons in *FilmIndia*'s November 1951 issue would suggest.[50] 'Retired Hurt' suggests battering of the principal architect of the bill, the eminent jurist Dr Ambedkar, an untouchable by birth, by the dominant forces in the majority Congress party who maintained their prejudices against untouchability. The tattered Hindu Code Bill is held up in the centre of the boxing arena by a pugilist, while a Muslim Congress member (supposedly polygamist) says 'Envious of Muslims, eh?' Prime Minister Nehru, the co-architect of the Bill, holds aloft the weapon that appears to have wounded Ambedkar and says, 'I am sorry you are going this way, Ambedkar!' The 'Hindu Code Debate?' depicts various Congress members shamelessly exposing themselves and proclaiming their masculinity to prove themselves to be high-caste men. Such cartoons document the cinematic meta-discourse tacitly supporting opposition to the Hindu Code Bill as unduly empowering minorities *and* women.[51] The tenor of this legal debate is of course to be understood as counter-weaving the discourse on minorities and women in the abduction context. At the very least, *FilmIndia*'s cartoons suggest the shaping of public, secular national identity by the ambiguities of a Hinducentric consciousness experimenting unhappily with modifying its theistic foundations[52] regarding gender and patriarchy.

One might call *Mr. And Mrs. 55* a cinematic text wherein rupture in the discourse of tradition and the ontology of the traditional man and woman tended to metamorphose into the discourse of romance, marriage and the 'family values' social. The last one on this list of 'filter' films I will discuss, *New Delhi* (1956),[53] provides a double prospect on the theme of ontic instability and indeterminacy that is tied to new nationhood and emergent citizenship. *New Delhi*, starring Vyjayantimala and Kishore Kumar, the Ginger Rogers and Fred Astaire of the Indian fifites, may be called the romance of performance. The film details the love of Janki and Anand, a South Indian Tamil 'girl' and a North Indian Punjabi 'boy,' set in the new nation's new capital, New Delhi. Anand masquerades as a Tamil speaker in a city where linguistic and regional prejudice has become intense enough that rental lodging is conditional upon being a co-regionalist or a co-linguist. The nation as home is obviously invoked, though strongly crosscut by ethnographic or heritage tourism shots of the city in the film's opening sequences, wherein architectural and historic sites dominate the camera in an attempt to establish the modernity, urbanity and historic cosmopolitanism of independent India's capital city. The 'tourism' angle never disappears as the romances in the film (Anand and Janki's, and Anand's sister Nikki and a young Bengali-speaking painter's) occur in heritage settings such as the Red Fort and other architectural registers of historic importance. The 'heritage' sequences also induce a theme of ontological instability of the 'common citizen' once again, because the sites' very publicness induces questions about the verifiability and enumerability of those one meets there when on a sight-seeing tour. The new nation is a new world of diverse anonymities.

In a 'tragic' pre-climax, *New Delhi* figures the death by drowning of Janki when her romance with Anand is discovered. Anand's autocratic and bossy father[54] vetoes both his son and daughter's inter-linguistic romances. The fictitious 'death' or suicide of the 'Tamil' Janki, as a result of her romantic scandal, is implicitly the scandal of abduction; her turning to a 'Punjabi' for a romantic partner is diegetically treated with the horror usually reserved until this point in Indian cinema for the fallen woman who transgresses ascriptive ethnic identities. After a tumultuous scene with her distraught father who wishes her dead rather than married to a Punjabi speaker, Janki is thought to have committed suicide by jumping into the river; only her shawl is found by the riverside. Her carefully contrived resurrection enables a rapturous ending to the story of abduction. Janki's 'death' is thus doubly obliterated, by the refiguration of community and by her reabsorption into the family. The advertisement for *New Delhi* declared that it is 'A Film on the *Emotional Integration* of India.' Indeed, the tacking of 'Emotional' before 'Integration' in the slogan is symptomatic: it figures that other integration that was not possible.

The Post-Nineties: *Gadar, Veer Zaara*

One of the great blockbusters of Indian cinema, *Gadar: Ek Prem Katha* (*Gadar; A Love Story*; 2001)[55] was a big budget film marked by 'catchpenny sloganeering and noisy melodrama'.[56] As Deepa Gahlot writes, 'It can't be denied that it was the blatant jingoism of Gadar that made it one of the biggest grossers of all time... .'[57] An example of *Gadar*'s revisionist memory of collective trauma is its representation of trains (see Figure 5).[58] A visually lurid recreation of the tense traumas of flight and survival during the Partition and its massacres, train stations in the earlier scenes of *Gadar*, and train journeys in the later scenes, rewrite the entire political narrative of the partition, relegating the Muslim to the category of national traitor, elevating the Indian Sikh to the role of national hero and savior, and fixing the denationalized woman as the porous body of communal conflict and contestation. Opening sequences show a Sikh family leaving Pakistan and providing poison as a safeguard against abduction to the daughters, the train full of refugees being attacked by armed Muslims, the daughters being raped or undergoing mutilation (it is unclear which) and so forth. These images are piled on each other till the train chugs into Amritsar station in India, where an incredulous Indian crowd watches the blood-bathed compartments rolling in, and the camera pans to disbelief in the extreme close-up shot of the eyes of the Sikh hero Tara Singh, who reads the Urdu words written in blood on the train: 'Indians, learn from us how to chop.'

This montage of ostensibly 'historic' events establishes the film's truth claims, which are enmeshed with the film's anti-Pakistan rhetoric and imagery thereafter. The Sikh hero's disbelief transforms into rage, triggering a rampage of killing Muslims in India. Now the hero sees the heroine Sakina, daughter of a fleeing Muslim aristocrat, in Amritsar station. Tara Singh is unable to cut down the 'Mussalmani' Sakina as his compatriots urge him. She is then left behind in another chaotic scene of trains and pell-mell refugees, and found trampled and bleeding on the station floor by Tara Singh. Now the camera closes up on Tara Singh's face and eyes to show him as a humane figure though a vigilante. Sakina recovers from her faint, and finds herself pursued by a gang of Hindu would-be rapists and murderers. As she flees, she finds herself on the tracks of the departed train where Tara Singh now stands, and as she faces him, they recognize each other. As he fends off the maddened crowd, it is revealed that Tara and Sakina had nursed an unsanctioned fascination with each other during pre-partition days. She is saved by him after much further bloodshed and despite his co-religionists' reminder than she is a 'Mussalmani,' a hated other. Tara Singh, whose eyes have glared and teared in turns, declares her a 'Sikh' woman by anointing her with his blood.

Sakina thus becomes Tara's 'wife,' and the next shot shows Tara and Sakina separated from the rioters and aligned against them in the frame.

Tara and Sakina marry despite his family's opposition. Sakina takes to the life of the Sikh woman and wife with gusto, there is much cultural tourism by way of songs and dances, a child is born. However, now she discovers that her parents are alive and well in Pakistan. When she visits Pakistan, her father refuses to acknowledge her marriage or her child. Sakina is now 'recovered' by her father, and Tara Singh and son must force their way across Pakistan to 're-abduct' (or 're-recover') her. Just in the nick of time, too, for Sakina is about to be remarried to a Muslim man, and is engaging a Qazi – a Muslim priest – in some heated theological debate about women's rights and exogamy according to Sharia law. Her family by this time even urges poison on her, in a not-too-subtle flashback to the opening scene and the Punjabi refugee women. In language reminiscent of Radha in *Mother India*, Sakina refuses death because she is certain her husband will come to take her back to India, and he must not be disappointed. In a firestorm of ethnocidal 'love,' Tara Singh streaks through Pakistan, blowing up bridges, trucks and people, and finally escapes with Sakina on a burning train which he hijacks and drives across the border. There are repeated shots of Pakistani armoured vehicles blowing up while Tara Singh single-handedly destroys the Pakistani army and drives the train to India, quite a rewriting of the train ride of the opening sequences. The body of the Muslim woman remains for Indian state and cinema the fractious locus for the identification of citizenry.

In *Veer-Zaara* (*Veer and Zaara*; 2004),[59] in which a remarkably similar scenario is displayed with inversions and greater graphic slickness – it is Veer Singh, the brave rescue pilot of the Indian army, who languishes in a Pakistani jail for his loyalty to Zaara Hayat Kahn, daughter of a Pakistani politician whom he came to re-recover but could not. The train station here is a scene of abduction by one's own men. Zaara crossed the border to bring her Punjabi Sikh Nanny's ashes to India, as per her Nanny's wishes. The Nanny's story is never detailed; we just know that she migrated with the Muslim family to the Pakistani side of the border, and had wished to be 'returned' to the land of her birth after her death. Zaara's story is palimpsestic in its encoding by the prior history of another, older woman who was taken to Pakistan, presumably during partition. Later we will see Zaara too as an older woman who has chosen India as her home, despite having been born in Pakistan – a reverse image of her nanny. Zaara demonstrates affective assimilation with 'Punjabi' India when she meets Veer's family, after being rescued by him from a hillside accident, a leave for Veer having been conveniently due just around this time. Veer's foster father – a very 'Punjabi' ex-mega-hero Amitabh Bachchan – affectionately tells her that she is a 'true' repository of Hindu traditions. Thus Zaara's assimilation is to be contrasted with the relative non-assimilation of another 'translated' woman, her Nanny.

Like Sakina, Zaara heads back for Pakistan quite lightheartedly, but as Zaara and Veer ascend the bridge between platforms, Veer says in an uncanny echo of partition refugee anxieties: 'Actually, there is a cut-throat race for seats.' Zaara's face is shown as freezing just as Veer speaks, and we encounter a tall man walking up to meet them and us, dressed in a black Sherwani that marks him instantly as anachronistically 'Islamic,' though Veer and Zaara wear contemporary clothing. This is Raza Sharadi, Zaara's fiancé, Veer learns. However, the nearly sociable encounter at the train station, in a thematic, social and aesthetic inverse of the traumatic station scene in *Gadar*, is the beginning of Zaara's re-abduction. But here we must linger a little over the earlier tale of border-crossing, if not of abduction.

Zaara crosses the border in the first place, in legal conformity with the Indian state but disobeying her family and community's wishes. While Zaara's passage to India is politically and legally unmarked and unremarkable until Raza appears at the other end of her trajectory, the Nanny's much earlier and possibly cataclysmic passage is even more unmarked. Zaara can be reabsorbed, clearly into the 'lost' Indian side of her Punjabi self, via Veer Singh and his Punjabi relations who immediately identify her as a returning bride, a sort of returned object of abduction, but the Nanny's near-lifelong existence and exile in Pakistan is a story only of rupture and mysterious surrogacy, in suturing which Zaara's life enters simultaneously into rapture and the rupture of hostile state relations. As Zaara is handed over – 'transferred' from Veer to Raza at the train station – the camera cuts to a limp handshake coming undone between Raza and Veer, superimposed over the figure of Zaara standing between the two men. The story of abduction is then a story of quadruple abduction: it was the Nanny, unidentified and unidentifiable, who began the chain of actions whereby Zaara crosses the border and is recaptured; then Veer crosses the border and is unable to return, like the old Nanny.

The greatest *legerdemain* of *Gadar* and *Veer Zaara* is in their manipulation of a critique of the state that would at first glance appear to be progressive. Scholarship has highlighted the unfairness of some recoveries: "abduction' as defined by the act of 1949 assumed that any and every woman located in the home or under the control of a family or individual of the other community, was eligible for recovery, regardless of any indications to the contrary.'[60] *Gadar* might be seen as playing out this critique. It makes feminist critique serve for contemporary anti-Pakistan and anti-Muslim propaganda. In making melodrama of a 'progressive' recognition of state-sponsored excesses of identifying citizens – though the only state held responsible is Pakistan – *Gadar* makes a calculated bid for exploiting the excesses of spectatorial identification with characters of cross-border romance seen as victims of (Pakistani) state-sponsored identifications. These excesses reify – at the peril of embedding the present in the past – the monumentality of the singular event motivated by desire against the law.

That *Gadar*'s story of redone recovery – or recovery done twice – is a jingoistic appropriation of national space vis-à-vis the woman's body (if the women of Pakistan want to return to their Indian lovers, shouldn't Pakistan itself regret its rapturous rupture?) might take a little while to uncover. In *Veer-Zaara* a very similar double recovery adopts similarly duplicitous modes of writing political structures as individual destinies whose triumph over nation-state politics drives aground more completely any redemptive plot of neighborly understanding: the 'progressive' transnational romance legitimates the distorting representation of the ethnic other whose past is read as the problem of the national present. The gender of citizenship is the fault-line along which the failed dialectic of structure and event in historic memory diverges to make Indian cinema's representation of romantic rapture analogous to that of political rupture.

Chapter Nine

'IT'S ALL ABOUT LOVING YOUR PARENTS'[1]: LIBERALIZATION, HINDUTVA AND BOLLYWOOD'S NEW FATHERS

Meheli Sen

The becoming cultural of the economic, and the becoming economic of the cultural, has often been identified as one of the features that characterizes what is now widely known as postmodernity. In any case, it has fundamental consequences for the status of mass culture as such.[2]

In the battle between love and fear, fear will always win.[3]

India's socio-economic and political arenas underwent unprecedented transformations over the course of the 1990s. In fact, the national public sphere went through changes that altered the fabric of the nation and state in ways that were radical and irreversible. The most salient and powerful transformations were tethered to two processes: the advent of economic liberalization and the concomitant and meteoric rise of Hindu nationalism. Despite the suddenness with which the two phenomena appeared to annex the affective and political energies of the nation, their genesis was in fact in the making for several decades.[4] For my purposes, however, the break that characterized the 1990s to the present is most crucial to underscore.

In July 1991, after a few decades of tentative pro-liberalization rhetoric and under heavy pressures from international lending agencies such as the International Monetary Fund, the Congress government under Prime Minister P V Narsimha Rao undertook concrete steps to liberalize the Indian economy. Economists and 'trade pundits' formed a powerful consensus with the elite bourgeois groups, and liberalization was offered as 'the' mantra for growth and development of the 'sleeping giant;' the frustrations and disillusionments that informed the 'failure' and 'stagnation' of the planned economic structure and state control were sought to be conjured away by the genie of laissez faire.[5]

While the Congress government initiated these processes, it was unable to capitalize on the changes that liberalization both implied and concretized; as the party of the independence movement and of the Nehruvian planned economy, its public image was too strongly associated with the 'past' that the nation was supposedly desperate to overcome. The BJP – Bharatiya Janata Party, the political party of Hindu nationalism, usurped the public terrain as the force that could galvanize both the economy and the Hindu majority of the nation. Thus, 'Hindutva' – or Hindu-ness – in its latest avatar, came to be constitutively tethered to the exultant discourses of economic liberalization. Arvind Rajagopal provides an excellent reading of BJP's canny annexation of the rhetorical terrain unleashed by liberalization:

> Hindu nationalism worked at two levels, on the one hand offering the cultural and ideological accompaniment to liberalization for middle and upper classes, and at the same time translating it into a religio-mythic narrative that would win popular consent...The alliance between economic liberalization and Hindu nationalism was opportunistic and unstable, but nevertheless, in the context, developed a considerable force and momentum.[6]

Hindu nationalism and its multiple incarnations have elicited much scholarly inquiry.[7] In the simplest of terms, the move towards Hindutva meant a recasting of India as 'Hindu Rashtra,' obliterating India's long standing, if barely understood, commitment towards secularism.

It is crucial to understand Hindutva as more than simply a religio-political movement that gained visibility at a particular historical juncture. Hindutva – in its myriad guises, forms and habitats – fundamentally and constitutively transformed the socio-cultural fabric of the Indian nation-state. It not only changed how people thought of themselves and each other, but it also altered the collective imaginary of nationhood. The many arms of Hindu nationalism interestingly became fervent proponents of the economic reforms. The decade of the 1990s saw a curious echo chamber effect between economics and ideology, such that, 'each tells the story of the other, ideology that of the economy, and the economy that of ideology.'[8] Liberalization comes to be as much a 'cultural' imperative as a matter of restructuring the national economy. Conversely, Hindu nationalism self-consciously became the handmaiden of the free market ethos that characterized much of the period.[9] Together, they formed the dyad that best encapsulates the decade politically, economically and culturally.

However, apart from the mutually beneficial, semi-symbiotic relationship described here, Hindutva and liberalization shared other, more profound similarities. Each of these processes contained within itself a curious paradox: while some of its consequences and effects were concrete and tangible – and thus effective – others remained peculiarly diffused and imprecise, and in turn efficacious for this imprecision. This paradox is best evidenced at the level of the dispersal of specific ideas. For example, economic liberalization did not simply mean that internationally visible logos such as Nike and Coca-Cola flooded the market; it simultaneously ensured that these labels and the meanings that accrue to them were rendered both invisible and 'valuable.' By a similar token, Hindu nationalism did not just affirm a certain kind of religiosity; it also brought in its wake an increased investment in seemingly unrelated institutions, such as the Hindu feudal family. I argue that the success with which the dyad informed the diverse components of public culture in India could be understood if we remain sensitive to this duality of its operation – a simultaneous tendency towards concretisation and abstraction.

I contextualize Bombay's new melodramas within this historical moment. Bombay or Bollywood – its new avatar – fashioned a new kind of cinema to respond to the compulsions of this era. With the hindsight now available to us, we can clearly delineate the changes that have animated the industry and its products in the last decade. Before discussing this genre and the films themselves, however, it is useful to reflect more generally on Bollywood's negotiation of nation-ness in the 1990s.

Whose Imagined Community? Bollywood in the Era of Liberalization

It has been repeatedly argued that Hindi cinema is the most salient bearer of nation-ness and national identity in India.[10] This ability to 'imagine' the nation – inscribe it textually, as it were – functions as the strongest legitimation of Bombay cinema's claim to the status of 'a national cinema proper.' Not surprisingly then, the popular Hindi film did not remain insulated from the changes that were sweeping across India over the 1990s.

In terms of formulating a new terrain of visualities, liberalization heralded the arrival of satellite and cable television, and soon hundreds of channels, carrying information and entertainment from all over the globe were beamed into Indian middle-class living rooms. While the state-owned Doordarshan scrambled to overcome its torpor and cultural conservatives blustered at the cultural 'invasion', the film industry found an ally in the satellite channels. Simultaneously, seduced by the possibility of a massive transnational market, Hindi cinema went aggressively global; an increasing number of primarily big-budget Hindi films began to be screened for international audiences. The Indian diaspora has been growing in leaps and bounds over the last several decades, however, it only became a viable target audience for the Bombay industry starting in the 1990s.[11]

Given the potential for earning foreign revenue that the free market enabled, the industry began to woo diasporic audiences with a zeal that was unprecedented. This commitment towards expanding its audience base meant that Hindi cinema had to transform itself in crucial ways. The two most significant changes involved: first, the Bombay product had to somewhat revamp itself to compete as an equal in the global marketplace of images,[12] and second, the diasporic citizen had to be interpellated as an 'Indian' subject within the filmic fantasy.

Feudal Family Romance: Why Patriarchy?

As is clear from my brief and schematic discussion, the massive upheavals that made the 1990s an epochal decade for the nation-state also transformed its most powerful and beloved cultural artifact – the Hindi film. While, some of the changes inflected the workings of the industry, others animated specific genres and films. The Hindutva-liberalization dyad, which gathered considerable ideological and rhetorical momentum over the decade, exercised a profound influence on Bombay cinema.[13]

The Hindutva-Liberalization dyad contained within itself a plethora of meanings and ideas and not all of these were immediately discernable. The national public sphere—all terrains for the dissemination of properly national discourses, including obviously the popular film—was brought into the dyad's orbit of influence. The dyad managed to perform a superstructural overhaul: the ideological matrix of the national public sphere became, at least for a while, completely enthralled by the all-pervasive, mesmerizing appeal of the dyad.[14]

It is this recasting of the larger public sphere that we must be attentive towards, while reading Bollywood's new romance with melodrama. The family melodrama became, over the 1990s, Bollywood's answer to the violence that characterized other genres – notably the hypermasculine action film or the nationalistic genre. While melodrama has always been Hindi cinema's staple generic modality, the narrative centrality of the family had become somewhat obscured in the 'blood and gore' decade of the 1980s. The 1990s witnessed the family melodrama's triumphant return, complete with overwrought emotional registers, soulful music and 'excessive' mise-en-scène.[15]

A certain fantasy of the Hindu feudal family unequivocally occupied the core of this new melodrama. Melodrama persistently displaces all socio-cultural struggles into the domain of the family. Hindi cinema, too, 'projects the imagined nation on the terrain of the family, heterosexuality, and community through contestations that throw into relief its social structures and realignments.'[16] The moment of the 1990s refurbishes this axiomatic formulation: the historical juncture was fundamentally novel, thus Bollywood fashioned a new family to articulate the nation's contemporary vicissitudes. I argue that the most relevant bearer and – perhaps more importantly – arbiter of the nation/family's vexed conflicts is the Father; the Phallus, Paternity and Patriarchy coalesce in a marvelously overdetermined manner in Bollywood's new family romance.

While scholars have noted Bollywood's renewed investments in 'tradition,' the family, etc.,[17] the salient figure of the new, Hindu Father has been subsumed under generalised discussions of 'patriarchy,' which do not do justice to the complex miscellany embodied by the figure. This patriarch draws on the new discourses of Hindutva in multiple ways: at the level of plots, his claim to the films' moral/ethical centers is generously inflected by his religiosity. On a more abstract register, he gathers around himself the deeply masculinist discourses that are espoused/disseminated by the Hindu Right. I would argue that the Father deserves special attention – not only as the most vital carrier of 'tradition', but also because he often emerges as a powerful repository of 'modernity' – which, in this context, refers to the multitude of meanings that inform popular understandings of globalization/neo-liberalism. The meanings, which gather around Bollywood's new patriarch, are flexible and varied, and an inquiry into these can give us a point of entry into contemporary India's dominant cultural and ideological discourses.

I argue that this recent phase in Indian cinema has given rise to vastly reactionary narrative modalities. The new investments in the patriarch have specific ramifications for the representation of the individual citizen-subject, marginalized groups, as well as the heterosexual couple and/or the nuclear family. However, the 1990s also witnessed the triumph of liberalization – with its attendant emphases on consumer choices and the overvaluation of the bourgeois citizen as consumer.[18] Within this matrix, the individual's right to 'choice' emerges as an important locus of meaning. By choice, I am referring to a broader cultural logic of a free-market economy, i.e., the system that determines subjects' right to choose between multiple commodities also governs other aspects of existence. The logic of consumption becomes an overarching framework that organises all aspects of life. However, through textual analysis of several recent commercial hits, I demonstrate that the Father and the discourses that he embodies, in fact legitimize a certain delimitation of 'choices;' in effect, this new patriarch renders the idea of choice or will obsolete. These choices and their inevitable frustrations mostly involve romantic/sexual decisions; the Father and his rhetoric fundamentally seek to oversee the domain of (hetero)sexuality. Thus, the desire of the individual subject-citizen and the authoritarian might of the Father are held in tension in many of these films.

My focus on the patriarch is aligned to the nation's larger investment in a fundamentally masculinist historical moment. The discourses that dominated the Indian public spheres in the 1990s were tethered to constitutively phallic constructs. For instance, a certain aggressive militant Hindutva gathers within itself other resonances that can be characterized as 'male;' the epic hero Ram's transformation from a gentle god to an aggressive crusader, the promise of a 'hard state,' a tough military stance against Pakistan, an enormous financial and affective investment in India's future as a nuclear power, a hawkish crackdown on minorities and illegal immigrants – all of these imperatives can be read as significant components of an overarching Phallic regime. This was a time when India embraced a specific kind of masculinity, the rhetorical dispersal of which was along several axes. Certain representations come to be salient in certain ideological climates. And it is in this larger context of the political economy that the figure of the Bollywood Patriarch is locatable. In a national/cultural terrain geared toward romancing authoritarian power, the figuration of a triumphant symbolic Father is no accident.

A key analytical vector of this inquiry is the stardom of Amitabh Bachchan. While much scholarly work has focused on Bachchan's performance of the 'Angry Young Man' in the 1970s and 1980s, his more recent phoenix-like return from the ashes of a flagging career has not elicited as much critical discussion.[19] Partially, this is an effect of the roles he has chosen in this second stage of his career: while the first phase enabled scholars to read an 'aesthetic of mobilization'[20] in his 1970s hits, his more recent avatar has become a profoundly visible spokesperson for elite authoritarianism. However, I argue that the compelling force gathered by his persona owes much to his earlier stardom. While the roles/characters Bachchan has played in recent years may be far cries from the proletariat hero in *Deewar* (The Wall, 1975), *Lawaaris* (The Bastard, 1981), or *Coolie* (1983), the compelling meanings that gathered around that figure continues to inflect Bachchan's recent performances. The mannerisms – the hooded eyes, the deep voice, the suppressed violence and the curious stillness[21] that gave his violent and ravaged body so much of its power at that fraught moment in history are being redeployed, only to significantly different ends. In this context, it is fruitful to note that Bachchan is almost always a 'parallel text,' that is, he is able to 'move in and out of the film as a star whose presence transcends the text.'[22] It has been contended that Amitabh Bachchan's brutalized body inscribed the violence and trauma of the emergency years; I argue that his stardom continues to resonate with India's political present. In fact, one could map the nation's multiple schisms onto the contours of his long and successful career. Bachchan is the star-text whose body and performance most powerfully registers the multiple tenors of Liberalization-Hindutva dyad in the 1990s and beyond. In a provisional taxonomy, I discern three somewhat discrete configurations of Bollywood's patriarch; interestingly, Bachchan has embodied all three types.

The Phallus Unveiled and the Phallus (Dis)guised: Fathers, Sons and Lovers

The first of these patriarchs is Phallic in the most immediate sense – the locus of authority that is most transparently aligned to a certain glamorised conceptualisation of a revamped feudalism. What I argue sets this father apart from Hindi cinema's earlier paternal figures is both the deep reverence with which he is figured and the equally profound desire to surrender to his regime. Oppositions become mere smokescreens; concealed behind the spurious resistance is a deep desire for non-modernity, to inelegantly rephrase Prasad.

Mohabbatein (Loves, 2000) was the first indication of things to come, as Bachchan's much hyped 'comeback film.' It was also the film that I argue, inaugurated the cleverly veiled thematics of surrender, collusion and compliance vis-à-vis the renewed investment in the patriarch and the stardom of Bachchan.[23] In this film, Narayan Shankar (Bachchan) is the headmaster of Gurukul – the exclusive private college for young men. As a premier educational institution of the country, Gurukul's stature and standing has much to do with its principal's formidable reputation. Conversely, Shankar's authority is buttressed by the school's impressive status and the successful lineage of its students.

I further argue that despite the importance of Raj Aryan (Shahrukh Khan) in the plot, Shankar remains indubitably the flawed 'hero' of *Mohabbatein*. This centrality has to do with narrative imperatives as well as the visual regime within which the film situates the star Bachchan. Shankar is the focal point of the text's fetishisation of feudal authoritarianism. This positioning is amply demonstrated in the film's pre-credit prologue, when three young students, Karan (Jimmy Shergill), Vicky (Uday Chopra) and Sameer (Jugal Hansraj) first arrive at Gurukul. The spectator participates in the point of view shot that first enables us to witness Shankar's physical bearing through an open window as the patriarch pays his daily obeisance to the sun. Thus, we share the reverential gaze of the young men, as Shankar's body is fragmented into component parts of eyes, hands, etc., over several shots—a dramatic jigsaw that finally culminates in the iconic presentation of Bachchan's entire body. The specular/visual mechanisms deployed in this expository occasion remain crucial, because these strategies of representation sustain throughout *Mohabbatein*'s staging/placement of the Bachchan persona. As Shankar turns around, resplendent in the rays of the early morning sun, the camera tracks in slowly to augment the iconicity of the image; with non-diegetic drums on the soundtrack to signpost the significance of the moment, Shankar walks toward the camera in spectacular slow-motion.

This initial frontal/iconic staging of Shankar's body congeals in the very next sequence when the stern headmaster meets his charges in the massive assembly hall. As he effortlessly dominates the imposing contours of the room, Shankar introduces his phallic regime by invoking the hoary trinity that defines Gurukul: Tradition, Honour and Discipline. In this sequence, Shankar delivers a series of barely veiled threats regarding the dire consequences of transgressing the Law of the Father. Mise-en-scène, cinematography and editing are absolutely instrumental in concretising the meanings of the sequence: the students stand en masse dressed in identical uniforms; they are an undifferentiated block of bodies captured by a craning, tracking, extremely mobile camera. Shankar, on the other hand, stands apart on a podium gazing down at his students, carefully dressed in monochromatic somber black. The lighting remains warm, and Shankar is framed by the rays of a painted sun, the often-visible logo of Gurukul, which lends to him a literal halo. The faceless, generalized crowd underscores Shankar's monumental singularity – he remains very much the phallic spectacle obsessively centered by the framing in this sequence. The cinematic apparatus presents this splendor of fascist authoritarian will: we share in the awed contemplation of phallic power via a careful deployment of shot composition, camera movements and points of view. *Mohabbatein's* frank reverence for the Bachchan/Shankar brand of masculinist aggression does not end here; whenever Shankar is framed, the film does so in a manner that underscores the grandeur and majesty of his persona – he is insistently framed through large arches, magnificent corridors and against imposing edifices.[24] Shankar's awesome might and presence is inflected by his deep religiosity: a devout man, he insists on a strict observance of Hindu rituals. This is where the film lays bare its allegiances with the meanings harnessed by the Hindu Right; Shankar's heroism is considerably mediated through his embodiment of a specifically Sanskritized, upper-caste Hindu masculinity.[25]

Into this domain, overseen by the relentless, unchanging Law walks Raj Aryan, 'with a violin in his arms and a smile on his lips.' As an errant son, he immediately seeks to topple the patriarch from the pedestal, and literally and figuratively break the gates that enclose all within Gurukul. In fact, the rest of the text is meant to be read as a battle of epic proportions, a clash of wills that pits 'love against fear'. Aryan's transgressive strategies are fairly transparent and range from wheedling permission for his students to find employment outside the institution's robust gates, to sneaking women into Gurukul from a neighboring college for a dance party.[26] This last misdemeanor prompts a demand for Aryan's immediate resignation, for it is fundamentally the domain of sexuality that the Phallic Father seeks to oversee. As a defiant Aryan cites his contractual right to remain at Gurukul, we become privy to the history of enmity that binds the two protagonists inexorably to each other.

We learn that Raj Aryan Malhotra was a former student of Gurukul, who had audaciously fallen in love with Shankar's daughter Megha (Aishwariya Rai). Enraged by this unacceptable display of desire, Shankar had unceremoniously expelled Aryan from Gurukul without so much as a meeting. Megha had committed suicide in anguish and this tragic event has hardened Shankar further, instead of softening his aging mien. Before we move on to the nature of the lovers' rebellion however – as a wraithlike Megha resolutely joins Aryan after the declaration of war – we must dwell briefly on what is arguably the affective core of the text: Shankar's obsessive desire for his daughter and its corollary, the desire to police his daughter's sexuality. We first see Megha alive through Shankar's flashback, as she offers morning prayers at a shrine. She greets her father affectionately and the spectator is allowed a glimpse into an affective realm where Megha operates not as a daughter, but as a surrogate for her mother. Like a dutiful wife, she takes care of her father's personal needs, keeps his house for him and indulges his whims. In a particularly revealing moment, she masquerades as a bride with a veil and 'mangalsutra,' which had once belonged to her mother. Shankar contemplates his daughter in her bridal finery and proclaims that his 'daughter is more beautiful' than her mother ever was.

After this rather frank verbalization of desire, Shankar finds Megha's love for Aryan unacceptable, when she confesses to her misdemeanor at his feet. She is left to grieve alone, as Shankar rushes out to take punitive action against the imposter who has challenged his primary claim over his daughter's body. While Megha initially appears to accept her father's inexplicably harsh verdict – she tells him she is happy if he is, sitting on his bed in an intimate glow of light – she nevertheless asserts her agency by refusing to live without Aryan. In Shankar's fantasy, she tells him she loves them both and returning the 'mangalsutra' to him, jumps to her death. The refusal to live without Aryan is, significantly, also a rejection of Shankar's desire – hence the meaningful black beads of Hindu matrimony are returned to him. This tragic event, then, is Shankar's albatross and Aryan's Holy Grail –the love of a woman who has paid with her life for having failed to privilege one of them above the other.

After the narration makes us privy to this Oedipal history, the spectator is urged to read the rest of *Mohabbatein* as a massive confrontation between the Phallic Father and the errant Son – two differently configured masculinities, a clash of wills wherein at stake are abstractions such as 'love,' 'fear,' and 'transformation.' While a resolute Aryan vows to irrevocably transform the terrain of the Father that Megha has sacrificed herself for, the patriarch responds with an answering battle-cry from an undying fountainhead of hatred: this confrontation, he declares, has given him 'an old man of fifty five, a reason to fight all over again.' Hence, the text positions us to read the rising action and dénouement of the narrative as a series of skirmishes between two contradictory but equally implacable masculine positions.

However, this carefully erected edifice of opposition, contradiction and difference – conflicts that the text configures as dialectics between two apparently incommensurable poles – crumbles decisively at the climax when the futures of Vicky, Sameer and Karan come to be threatened. For having flouted one too many rules of Gurukul, Shankar expels the young men as much for their lack of contrition as for the transgressions themselves. Anguished but helpless, Aryan comes to him to concede defeat and beg for his students' lives. Shankar gloats at this victory of fear over love, only to be reminded of his own losses by the younger rival. What remains startling about this climactic confrontation is not so much the hyperbole of the dialogue, as the surprising inversion of terms via which Aryan delivers his final blows. Aryan confesses that he had not come to fight at all; what was being interpreted as opposition and rebellion was merely a desire to demonstrate the power of love. Aryan has returned for 'the father of the girl [he] loved…to break the shell of hardness that surrounds' him. Moreover, he has come back for Megha, to show Shankar that she exists wherever there is love; he has also returned to 'complete Megha' because she remains incomplete without both of them. Finally, Aryan delivers the harshest sentence – he condemns Shankar not only to the loss of a daughter, but also the loss of a son – himself. From Aryan's perspective, Shankar remains a 'stubborn defeated man…who has turned his back on the two people who love him most', i.e., Megha and himself.

This, then, is the surprising twist of *Mohabbatein*: the discovery that conflict, struggle, dissent and defiance merely veiled a profound desire to surrender, to comply and collude – in other words, to love. While much of the film traces the ostensible difference between the two principal male protagonists, the closure disperses a different set of meanings. While paying obeisance to the sun, Aryan had asserted his right to do it his 'own way;' at the conclusion, he admits that his goal has been an aspiration to reconciliation, to an ironing out of difference.[27]

Having witnessed this 'climax', the spectator is prepared for Shankar's final speech, which, unsurprisingly, is delivered within the imposing assembly hall. In his final discourse, Shankar accepts the error of his ways, accepts that 'tradition, honour and discipline,' the three pillars on which he has built and nurtured Gurukul, are inadequate for a successful life. Life, he concedes, 'is all about giving and receiving love.' Having experienced this epiphany, Shankar willingly passes on the baton to Aryan, because he wants to hereafter, 'proudly declare that a Raj Aryan exists within each of my students.' Thus, the closure is about the old generation changing its traditions 'so that a new generation can create its own;' it is about the transgenerational transmission of patriarchy – the family of the Father dissolving into families of brothers. It is crucial to understand the tenor of the conclusion, if we are to remain sensitive to the meanings dispersed by *Mohabbatein*: Shankar is emphatically 'not a villain' in this text; he remains a misguided, but noble patriarch, who has simply failed to recognize the rightful son. He is not diminished by his 'defeat'; in fact, the majesty of his persona is augmented by the graceful (if belated) willingness to usher in the changes that are heralded by Aryan. Aryan, now the worthy heir to the Father's mantle, finally seeks and receives the blessing that he has craved all along. Father and Son mirror one another in a profoundly mimetic moment of mutual recognition. This is the occasion when the text seamlessly brings together the contradictory valences of liberalization and the Hindu right; the opposing male protagonists have embodied two discursive strands, and now they appear before us reconciled, united, unified. Contemporary India's myriad schisms and fissures are thus magically conjured away.

Adding to the startling transformation of rebellion into reconciliation is the figuration of a transgenerational erotic triangle. The final shots of *Mohabbatein* feature Father, Daughter and Lover together walking toward Gurukul's imposing contours; Megha is finally 'complete,' an effect of the collusion between two differently garbed patriarchies. She wears her mother's 'mangalsutra' as a gesture of acceptance of Shankar's desire; she walks between the two men, no longer haunted by their difference but now finally secure in their fundamental sameness.

Mohabbatein is remarkable for its reverential presentation of Phallic power; it transforms a non-modern, authoritarian ethos into a fetishized spectacle. The text's success hinges on a monumental masquerade – the performance of 'difference,' the narrative emphasis on conflict, which we only belatedly recognize as a thematic of collusion and compliance. This novel inscription and elabouration of patriarchy is what defined post-1990 Bollywood. Embodied by Bollywood's new fathers – but also its new sons and lovers – the patriarchal consensus reinvents itself in the decade through new guises and manners that are not necessarily immediately recognizable as such. And this is the juncture in which the liberalization-Hindutva dyad gains its salience. *Mohabbatein* is a deeply conservative film but appears not to be; our identification with Aryan makes us complicit in an ideological nexus that is far subtler and thus more effective, than an alliance with Shankar's more open chauvinism would entail. The spectator is left enthusiastically cheering for the harried lover, willing for him to 'win' the battle of love against oppressive, feudal forces only to realise that the battle has already been won elsewhere.

Mohabbatein was also the first film that was able to capitalize on the phallic potential inhabiting the Amitabh Bachchan star text. Hereafter, Bachchan would embody the phallus in countless films, many of which would create box office history both within the sub-continent and in diasporic hubs worldwide. Bachchan would soon become the contemporary moment's most emblematic Father.

The Family of Business and the Business of Family: Fathers, Big Business and Errant Sons

If a certain kind of patriarch(y) is revered, fetishised and simultaneously veiled in recent popular cinema, modernity—or more accurately, a particular vision of globality – is also inducted into this discursive domain as a necessary ally. I have argued that Bollywood's plush family dramas pitted the patriarch and his discourses against a younger figure – the Son or the Lover who could carry on the patriarchal baton without ever appearing to do so.

However, at this time the Bombay film also imagined another patriarch – a new Phallic Father who is 'himself a signifier of modernity.' This modern-global figuration of phallic authority gathers much of his political and emotional charge from his ability to speak from positions that are emphatically those aligned to the new India being envisaged by the bourgeoisie at this time. This Father is aligned to the world of big business – ranging from heavy industry to corporate finance. In the era of economic liberalization, the new India being visualized by its proponents relies heavily on discourses of corporate competence, on an assemblage of images that resonate with India's triumphant entry into the global market. Bombay film was also fashioning a new iconography to legitimise/celebrate India's new economic culture. From a figure that articulated feudal authoritarianism and 'traditional values,' the Patriarch morphed into a corporate colossus, effortlessly and comfortably at home in Bollywood's imaginings of a market driven economy. Indeed, 'at-home-ness,' becomes his special weapon; the ease with which he presides over public and private spaces, the aura of inhabiting the home and the outside world with power and grace come to be hallmarks of the revamped Father. However, his most efficacious source of power is aligned to the particular economics he straddles – his control of capital.

The world of the Hindi family melodrama is awash with wealth; from consumable objects that are dispersed throughout the filmic frame to the championing of consumption as lifestyle, this cinema is wholly invested in the euphoric rhetoric of the market. One of the key factors in the creation and maintenance of this mise-en-scène of plenitude is the absolute erasure of labour. Completely unmoored from the domain of production, consumer objects/lifestyles float freely through the films, securely legitimised by narrative/national ideology.

It is in this context that a film like *Ek Rishtaa: The Bond of Love* (2001), directed by Suneel Darshan, becomes exceptional. *Ek Rishtaa* is one of the only films of the period that locates industrial labour and capital within the story of a family. The film is heavily melodramatic both in terms of style and content, with a florid, excessive mise-en-scène and many emotionally charged moments of confrontation. It tells the story of the rise, fall and eventual victory of patriarch/industrial tycoon, Vijay Kapoor (Amitabh Bchchan). In a marvelously adroit sleight of hand, *Ek Rishtaa* extends the domain of the organic, extended Hindu family to include the factory, its spaces/modes of production and its members, the urban industrial labour pool. The melodramatic mode operates on a much broader canvas, as 'outsiders' are inducted into a system of synthetic kinship. *Ek Rishtaa* personalizes the impersonal workings of industrial and late-industrial capitalism primarily through the figure of the patriarch and by deploying the family as a metaphor in order to contain and neutralize threats that beset him from both within and without.

The film opens with a huge baroque mansion being threatened with liquidation via an auction notice from the state. The plot is largely narrated through a flashback as the ailing Vijay Kapoor mulls over the events that have led to his present state of ruin. The very first public memory is that of a business symposium where the respected industrialist delivers a speech outlining his vision of a successful business enterprise. Immaculately clad in a designer suit, Vijay Kapoor intones in his deep baritone:

> Behind every successful industry or enterprise there are three crucial components – the owner, the management and the workers. Often workers will have complaints against the company. Owners often have problems with workers; management and workers cannot agree. But the owner is responsible, answerable for the company. In a situation like this, if a monthly meeting is organised between all three divisions – where they can have straightforward conversations – then a *relationship* will develop between the owner, management and workers. Then the whole establishment comes to be well organized – *woven into a strong family*. And as far as I know *no family in the whole world has ever gone on strike!* If owners are able to do this (organizing), the problem of sick industries will be resolved forever.

While the glib naïveté of this reading of industrial conflict and ailing industries may seem laughable at first glance, the ideas propounded in the speech fit perfectly into the narrative organisation of *Ek Rishtaa* where Kapoor's business and family come to be organized along similar lines. Vijay Kapoor's business is a 'Hindu Family Business,' in which the control of capital and resources – much like a Hindu extended family – is fairly centralised, with a strict vertical hierarchy of power and authority. The conflicts of *Ek Rishtaa* arise when the line between 'organic family' – father, mother, children – and 'synthetic family' – industrial workers and other outsiders as kin – disappears completely. The entire film is structured as a series of crises that beset Kapoor as he struggles to keep his 'family' (both real and metaphorical) together. As Father/Owner – and in the film the roles constantly slip and slide together – he is 'responsible and answerable' for the health of his empire.

A close reading of the factors/agents of threat to Kapoor's universe enable us to unravel the film's rather complex figuration of the family business. Trouble begins simultaneously on two fronts – his son Ajay (Akshay Kumar), returns with a business degree from the United States and his own ambitions and Preeti (Juhi Chawla), his pampered daughter, falls in love with Rajesh Purohit (Mohnish Behl), an employee of managerial rank. Much impressed by Rajesh's honesty and integrity, Vijay Kapoor blurs the division between employer and employee even further, by conferring upon him the title of his 'son' as he marries Preeti and invites the couple to live in his home.

Ajay, on the other hand, dreams of starting his own information technology business and seeks his father's financial and emotional support. Vijay does not believe that any business can flourish without experience and urges Ajay to join his own company instead. The clash of opinions and desires between father and son are presented as a face-off between 'experience' and 'education.' Interestingly, the conflict here is also one that India is struggling to resolve in the present moment: what we have here is the transition – the moment of dislocation – between an economy of 'high capitalism' – characterized by heavy industry and manufacture, and, an economy of 'late capitalism,' where capital is globalized and labor, manufacture and distribution/consumption have become entirely separated from one another. The narrative of *Ek Rishtaa* attempts to allegorize the alternatives that confront newly liberalized India[28] – the choices between 'Fordism and flexible accumulation.' to borrow a phrase from David Harvey – through a melodramatic confrontation between two generations.[29]

Initially obedient to his father's dictates, Ajay acquiesces and joins the company. Vijay however, insists that his son reach the pinnacle of the company pyramid through hard work and experience; simple inheritance ought not to bestow upon Ajay an entitlement of privilege. Having internalised this noble work ethic, Ajay begins at the bottom of the totem pole – in the factory floor as a machine operator. When an altercation with union leader Hari Singh for violence and gambling in the factory precipitates a strike, a furious Vijay reprimands Ajay by pointing out that he has not suffered a strike in 25 years because he has learned to live with and has negotiated with union leaders – as necessary evils. He proudly declares that he uses the union leaders 'as dogs... and I keep them at my feet.' Following a humiliating public apology ordered by his father, Ajay resolves to start his own business, in spite of Vijay's disapproval.

This then is the first threat of dismemberment; and as the conflict gathers momentum, Ajay borrows money from the market to start his own IT firm. This leads to another momentous confrontation between father and son, as Vijay balks at the idea of his son taking a loan from 'outsiders.' After several highly dramatic altercations and melodramatic twists aided and abetted by Rajesh's ingratiating presence, Vijay orders his son to leave the mansion: 'In this house every word I speak is the Law. I'm now ordering Ajay to leave this house. Get out of here!' he thunders in front of a stunned family. A devastated Ajay leaves home despite entreaties from Protima (Rakhee) and his siblings. He marries Nisha against her father's wishes and they set up a nuclear home; Ajay also starts his firm. Ajay's many transgressions straddle the 'inside' and 'outside' dynamics that the film sets up in crucial ways. First, Ajay wants to break away from the family business; in the film's terms, this is tantamount to breaking away from the family itself. Second, he jeopardizes the factory by antagonizing the evil union leader, Hari Singh. He constantly pits his education against his father's vast experience in the workings of industry. But finally his most serious offense is understood by Vijay as an attack on his selfhood and authority as patriarch. Ajay is not only disrespectful towards his father, but he also insults Rajesh – the outsider whom the patriarch has adopted as son. Rajesh's supposed humiliation finally becomes the catalyst for Ajay's eviction from home. All members of the family pay this price because Vijay Kapoor's conceptualization of family and business must be maintained at all cost.

The second threat is posed by Hari Singh – the smarmy labour leader who joins hands with Rajesh to ruin the family/business. Here too, Hari Singh's status as labour leader is mediated through his connections with family.[30] Rajesh is the typical villain who enters the home as Preeti's husband and adopted son and subsequently betrays the family's trust in the name of 'doing business.' He, more than any other agent, destroys the family from both within and without by stripping Vijay Kapoor of his company's control. Kapoor is harassed by creditors and pushed towards the brink of bankruptcy; the patriarch is able to negotiate threats as long as they come from the outside; estranged from his biological son and devastated by his adoptive son's betrayal, Kapoor falls seriously ill. The potency of this patriarch is heavily mediated by his control of capital and labour; once these cease to scaffold his authoritarian persona, he literally collapses. The financial doom heralds the possibility of both home and factory being auctioned off. At this juncture the synthetic family envisaged by Kapoor starts crumbling, and, it becomes necessary to re-sketch lines between private and public, insiders and outsiders, the home and the world. At this moment, the film returns from flashback to a narration in the present tense.

Ajay rushes home to support his father in his darkest hour and vows to save the family home and factory – his father's 'honour.' The biological family rallies around the patriarch and looks ready for a new consolidation. However, another crisis forestalls the process: Nisha, Ajay's pregnant wife demands that he choose between their conjugal home[31] and his natal family because she is unwilling to share his love with others. Nisha is squarely placed in the domain of affect and, as such, the threat she presents would involve only the personal, private sphere. However, *Ek Rishtaa*, as I have outlined above, elides the distinctions between business and family such that each term comes to define the other. Thus, Nisha, the wife speaks the language of business transactions: she insists that Ajay rebuff his natal family in exchange for her love. She withholds her affection because in her understanding Ajay violates the contract between them that they would both leave their natal homes to build a home together. Ajay refuses to break old relationships to sustain a new one, and a distraught Nisha returns to her father's home. This sets up a parallel narrative of dismemberment as the Kapoor clan struggles to come together and overcome the colossal odds that beset them. Preeti returns to her father's home as well, unable to make Rajesh recognize the error of his ways. Rajesh, on his part, insists that he has not acquired the money by unfair means (i.e., he was not doing anything illegal when he abused the power of attorney); he has merely done 'business with a foolish, weepy family.' Though within his legal rights when he appropriates Kapoor's money and assets he breaks a much more serious law: for *Ek Rishtaa*, the Law of the Father far supercedes the law of the land,[32] and it is for the transgression of the former that Rajesh must be brought to justice.

The narrative sets up a series of bipolar oppositions between 'good' and 'bad' family business: while Vijay Kapoor's business ethic is built on strong principles of honesty, trust and kinship, Rajesh's business acumen is unworthy, for it rests on his clever tongue and his capacity for treachery. Ajay is young and impetuous and lacks the necessary experience to make things work. Hari Singh is merely a mercenary pawn who can be bought and sold. And Nisha and her father dishonour the sacred ties of business and family by swapping one for the other – never mind that Kapoor himself does the same on several occasions. These then, are the crises that confront the embattled Kapoor clan. While the threats posited by the film can be read as a series of slippages between family and business, the resolutions offered are startling insofar as they refuse to engage the questions raised by the film. Threats are either brutally neutralized or magically conjured away.

The factory/family must be restored to the patriarch and the hierarchical organisation of these institutions must be recuperated under the aegis of his authority. Led by a repentant Hari Singh – who realizes that 'if the master's home is in darkness, there cannot be any light in worker's homes' – and Ajay, the workers storm and vandalize Rajesh's home over a long, drawn out climax. Threatened with lynching, a terrified Rajesh seeks refuge in the only haven of safety –Vijay Kapoor's office. As he begs for Vijay to save his life, the Patriarch – now re-enthroned on his rightful chair asks: 'How much would you say is the price of your life?' Since refusal to pay back would mean death, Rajesh relents and promises to return Kapoor's money/property/factory and other assets. Vijay Kapoor metes out punitive justice that is entirely pre-modern and extra-legal. The police do not make an appearance to protect Rajesh or his rights as citizen. This is the moment at which *Ek Rishtaa* finally embraces the non-democratic ethos it has cleverly veiled; the final dénouement, the brutal use of industrial labour to stage a violent coup lays bare the film's ideological propensities. The Patriarch's spectacular vindication and revenge collapse the family-business dyad one last time as he is rehabilitated as both Father and Owner. Rajesh thus learns the family business by paying a high price; the proximity to death 'cures' him, as it were, and the Kapoor family welcomes him back as repentant son and grateful employee. However, his punishment gains another dimension as Preeti refuses to forgive the pain he has caused her family. The film does not attempt to recuperate the couple.

Ajay's ambition – his dream of starting his own IT firm – is simply disavowed. Since the joint Hindu family business gathers its power from the Patriarch's position at the helm as both father and owner, Ajay's defection would leave him semi-castrated, maimed. Vijay Kapoor must, of necessity, continue as lord and master of both home and factory for his authority to be reinstated in full. Interestingly, this also translates as the triumph of high capitalism over late capitalism. In Bollywood's grammar, corporate finance must wait in the wings until an older model of manufacture and development is ready to relinquish the reins. While this is not a reflection of any visible reality in India, the popularity of films like *Ek Rishtaa* reflects the larger need for the sustenance of such a myth.

Nisha and Ajay had been unable to reconcile and their separation causes each of them much pain. *Ek Rishtaa* however, cannot allow this particular couple to remain unconsolidated. As the son and heir, Ajay would carry the family line forward; hence his offspring must be brought back into the fold. Furthermore, the desire of the modern couple for privacy has already been articulated by Nisha, and in order for *Ek Rishtaa's* grammar to work, this desire must be neutralized. Rejoining the Kapoor family with her newborn son, Nisha apologises to her parents-in-law for her desire to build her own, independent nuclear home. This individualistic desire, she says contritely, was a result of her flawed upbringing *sans* a mother; in other words, having grown up in a nuclear and thus 'incomplete' family, Nisha had been unable to appreciate the fulfillment and generosity inherent in an extended family. Thus Ajay and Nisha both willingly relinquish their dreams of branching out on their own; in *Ek Rishtaa's* spectacular recuperation of Patriarch(y), the individual citizen-subject, the modern heterosexual couple, urban labour, modes of production – the very desire for modernity in its multiple guises – are simply subject to erasure. The Hindu family business cannibalises all else; the patriarch Vijay Kapoor renders all dissent obsolete. In *Ek Rishtaa's* ideological and narrative syntax 'the feudal is the modern' – thus the very terms of articulating a dialectical relation are disabled, if not overturned.

There is a kind of plenitude in this operation of neutralizing dissent. The film manages its own contradictions with a kind of competence that is remarkably consistent. As Vijay Kapoor adds an 's' to a sign reading 'Vijay Kapoor and Son(s) Industries', he effortlessly inducts Rajesh, Ajay, Hari Singh, the labourers, and even Nisha back into the Family Business. *Ek Rishtaa's* success as a text is secured by this competence – it never slips up and exposes the labor that goes into the management/erasure of oppositional discourses.

The Abject Father and the Poetics of Suffering: *Baghban*

Ravi Chopra's *Baghban* (The Gardner, 2003) undercuts and even reverses many of the meanings that gather around the Phallic patriarch in the 1990s family melodramas. As mentioned above, the authoritarian stature of the Patriarch in films like *Ek Rishtaa* and *KKKG* is buttressed by the Patrriarch's control of wealth and capital. A complex series of narrative and ideological scaffolds maintain and uphold, as it were, the massive construct of the patriarch. The dispersal of Amitabh Bachchan's massive star-presence also undoubtedly contributes to the visual and ideological strength garnered by the Father. And this is partially the reason for *Baghban's* emotional power: here again we have Bachchan as Raj Malhotra the father, but a different set of meanings accrue to his character in this film. How these alternate meanings are arrived at, is of special interest to this discussion of patriarchy in the 1990s.

Baghban's most powerfully iconoclastic gesture is to humanize the patriarch. In lieu of narrative and style colluding to 'produce' the spectacle and splendor of phallic authority, *Baghban*, in a certain sense, cuts the father down to size. Raj Malhotra is a middle-class man, who works in a bank and by his own admission, 'is used to working under a boss.' The transformation of the Bachchan father from capitalist mega-magnate to service sector employee considerably impacts the meanings – both affective and narrative – that attend to this figure. Malhotra is a 'common man,' insofar as Bachchan can embody a certain quotidian, middle class subject position. He is loving, accessible and is entirely devoted to his wife Pooja (Hema Malini) and his grown up children. Hence, the nature of allegiance demanded by the father is also markedly different: Raj Malhotra asks for love, not obedience.

This middle-class-ness perhaps also accounts for Malhotra's modernity – he is, quite emphatically, a bourgeois subject. While his profession and general demeanor signposts this, what fundamentally corroborates it is his relationship with Pooja. In a remarkable departure from the standard Hindi film's desexualisation of parental figures, *Baghban* represents Raj and Pooja as a modern companionate couple. The film begins with their fortieth wedding anniversary, and, takes great pains to establish the mutual attraction and romance that animates their marriage; the romance between Raj and Pooja is a primary conduit of meaning for *Baghban*. This love story, in fact, forms the affective fulcrum for the text; it is their separation that will propel the narrative forward. In tandem with this configuration of the modern couple, Raj and Pooja are never shown to regulate their children's lives; in fact when Aloke (Salman Khan), their *de facto* adopted son, calls from London to seek permission to marry his girlfriend Arpita (Mahima Chowdhary), they joyfully give their blessings and consent. The film provides many such instances Raj and Pooja's warmth, generosity and supportiveness of their children's desires. Raj depletes his life's savings in order to fulfill his children's needs, on an assumption that they are his 'fixed deposits,' his assets to count on after retirement.

The fundamental crisis of the narrative revolves around Raj and Pooja's desire to move in with the children after Raj's professional retirement. Finding themselves increasingly lonely for their companionship, Raj and Pooja invite their three sons and two daughters-in-law to decide where they should live together as a family. This decision alarms the children considerably, since none of them are able to make room for the older couple in their carefully organized nuclear homes and hectic lives. Reluctant to reject Raj's proposal offhand, the younger generation devises a cruel strategy: they propose to divide the couple between them, and take turns in allowing each parent to spend a few months in their homes. In effect, this would mean that Raj and Pooja would be forced to live apart, after forty years of coupledom. The plan is predicated on a crucial assumption – that Raj and Pooja will never agree to the separation, and their request to move in will die a natural death. This however, does not happen. On the contrary, Pooja practically forces Raj to agree to this strange proposal; she is unable to gauge the enormity of her children's heartlessness and urges Raj to 'not suspect his children's motives.'[33]

Thus, in a melodramatic gesture par excellence, the second generation's cruelty and Machiavellian manipulations are counterpoised to the parents' warmth, love and 'goodness.' This is not the only instance of a bipolar confrontation between 'compassionate' and 'bad' modernities in *Baghban*, but it remains one of the most compelling emotional moments in the film. Amidst a great deal of sadness and despair, the couple goes their separate ways; in a moment of overdetermined pathos, their pet dogs go with the youngest son because Raj 'cannot bear to see them separated.'

Hereafter, the plot consists of a litany of deprivations and daily humiliations that Raj and Pooja endure in their uncaring children's homes. Ranging from Raj being disrespectfully asked to vacate the head of the table and relinquish the morning newspaper, to Pooja having to sleep in the maid's room because the granddaughter Payal (Reemi Sen) refuses to share her bedroom, *Baghban's* singular achievement is in organizing the suffering of the elderly parent in fairly convincing ways. Some privations are large and some not, but each moment of suffering cumulatively impacts the affective register of the film. However, the most gut-wrenching experience – for the protagonists and by extension for the spectator – remains the separation itself. Raj and Pooja's acute need for each other's company and presence accounts for the considerable emotional power of the text. And the fact that each must conceal their pain from the other, adds yet another layer of poignancy to an already overwrought scenario.

One of the most compelling instances of Raj's pain remains the moment when his eye-glasses break, for this leaves him unable to read Pooja's letter. Raj tentatively requests his son to get the glasses repaired but in yet another telling display of callousness is insensitively rebuffed. When his little grandson spends the money allotted for buying shoes in repairing the glasses, he is yelled at and beaten up by Reena (Divya Dutta), the daughter-in-law. The castration of the Father is complete – *Baghban*, the final text of the series, strips the Patriarch of wealth, power and even dignity within the domain of the modern nuclear family. An abject[34] figure of lack and suffering, this father must find solace outside of biological kin in a café run by a Gujarati couple Hemant (Paresh Rawal) and Shanti (Lilette Dubey). They call him 'mota bhai' (elder brother) and treat him with respect and kindness. The café becomes a surrogate home for Raj, and the owners and young customers, his kin. Meanwhile Pooja has no such respite and continues to suffer in her own exile, enduring insensitivity from her son's family.

We must pause at this juncture and evaluate the nature of Raj and Pooja's suffering. Clearly, being separated from one another by their 'uncaring' offspring is the first and unkindest gesture of all. Hereafter, everything that happens to Raj and Pooja – their daily tribulations within the cold contours of the modern nuclear family – comes to be framed within this larger narrative of suffering that is already in place. *Baghban's* masterful move is to organise the distinct occasions of suffering in a manner that collapses the distinctions between them. In other words, the mistreatment that Raj and Pooja receive at the homes of their sons – which the film expends significant narrative energy in presenting – comes to be a single narrative of 'bad modernity.' It is the coherence – the singularity, as it were – of this narrative of pain and endurance that demands further unpacking.

The seriousness of the offenses against the parental figures is wide-ranging. There is neglect and indifference, often coupled with aggressive or harsh behavior, but there are also demands of modern existence that the film circumscribes within the previously described metatext of suffering.[35] *Baghban* makes no distinctions between particular acts of insensitivity or cruelty undertaken by the children and the general vicissitudes of modern, metropolitan existence. Since the film organizes all these disparate moments and occasions within the metatext of suffering and endurance, it becomes possible to elide the distinctions between legitimate and illegitimate demands/treatment; the constitutive difference between inflicting pain/humiliation on an elderly parent and exercising one's basic rights as a modern subject collapses in such a melodramatic arrangement. In disempowering the Father and recasting him as a figure of abjection, the film mounts a critique of modern metropolitan life and the nuclear family that completely annihilates both, as emotionally bankrupt and devoid of human values. Invalidating the quotidian expectations/entitlements of modern subjectivity – by framing it within a larger narrative of filial cruelty – is only one avenue through which *Baghban* articulates this critique. A second avenue is explored through the good Son, Aloke, and his wife Arpita.

Aloke, the non-biological son comes to be a repository of 'good' values in *Baghban*. In vivid contrast to the morally dissipated representations of Raj's biological offspring, Aloke and his wife Arpita embody a refashioned modernity, one that is in tune with the parents' value system. This couple and the discourses they stand for, therefore, deserve some scrutiny. Aloke and Arpita have both studied in London; in Hindi cinema's shorthand, this comfort in inhabiting different national terrains and spaces makes them citizens of a global order. However, in spite of the 'western' allegiances Aloke and Arpita deeply cherish 'traditional Indian' values, among which respect for elders features predominantly. Aloke and Arpita repeatedly find themselves and their home 'empty and incomplete,' without the warmth and benevolent parental presence.[36] They plead for Raj and Pooja to grace their home for a few days, because, Aloke proclaims that it has been his dream to have his parents live with him. Moved by their love and generosity, Raj and Pooja concede to spend a few days at this 'ideal' nuclear home. Aloke refuses to leave their side, preferring to spend his nights at their bedside. This startling gesture not only privileges the bond with parents over the relationship with spouse, it also dismantles the very construct of privacy between the conjugal couple as obsolete.

This then is the family, and this is the modern couple 'worthy' of parental love. The trials and tribulations, the long months of painful separation that Raj and Pooja undergo at the homes of their own kin are nullified and compensated for in Aloke and Arpita's house. This vision of a non-modern familial utopia, where the Father (and by extension, also the mother) is venerated as divinity comes to operate as yet another significant component of the indictment of modernity. *Baghban* is remarkable as a text for it performs an ideological gesture of great dexterity; it castrates the Father, disempowers him, and strips him of wealth, dignity and agency. In doing so, it inscribes the patriarch as a monumental figure of lack, as a victim par excellence. As an abject victim Raj Malhotra – always already Amitabh Bachchan as well – comes to be the hero, the primary locus of spectatorial identification. The tale of paternal suffering however does not conclude here; it closes on a reification of the non-modern – and this recuperation of the Father as Phallus is what I turn to now.

The warmth and affection Raj and Pooja receive at Aloke's home restores their shattered spirits somewhat. They return to their old home and community of friends, with their 'new' children in tow. The film could have ended here; this moment of reunion provides an occasion for a satisfactory closure, for the couple is restored to their former happy life. However, the text forcefully reminds us of what is at stake here – the Father must have his vengeance in order be completely reinstated. How *Baghban* arrives at this recuperative moment is worth dwelling on, because it forcefully affirms the terms of this analysis. Raj had once written of his suffering at the hands of his children; he had, in the long months of incarceration and anguish, transcribed his experiences on paper. This crucial testimony had been left behind in Hemantbhai's café, his former haven of peace and companionship. Via a complicated series of coincidences the manuscript is finally recovered and published as a book – titled *Baghban*. This resonance between book and film titles is no coincidence; the film is about nothing and no one else, but the Father – text mirrors testimony in powerful communion. The Father is the gardener – the compelling central metaphor of the film – the one who carefully and painstakingly tends to his saplings, only to be cast aside as the garden matures and begins to bloom on its own. Leaving this unworthy garden behind, the Father rises again to claim his rightful place and to judge and to assign guilt and punishment. The title – mirrored as book – reminds us that we, as spectators, have been the privileged recipients of the Father's Word. Raj Malhotra's book is nominated for the Booker Award. *Baghban* (the book) becomes logos (the Word) a text that holds within it the might of the Phallus. And what, we may ask, of the film? How can we tell the two apart? The point here is the absence of that gap – the collapse of the two texts – their singularity, as it were, is what makes the film compelling; what we have been privy to, we retrospectively recognize, is that narrative which refuses a radical separation from the Father's Word. Poststructuralist/ Feminist theorists have long remarked on the inherent masculinist underpinnings of Language, Philosophy, Culture, via the term phallogocentrism – the inherent power of the Word that is always already masculine. In a marvelously overdetermined manner, *Baghban* makes this connection between the symbolic authority of the speaker and the spoken word literal.

The authority of the Father's word – and this is a key signifier of his legitimacy – remains unexamined. The book is beyond scrutiny or assessment, because that would be unnecessary and indeed impossible, for it would have to mean a re-telling of the film itself. We, as spectators, already know the veracity of *Baghban's* narrative substance. However, the book does have a diegetic audience – the reading public who gather to pay homage to the Patriarch in the final moments of the film, at a reception organised to celebrate the success of the book. This public – along with the spectator – is the addressee of the text, is the privileged recipient of the Father's traumatic testimony. Indeed, the spirit of bearing witness to a long and agonizing journey is writ large on this sequence as Raj declares, 'I am not a writer...I have only written what life has taught me.' The reversal of the Father's fortune, the undoing of his abjection makes this a key moment in the film: the moment when the Father can reclaim the Phallus, the moment when the Patriarch – character, star and symbolic construct – will be reinstated by Hindi cinema. And *Baghban* closes with him in his moment of triumph and vindication. This is also the crucial occasion of assigning guilt and taking punitive action. As Raj Malhotra embraces Aloke as his rightful kin and heir, he also metes out crushing punishment to the biological sons.

After the speech, which he concludes by affirming his love for Pooja, Raj is asked by reporters what he would have done if *Baghban* were to be his own story. Unflinchingly Raj – now securely refortified – replies, 'Those children who are not able to give their parents love, or shelter or respect – I would never forgive them; I would punish and disown them.' The guilty sons and their spouses grovel for forgiveness, but even Pooja remains implacable. As the Father transforms from a kind, affectionate man to a vengeful god, the only ones within the hallowed circle of his embrace are Aloke, Arpita and his grandchildren. The repentant offspring remain forever banished for having locked horns with the Law. Modernity – as we understand it – is also deconstructed in the same moment.[37]

I have explored some of the transformations that attended to Hindi cinema in the 1990s and beyond. I have argued that the new idioms, the new languages of this cinema must be understood within a larger national-political context. This large terrain was itself being decisively reordered at this time – the rise of Hindutva and the liberalization of the national economy altered the public culture of India almost beyond recognition. While the visual texture of the popular film embraced new global technologies and disparate regimes of visuality such as the music video and the advertisement film, the content of Hindi cinema looked inward to focus on the family, nation, religion and tradition. This is why, I argue, that recent Bombay cinema is best analyzed by interrogating its allegiances with the liberalization-Hindutva dyad. Both of these processes harness a wide range of events and meanings, but the family melodrama managed to inscribe these in fairly consistent ways through its own visual and narrative grammar. I have further argued that a particularly compelling locus of meaning comes to be the Father – the figure who becomes salient in the dispersal of such terms as 'tradition', 'family', etc. A deep conformism, indeed conservatism, colors the ideological propensities of Bollywood's slick new products.

This Father ought not to be subsumed within generalised discussions of an abstraction called 'patriarchy.' As a central and iconic construct of this new melodrama, the Father is also a crucial carrier of modernity and globality – terms which have gained much currency in post-liberalization India. In other words, the comforting binaries that simplify our understandings of 'tradition' and 'modernity' as dialectical opposites have collapsed in this new Bollywood. The terms on each side of the binary now slip and slide into one another, such that a radical distinction becomes virtually impossible. Paradoxes abound, as a 'new tradition' seeks to replace the 'old modern'. However, this state of affairs – indeed this competence with which Bollywood continues to confound our critical paradigms – should not paralyze critique. The somewhat comforting critical position that enables a recuperation of another vague abstraction, 'people,' through the category 'popular' is no longer available to us. New Bollywood demands careful and sustained scrutiny. The Father – and his Sons – in all their masquerades, garbs and guises must be subjected to critical scalpels. If not, his regime will continue to interpellate us as scholars and spectators in an idiom that is deeply undemocratic.

NOTES

Chapter One. Bollywood, Nation, Globalization: An Incomplete Introduction

1 Virdi, Jyotika, *The Cinematic ImagiNation: Indian Popular Films as Social History*, NJ: Rutgers University Press, 2003, p. 192.
2 Jameson, Frederic, *The Geopolitical Unconscious: Cinema and Space in the World System*, Bloomington: Indiana University Press, 1995, p. 3.
3 Spivak, Gayatri C, *A Critique of Postcolonial Present: toward a History of the Vanishing Present*, Cambridge and London: Harvard UP, 1999, p. ix. Spivak's reference to 'a certain postcolonial subject' is directed towards the metropolitan postcolonial scholar.
4 Bhaumik, Kaushik, 'Lost in Translation: A Few Vagaries of the Alphabet Game Played Between Bombay Cinema and Hollywood,' In *World Cinema's Dialogues with Hollywood* (Ed.) Paul Cooke, Great Britain: Palgrave Macmillan, 2007.
5 Rushdie, Salman, *Midnight's Children*, Penguin: Delhi, 1991, p. 162.

Chapter Two. Sentimental Symptoms: The Films of Karan Johar and Bombay Cinema

1 A quick survey of box-office returns indicates that in 2006 *Pyaar ke Side Effects* (The Side Effects of Love, directed by Saket Chaudhury) and *Khosla ka Ghosla* (Khosla's Nest, directed by Dibakar Banerjee), with returns of 84 and 45 millions respectively were judged multiplex successes, while in 2007 *Life in a ... Metro* (directed by Anurag Basu), *Honeymoon Travels Pvt Ltd* (Reema Kagti) and *Bheja Fry* (Sagar Bellary) were considered hits with returns of 162, 115 and 79 millions respectively. All figures in Indian Rupees. http://www.boxofficeindia.com/showProd.php?itemCat=214&catName=MjAwNw==
2 This practice might be viewed as part superstition (the letter 'K' proved lucky for Karan) and part branding. The Hindi film industry is famously superstitious but as Ekta Kapoor's Balaji Telefilms showed, a preference for the letter 'K' also helped create one of the most recognizable brands on television. Johar is a big fan of Kapoor's whose soaps have revolutionized television programming. Her success might be attributed to a synergistic production model and efficiencies of scale applied to a winning 'formula.' These films resemble the 'KJo' film insofar as they are family sagas that combine elaborate displays of ritual and festivities with fairly racy, soap-style subject matter. For more on Ekta Kapoor's work see Shohini Ghosh, 'Married to the Family: Cultural Apprehensions in the

Narratives of Film and TV' March, 20, 2003 and Ipsita Chanda, 'Kyunki Main Bhi Kabhi Tulsi Thi: Opening and Using the Black box of Primetime Telereality.' *Journal of the Moving Image*, no 4, November (2005): pp. 77–100.

3 [http://www.boxofficeindia.com/cpages.php?pageName=overseas_earners].

4 [http://www.boxofficeindia.com/cpages.php?pageName=all_time_earners].

5 As such, the two categories have distinct genealogic affiliations. So for instance, if the 'hat-ke' film is aligned, as we saw above, to the art or parallel cinema in its attachment to realism and its investment in improving the tastes of the viewing public, we can trace its commercial instincts to the middle cinema movement of the 1970s and 80s which tried to bridge the art-commercial divide by making thoughtful fare addressed to the urban middle classes in India. These films are linked as well to programming on state-sponsored TV in the 1980s that emerged as an important venue for serials and films that combined formal inventiveness with progressive content. The 'KJo' film, on the other hand, selectively draws on the popular idiom that evolved in the 1970s and continued into the 1980s particularly under the aegis of directors like Yash Chopra, Prakash Mehra and Subhash Ghai but Karan Johar's highly self-conscious relation to this genealogy is a key component, as I shall show, of his aesthetic.

6 Of equal if not greater significance, at least from the perspective of popular appeal as judged by box office returns, is the rise of genre pictures including comedies, thrillers and action films. Comedy had until the last decade been a marginal genre, with comic routines being included in the catch-all masala film and yet some of the biggest blockbusters in recent years have included the comedies *Welcome* (2007) by Anees Bazmee which made an extraordinary 762 millions at the box office and placed second for the year 2007 and *Partner* (2007) by David Dhawan which made 621.2 millions and placed 5th. Equally noteworthy is the rise of the action franchise – *Dhoom* and *Dhoom 2* (2006) both directed by Sanjay Gadhvi with the latter dominating the returns for the year at 85.4 crores. Also significant is the spatial and regional segmentation of the Indian box-office. Thus *Vivah* (A Journey from Engagment to Marriage, 2006) by Sooraj Barjatya which made 326 millions and came in at No. 10 is considered a blockbuster on the merits of doing extraordinary well in the 'interiors' – i.e. smaller towns while *Bhool Bhulaiya* (The Maze, 2007) by Priyadarshan at 539 millions ranked 6 and was judged an extraordinary hit in West Bengal. What this rudimentary sampling bears witness to is a fragmenting of the national public such nationwide appeal is no longer the benchmark of a truly popular cinema. All figures can be found at [http://www.boxofficeindia.com/showProd.php?itemCat=212&catName=MjAwNg==].

7 In the introduction to their important volume, *Pleasure and the Nation: The History, Politics and Consumption of Popular Culture in India*, Rachel Dwyer and Christopher Pinney describe Indian public culture as a 'citational praxis' – what Sumita Chakrabarty has called impersonation and Homi Bhabha vernacular cosmopolitanism.' The outside indexed here is the West which is engaged with through signs and symbols, language and dress but with no particular attention or fidelity to the contexts of these signs. I am claiming here that we see in the KJo film, this mode of citation being applied to Hindi cinema. Rachel Dwyer and Christopher Pinney, eds. *Pleasure and the Nation: The History, Politics and Consumption of Popular Culture in India*, New Delhi and London: Oxford University Press, 2001, p. 12.

8 See www.passionforcinema.com and Iyer, Sandhya, 'Interview with Karan Johar.' [http://sandhyai.blogspot.com/2007/08/interview-with-karan-johar.html].

9 [http://www.mynameiskaran.com].

10 See Sangita Gopal and Sujata Moorti, 'Introduction,' in *Global Bollywood: Travels of Hindi Film Music* eds. Sangita Gopal and Sujata Moorti, Minneapolis: University of Minnesota Press, 2008 and Raminder kaur and Ajay J Sinha eds. *Bollyworld: Popular Indian Cinema Through a Transnational Lens*, London: Sage, 2005.

11 There is by now an excellent body of work on changing relations between the Indian state and Hindi commercial cinema and the emergence of the diaspora. Of particular interest are monographs like Jigna Desai, *Beyond Bollywood: The Cultural Politics of South Asian Diasporic Film*, London and New York: Routledge, 2003; Rajinder Dudrah, *Bollywood: Sociology Goes to the Movies*, London: Sage, 2006; Rachel Dwyer, *All You Want is Money, All You Need is Love*, Cassell, 2000; Gayatri Gopinath, Vijay Mishra, *Bollywood: Temples of Desire*, Routledge, 2001. Gayatri Gopinath, *Impossible Desires: Queer Diasporas and South Asian Popular Cultures*, Durham: Duke University Press, 2005. See also the following essays, Monika Mehta, 'Globalizing Bombay Cinema: Reproducing the Indian State and Family,' in *Once Upon a Time in Bollywood: The Global Swing in Indian Film*, Tsar, 2007; Purnima Mankekar, 'Brides Who Travel: Gender, Transnationalism and Nationalism in Indian Film,' *Positions* 7:3 Winter (1999), pp. 731–761; Patricia Uberoi, 'Imagining the Family: An Ethnography of Viewing *Hum Aapke Hain Kaun*.' in Dwyer and Pinney eds. *Pleasure and the Nation*, pp. 309–51 and Jenny Sharpe, 'Gender, Nation and Globalization in *Monsoon Wedding* and *Dilwale Dulhaniya le Jayenge* in *Once Upon a Time*, pp. 70–91. Mankekar and Mehta's work is distinguished by the articulation of the diegetic content of Hindi cinema with the political economy of liberalization. Thus Mehta argues that the granting of industry status to the film industry in 1998 signals a radical shift in state policy towards an industry which the state had historically kept at bay. This new intimacy between the state and the industry she suggests was aided by a common pursuit of diasporic capital. 'Family films' that projected a happy marriage between market forces and national traditions helped mediate new configurations of national identity in an era of globalization but the active promotion of such family fare by the state also enabled it to secretly regulate the industry. Mehta incisively notes a shift in state apparatus from a repressive to a generative mode. Mankekar focuses on the landmark film – *Dilwale Dulhaniya Le Jayenge* – to show gender and heterosexual conjugality ideologically structure the relation of nation to diaspora. Thus she shows that unlike a 1960s film like *Purab aur Pachchim* where nationalism is territorially defined, *DDLJ* allows its UK born and bred hero Rahul to be fully Indian but as in the older film, female sexual purity remains central to national identity.

12 The term Bollywood, in what is now an oft-told story, was once used by Indian film journalists and critics to signal the derivative (in relation to Hollywood) nature of Hindi cinema but somewhere in the 1990s, Bollywood lost its pejorative connotation and began to be attached to popular Hindi cinema. If the former use of the term stressed Indian cinema inability to sufficiently differentiate itself from the global dominant Hollywood, Madhava Prasad suggests that the embrace of this term in more recent years might signal the opposite – 'a difference internal to the dominant idiom, a variation that is related to but distinct from the globally hegemonic Hollywood.' Thus Bollywood now emphasizes Hindi cinema not as derivative of but as an alternative to Hollywood but in order to produce itself as difference. It does so by reifying certain characteristics of popular Hindi cinema including song-dance sequences, melodrama, song-dance. Prasad reminds us that such reifications are activated by the diasporic spectator and her desires and sentiments in relation to the nation. In Vijay Mishra's pithy phrase, 'Mother India resonates only in the Diaspora.' Thus Bollywood, consisting of not only the films but the congeries of products, services and practices referred to above, what Rajadhyaksha has called 'cinema effects'

emerges to connect homeland and diaspora in an ever tighter loop. By 2005, this reinscription received further legitimacy when Bollywood got its own entry in the Oxford English dictionary. Today, along with IT and outsourcing, Bollywood is emblematic of brand India. This has also meant that the term no longer refers only or solely to the films, rather to its allied products and derivatives. In a global context, it serves as a signifier for the nation such that an Indian restaurant in London can now name a particularly hot dish – Bollywood curry! To quote Ashish Rajadhyaksha again, Bollywood signals not only films but 'a more diffuse cultural conglomeration involving a range of distribution and consumption activities from websites to music cassettes, from cable to radio.' Such diffusion of the cinematic object across media is also not an entirely new development – the textual heteronomy of Hindi film form had traditionally enabled elements of cinema – songs, dialogues – to circulate outside the cinematic instance, but the frenetic capitalization of such modes of consumption is indeed more recent. Vijay Mishra, 'Bollywood: A Critical Genealogy,' Working Paper, Asian Studies Institute, February, 2008, pp.1–31, p. 7; Madhava Prasad, 'This Thing called Bollywood.' [http://www.india-seminar.com/2003/525/525%20madhava%20prasad.htm]; Ashish Rajadhyaksha, 'The Bollywoodization of Indian Cinema,' in *City Flicks: Indian Cinema and the Urban Experience*, Calcutta: Seagull Books, 2007, pp.111–137.

13 Vijay Mishra suggests that not a totally new phenomenon. See 'Bollywood: A Critical Genealogy.'

14 Rosie Thomas provides what remains one of the most succinct descriptions of the predominant form of post-independence Hindi cinema – the social, which is not quite a genre but a master genre. She notes that though there were distinct genres in the 1930s like mythologicals, historicals, stunt, costume and fantasy films, by the 1940s the 'social' began to emerge as a dominant form that included 'a wide spectrum from heavy melodrama to lighthearted comedy, from films with social purpose to love stories, from tales of family and domestic conflict to urban crime thrillers.' Quoted in Prasad, Madhava, *Ideology of Hindi Film: A Historical Construction*, Delhi: OUP, 1998, p. 46.

15 Hollywood 'realism' as we know is not so much the result of a documentary fidelity to a pro-filmic reality but rather the effect of a rational, probable narrative system that constructs and sustains its illusion. Hindi film form, on the other hand, seems to resemble the attractions driven narrative that Tom Gunning identifies as characteristic of early American cinema. Like the 'cinema of attractions' – it presents a series of spectacles that are not necessarily subordinated to or integrated by the story world. The song-dance sequence that has been an almost invariable feature of all Hindi popular cinema is a excellent instance of this 'illogic' – whatever the subject of the film, it will include these performance sequences that may or may not or may to a variable degree be justified by the story world. That does not mean that these sequences do not contribute to the cinematic experience but only that their efficacy cannot be gauged solely from the vantage of the narrative. The same is true of filmi dialogues which while spoken by particular characters cannot be thought of as expressive of their unique selves – rather dialogues solicit pleasures and affects of their own and while the star's voice, diction and enunciation contributes to these pleasures and the narrative context no doubt excites such speech, dialogues are hardly the means to deciphering the psychology or even the traits of a particular character. Therefore to complain that dialogues or song-dances are not justified by the story world is to judge Hindi film form by rules that are not internal to it. Bordwell, David. *Narration in the Fiction Film*. Madison: University of Wisconsin Press, 1985; Gunning, Tom. 'The Cinema of Attraction: Early Film, its Spectator and the Avant-Garde,' *Wide Angle* 8 (3–4), 1986, pp. 63–70.

16 Gopalan, Lalitha, *Cinema of Interruptions: Action Genres in Contemporary Indian Cinema*, London: British Film Institute, 2002.
17 Ganti, Tejaswani, *Bollywood: A Guidebook to Popular Hindi Cinema*, New York: Routledge, 2004.
18 Vijay Mishra makes a somewhat related argument in 'Genealogy' though he views such memorialization as a hollow iteration, 'pure form' whereas I argue that such Hindi cinema is formally cited and then reconstituted.
19 I am using 'excess' in the sense that Kristin Thompson gives to the term, elements in a film that have purely perceptual, as opposed to narrative and stylistic, salience. They are not narratively or stylistically necessary though they do contribute to the overall value of the film.
20 This framing of film form as generating 'national-difference' in a global arena is allied to the pioneering work of Sumita Chakravarty who looks at Hindi cinema's relation to nationalism and national identity. See *National Identity in Indian Popular Cinema, 1947–1987*, Austin: University of Texas Press, 1993. Also see Jyotika Virdi's *The Cinematic ImagiNation: Indian popular films as social history*, New Brunswick, N.J.: Rutgers University Press, 2003.
21 Quoted in Anupama Chopra's *King of Bollywood: ShahRukh Khan and the Seductive World of Indian Cinema*, New York: Warner Books, 2007, p.144.
22 Biswas, Moinak. 'Mourning and Blood Ties: Macbeth in Mumbai.' *Journal of the Moving Image*, 5, December (2006): 78–85, p. 82.
23 There are a number of fine essays on Amitabh Bachchan in particular and this era in general. Among them, Anupama Chopra's *Sholay: The Making of a Classic*, New Delhi: Penguin Books, 2000 and Connie Haham, *Enchantment of the Mind: The Films of Manmohan Desai*, New Delhi: Roli Books, 2006 provide a nice overview of the 1970s by focusing on two key directors from this time. See also Ranjani Mazumdar's essay on Bachchan entitled 'From Subjectification to Schizophrenia: The 'Angry Man' and 'Psychotic' Hero of Bombay Cinema,' in *Making Meaning*, pp. 238–64 and Prasad's chapter entitled the 'Aesthetic of Mobilization,' in *Ideology*, pp. 138–59.
24 A film like Manmohan Desai's *Amar, Akbar, Anthony* (Amar, Akbar and Anthony, 1977) might be viewed as a parody of the excesses of Hindi cinema including certain well-worn plot-devices like brothers separated at birth, ideologies like nationalist integration, as well as emerging industry practices like the 'multistarrer' film where producers hoped to ensure returns by packing a film with stars.
25 See Prasad's chapter entitled 'The Middle Class Cinema' in *Ideology* pp. 160–187 for an excellent reading of the films of this era.
26 See Ajanta Sircar's excellent analysis of this film in 'Love in a Time of Liberalization.' In *Journal of Arts and Ideas*, 32–33, April (1999): 35.
27 This term is Ravi Vasudevan's. See Vasudevan, Ravi, 'The Melodramatic Mode and the Commercial Hindi Cinema,' *Screening World Cinema: A Screen Reader*, Eds. Catherine Grant and Annette Kuhn, London and New York: Routledge, 2006, pp. 104–126.
28 In *Roja* and *Bombay*, the extended versus the nuclear family, tradition versus modernity is spatialized along a rural/urban divide. The couple has to leave the village in order to live out its progressive destiny. While this divide is picturesquely contained in *Roja*, the regressive parents have to be left behind to die in *Bombay* so that the couple Arvind and Shaila might enter a brave, new secular day. In *Dil Se*, Amar puts both his family and country at peril for love. Interestingly, *Dil Se* which failed in India but was one of the first films to make it to the Top 10 in the UK box office, is also a diasporic hit and like the KJo film, it under-privileges the nation. The films of Mani Ratnam have been the subject

of many fine essays including Madhava Prasad, 'Signs of Ideological Re-form in Two Recent Films: Signs of Real Subsumption', in *Making Meaning*, pp. 145–167; Lalitha Gopalan, *Bombay*, London: British Film Institute, 2006; Ravi Vasudeven, 'Bombay and its Public,' *Journal of Arts and Ideas*, 29, 1996, Nicholas Dirks, Basu and Ananya Kabir.

29 See Madhava Prasad, 'Realism and Fantasy in Representations of Metropolitan Life in Indian Cinema.' In *City Flicks*, pp. 82–98.
30 See Ranjani Mazumdar, *Bombay Cinema: An Archive of the City*. Minneapolis: University of Minnesota Press, 2007, p.118; Sheena Malhotra and Tavishi Alagh, 'Domestic Dramas in Hindi Films Post 1990s,' South Asian Popular Culture Vol. 2, No. 1, April 2004, pp.19–37; Mankekar, 'Brides Who Travel,' and Sharpe, 'Gender, Nation.'
31 Prasad, *Ideology*, p. 49. In other words, though a commercial cinema, Bombay film was not yet entirely subject to market forces and was subject as a result to considerable inefficiency. The call for reform within the industry held Hollywood style efficiencies as a standard. Ram Gopal Verma might be viewed as one such modernizer. He simultaneously wants to streamline the product and the process. Thus he makes genre films – gangster, horror etc. His production firm is appropriately called The Factory.
32 [www.mynameiskaran.com], 7/3/08.
33 Vasudevan, Ravi, 'The Cultural Space of a Film Narrative: Interpreting *Kismet*.' *Indian Economic and Social History Review*, Vol 27, 2, 1991, 171–185, p. 181.
34 Lorenzon, Mark and Florian Arun Tauebe, 'Breakout from Bollywood: Internationalization of Indian Film Industry' DRUID Working Paper Nos 07–06, p. 13–14.
35 ibid. p. 21.
36 ibid. p. 22.
37 Prasad, *Ideology*, p. 49.
38 The parents really are superfluous and if anything subplots involving them really add to the length of a film that has already been widely critiqued for its extraordinary run-time. Interesting, all the fanvids on youtube which re-edit the film entirely leave out the parents.
39 For the relation of family ties to globalization see Jyotsna Kapur and Manjunath Pendakur's 'The Strange Case of the Disappearance of Bombay from its Own Cinema: A Case of Imperialism or Globalization,' in *Democratic Communiqué* 21, No. 1, Spring 2007: 44–59.
40 Mankekar, 'Brides Who Travel,' p. 744.
41 There is a rich body of work on melodrama including Peter Brook's classic, *The Melodramatic Imagination: Balzac, Henry James, Melodrama and the Mode of Excess*, New Haven: Yale University Press, 1976; Thomas Elsaessar's essay, 'Tales of Sound and Fury,' in *Imitation of Life: A Reader on Film and Television Melodramas*, Ed. Marcia Landy, Detroit: Wayne State University Press, 1991; Christine Gledhill's *Home is Where the Heart Is: Studies in Melodrama and the Women's Film*, London: British Film Institute, 1987; Ben Singer's *Melodrama and Modernity*, New York: Columbia University Press, 2001; and Linda Williams, *Playing the Race Card: Melodramas of Black and White from Uncle Tom to O.J. Simpson*, New Jersey: Princeton University Press, 2002. For work focused specifically on Indian cinema seen Prasad, *Ideology*, Chakrabarty, *National Identity*, Virdi, *The Cinematic ImagiNation*. Also see Ashish Rajadhyaksha, 'The Epic Melodrama: Themes of Nationality in Indian Cinema,' *Journal of Arts and Ideas*, 25/26 December (1993): 55–70 and Vasudevan, 'The Melodramatic Mode.'
42 Williams, *Playing the Race Card*.
43 Melodrama is said to thrive on repression, see Elsaessar above.

44 Chow further argues that while the sentimental is no doubt regressive and filial piety merely serves to consolidate and transmit certain ways of life, in a film that otherwise achieves contemporaneity, the sentimental is indeed a point of rupture. It is a gesture towards another time, it manipulates the viewer into accepting other affects. Chow, Rey, *Sentimental Fabulations: Contemporary Chinese Films*, New York: Columbia University Press, 2007, p.18 (italics in original).
45 ibid; p. 23.
46 Vasudevan, 'The Politics of Cultural Address in a Transitional Cinema: A Case Study of Indian Popular Cinema,' in *Reinventing Film Studies* Eds. Christine Gledhill and Linda Williams, London: Arnold; New York: Co-published in the United States of America by Oxford University Press, 2000, pp.131–164, p.138.
47 This kind of flashback reverses the logic of what Corey Creekmur suggestively calls the 'maturation dissolve.' See 'Bombay Boys: Dissolving the Male Child in Popular Hindi Cinema,' in *Where the Boys Are: Cinemas of Masculinity and Youth*, Eds. Murray Pomerance and Frances Gateward, Detroit: Wayne State University Press, 2005, pp. 350–376.
48 Frontality – or when a character directly addresses the spectator – critics have argued is a durable representational convention of Indian cinema carried over perhaps from painting via folk and Parsi theatre to the cinema. Rather than viewing frontality as some essential marker of aesthetic difference, critics have suggested that Indian cinema combines modes – frontal and realist – as a 'rhetorical strategy which makes the cinema both attractive as something new in the field of the visual, and culturally intelligible because it incorporates a familiar visual address.' Quoted in Prasad, *Ideology*, p. 23. For more on Frontality in Indian cinema see Gita Kapur, 'Mythic Material in Indian Cinema,' *Journal of Arts and Ideas* 14/15, 1987, pp. 79–108; Anuradha Kapur, 'The Representation of Gods and Heroes: Parsi Mythological Drama of the Early Twentieth Century,' *Journal of Arts and Ideas*, 23/24, January 1993, pp. 85–107; and Ashish Rajadhyaksha, 'The Phalke Era: Conflict of Traditional Form and Modern Technology,' *Journal of Arts and Ideas*, 14/15, 1987, pp. 47–78.
49 For the concept of cognitive mapping see Frederic Jameson, *The Geopolitical Aesthetic: Cinema and Space in the World System*, Bloomington: Indiana University Press, 1995.

Chapter Three. Is Everybody Saying 'Shava Shava' to Bollywood Bhangra?

1 See Mishra, Vijay, *Bollywood Cinema: Temples of Desire*, London: Routledge 2001, Prasad, Madhava, *Ideology of the Hindi Film: A Historical Construction*, USA: Oxford University Press: 2001, Vasudevan, Ravi, ed, *Making Meaning in Indian Cinema*, New Delhi: OUP India, 2000.
2 Mishra, Vijay, *Bollywood Cinema: Temples of Desire*, London: Routledge, 2001, 238.
Apart from India, Bollywood's spectatorship includes the Indian diaspora in African, West Indies, Fiji, North American, Canada and the Middle East as well as other third world nations in which it is hugely popular. With globalization, Bollywood flows into the first world have made a crossover impact on the Euro-American cultural mainstream as well. Ashish Rajadhyaksha uses the term Bollywood to differentiate contemporary Hindi cinema targeted at a global market to the India bound Bombay cinema before its global flows. I am using the term to include commercial Hindi cinema of both periods.
3 Sumita Chakravarty, *National Indentity and Indian Cinema, 1947–1997*. Austsin: University of Texas Press, 1998.

4 For example, Alison Arnold in argues that pre 1965 production represents 'the genuine artistic endeavor of a body of musically trained, creative composers to develop a modern, native music of national appeal at once popular, eclectic and yet fundamentally Indian.' (Arnold, Alison E, Aspects of Production and Consumption in the Popular Hindi Film Song Industry, Austin: University of Texas Press, 1992, pp. 122–36). With his exposure to Western orchestras accompanying silent films, Prabhat was the first to use instruments such as the piano, the Hawaiian guitar and the violin in his compositions. Naushad was the first to combine the flute and the clarinet, the sitar and mandolin and also the one who introduced the accordion to Hindi film music.

5 Prasad 1998.
Compare, for instance, the Bengali auteur Satyajit Ray's contempt for the six song and dance formula of Hindi films with Sudipta Kaviraj's reading of the critique of the city in the *zara hat ke zara bachke yeh hai Bombay meri jaan* song. It is quite obvious that raised on a staid European diet with strict demarcations between cinematic genres, Ray was confused by the *masala* film. Functioning with the ethic of unity governing Western narrative, Ray was unable to comprehend the presence of motifs that disrupt narrative progression without contributing meaning to it.

6 Trivedi 2006, Kaviraj 2004.

7 *Ramlila* is a seven day ritual performance that enacts sections from the epic *Ramayana* before the annual festival Dusherra. *Nautanki* is a form of folk theatre popular in North India and *Tamasha* is Marathi folk theatre.

8 Prasad 1998.

9 Skillman 1985, p.153.Not only in film, Bollywood song has provided a popular cultural language in which rituals of romance and courtship might be performed in public space in a society where such expressions are in general discouraged. Bollywood music and ghazal constitute a legitimate national mode for articulating romantic sentiments. Bollywood song has been one of the few means through which rituals of romance might be enacted discreetly and obliquely in public space. Much as in the Bollywood film, Bollywood music constitutes a language of indirection through which private thoughts and emotions might be articulated in words.

10 Trivedi 2006.

11 *Bambaiya* is a derogatory Hindi term used to refer to the kitschy, hybridized culture of the metropolis. Hindi cinema's mediation between Indian classical and folk traditions has been noted by Mishra, Saari and Lutze.

12 Partha Chatterjee notes that Master Ghulam Haider changed the conception of Hindustani film song by 'wedding strong assertive melodic lines with an articulate beat usually derived from the store-house of pulsating Punjabi rhythms'. Haider is best known for setting a new trend in *Khazanchi (1941) by* combining popular ragas with the rich verve and rhythm of Punjabi folk music. His prodigy Noorjehan is best known for her Punjabi songs and the most popular playback singer of Hindi cinema, Mohammed Rafi began his singing career with the Punjabi song 'Soniye Hiriye, teri yaad ne bahut sataya' for the movie *Gul Baloch* (1944). Master Ghulam Haider was a *mirasi*, the minstrel caste to which some of contemporary Bhangra artists belong, Manohar Deepak introduced the 'Bhangra in the film industry with B.R. Chopra's *Naya Daur* (1957). See Partha Chatterjee, 'When Melody Ruled the Day,' in *Frames of Mind: Reflections on Indian Cinema*, Ed Aruna Vasudev.

13 The term Bollywood, believed to be coined by the Anglophone global and national media, has been interrogated by a number of scholars in film studies. Making a clear distinction between Indian Cinema and Bollywood, Ashish Rajadhyaksha uses the

latter term to refer to mean culture industry that has emerged in the 90s. Tracing its origins back to Wilford E Deming's coinage of Tollywood in 1932 and the resourceful reporters of a Kolkata youth magazine *Junior Statesman*, Madhava Prasad establishes its relation to the structural bilingualism of the Indian nation state, which he defines as 'a state of affairs where the multitude of Indian languages (here counted as one) are held together by a metalanguage in which alone the national ideology can be properly articulated'. Vijay Mishra uses Bollywood in the title of his book but uses it to refer to Bombay Cinema. While I provide a few examples from Bombay cinema, my essay engages with the centrality of Punjabi music to films in the 90s.

14 *Geet* is song, *qawwali* is a form of Islamic spiritual music, *sufiana kalam* is Sufi spiritual music. Though Bhangra refers to specific performative and musical genres, I will employ the term in this article to include all Punjabi language compositions used in contemporary Bollywood cinema including *geet* and *sufiana kalaam* apart from the Bhangra *boliyaan*. Part of my argument is that differences between different genres of Punjabi music and Bhangra have been erased in the construction of the Bollywood Bhangra formula.

15 'It is unfortunate that people who know nothing about music have started performing on the stage with semi-naked girls. Such people have given a major setback not only to Panjabi culture, but also to the rich music traditions of the region,' said noted film music director Uttam Singh in an exclusive interview to Times News Network. [http://www.sikhi.com/modules.php?name=Forums&file=viewtopic&p=3789].

16 Shohat, Ella and Robert Stam, *Unthinking Eurocentrism*, UK: Routledge, 1996, p. 145.

17 Ibid.

18 Mayne, Judith, *Cinema and Spectatorship*, UK: Routledge, 1993, p. 78.

19 Daler Mehndi is considered the best exponent of Bhangrapop whose album *bolo ta ra ra* (1995) selling more than a million copies in Kerala alone challenged the hegemony of film music.

20 Bachchan's dancing skills that may not necessarily meet Western standards as Richard Corliss reports. 'I showed my dance-savvy wife Amitabh's 'Shava Shava' number from the 2001 blockbuster '*Kabhi Khushi Kabhie Gham*:' goofy and elaborate, with Amitabh switching in a wink from patriarchal elegance to jerking his body like a deranged marionette as 112 partygoers cavort around him. I'd hoped Mary would be beguiled. Instead, she remarked that the choreography was 'sub-West End.' Ouch: the ultimate insult, as anyone who has seen Brits try to match the muscular precision and ease of Broadway terpers will realize.'

21 *Naqqal*: Imitation.

22 Corliss acknowledges his ignorance of Bollywood gestural code. 'We could both be wrong. Indian choreographers and actor-dancers could be working in some gestural code we don't understand. They could have seen Astaire and Rogers and rejected a dance style we find sublime. In the Indian tradition, their form of dance could be tripping the light fantastic above ours, not clodhopping beneath. But Indian film imitated and transformed virtually every other aspect of Hollywood movies. Why wouldn't they dance the way Astaire or Travolta did, except that they couldn't?'.

23 An item number is a dance sequence of raunchy movements and risqué lyrics with little relation to the plot line, which aspiring starlets use to debut in Bollywood. In keeping with Bollywood's libidinous role, an item number is normally added on to generate publicity, guarantee the film's box office success and ensure repeat viewings.

24 *Diwali* is a Hindu festival celebrated by lighting earthen lamps to reenact the welcome given to the exiled king Rama by his subjects when he returned to Ayodhya after 14 years. *Karva Chauth* is a North Indian festival falling on the fourth night (day) after the Full Moon in Kartik month (of Hindu calendar) when married women observe a fast to

pray for the life and health of their husbands. Bollywood's wedding rituals happen to be gloriously Punjabi as much for their spectacular appeal as the Punjabi dominance in the diaspora. While multiple ethnolinguistic narratives might be available internally and externally for the celebration of family values and are being excavated by Bollywood in their special regional nuances, they become attached to *punjabiyat* due to its domination of the Bollyscape. But ritual celebration comes to be attached with the Punjabi diaspora in particular due to the Punjabi diaspora's greater cultural retention, unbroken contact with homeland and its careful nurture of 'the myth of return'.

25 Mishra, Prasad, Trivedi, (1993, 1998, 2006).
26 1993: 200.
27 Mishra, 1993, 254.
28 Mishra, 1993, 260.
29 Rajadhyaksha, 2003.
30 *Femina*, 2005.
31 Rajadhyaksha, 2003.

Chapter Four. Bollywood Babes: Body and Female Desire in the Bombay Films Since the Nineties and *Darr, Mohra* and *Aitraaz*: A Tropic Discourse

1 Prasad, 2003, p. 2.
2 Pendakur, M. and Subramanyam, R. 'Indian Cinema Beyond National Borders,' in J. Sinclair, E J and S Cunningham (Eds.), *New Patterns in Global Television*, Oxford: Oxford University Press,1996, p. 77.
3 For a detailed discussion, see Mishra,Vijay, *Bollywood Cinema: Temples of Desire*, London: Routledge, 2001, pp. 238–241.
4 Mishra, 2001, p. 237.
5 Radhakrishnan, 1996.
6 A significant phenomenon in the Bombay film industry since the nineties is the proliferation of over westernized starlets, who replace the 'stars' in age and appearance.
7 Niranjana, Tejaswini, "Roja Revisited" Economic and Political Weekly, 1994, p. 1299.
8 Culllity, Jocelyn, Prakash Younger , "Sex Appeal and Cultural liberty: A Feminist Inquiry into MTV India", *A Journal of Women Studies*, 25. 2 2004 (96–122), p. 2.
9 Nayar Sheila, "The Value of Fantasy: Indian Popular Cinema through Western Scripts", *Journal of Popular Culture*, Summer 1997 vol. 31 73–90.
10 Nayar, 1997.
11 Mulvey, 'Afterthoughts on 'Visual Pleasure and Narrative Cinema' Inspired by King Vidor's Duel in the Sun (1946)', in *The Visual and Other Pleasures*, London: Macmillan, 1989. Although Mulvey's psycho-analytical model will be interrogated in the subsequent section, some of her observations are valuable in the context of understanding the female visual experience.
12 Mulvey, 1989, p. 74.
13 Mulvey, 1989.
14 Majumdar, Neepa, "The Embodied Voice: Song Sequences and Stardom in Popular Hindi Cinema." *Soundtrack Available: Essays on Film and Popular Music*. Ed. Pamela Robertson Wojcik and Arthur Knight. Durham, NC: Duke UP, 2001, p. 167.
15 Vasudevan, R, "The Melodramatic Mode and the Commercial Hindi Cinema: Film History, Narrative And Performance In The 1950s." *Screen* 30, 3: 29–50, p. 44.

NOTES

16 Vasudevan, 44.
17 Vasudevan, 45.
18 Mishra, 127.
19 It is a point discussed elaborately in Priya Jha's 'Lyrical Nationalism: Gender, Friendship, and Excess in 1970s Hindi Cinema,' in *The Velvet Light Trap* 51 (2003) 43–53.
20 Dhami, N, *Bollywood Babes*, USA: Yearling, 2006, p. 30. (Emphasis mine).
21 Creekmoor in Pamela Robertson Wojcik, and Arthur Knight, Eds. *Soundtrack Available: Essays on Film and Popular Music*. Durham, N.C.: Duke UP, 2001.
22 Bagchi, Amitabha, 'Women in Indian Cinema.' Can be accessed at [http://www.cs.jhu.edu/~bagchi/women.html]
23 I have already stated earlier that this mode pf interpretation may not be essentialized and will reflect the understanding of the female urban spectator.
24 Bagchi. The reference is to her performance to *Tip Tip Barsa Pani*, another sexually explicit song and dance sequence.
25 The front blurb of the video release of the film by Zee TV, New York.
26 Tejaswini Ganthi WNYC Interview, 2007.
27 'Mallika Sherawat, self-defined 'Audio Visual Viagra', is *bindaas* when you tell her the promos of her new film *Murder* are hot. 'Showcase *aisa hai to socho godown mein kitna hoga* (if the showcase flaunts so much, think what the godown has in store)!' she quips' Vinayak Chakhravorty *Hindustan Times.com*.
28 Cullity and Younger, 2004, 101.
29 For the feminine principle behind gaze I am borrowing from Lacan, *The Four Fundamental Concepts of Psychoanalysis*.
30 The actress Priyanka Chopra, we are told, had a hard time playing this scene, even after she trained herself on Sharon Stone in *Basic Instinct*.
31 My reference is to *kitsch* as a term for the postmodern strategy by which the object for cultural consumption draws attention to its own artificiality, often fakeness. For a discussion of the kitsch in Bollywood films, see Mishra 2001, p. 243.
32 Mulvey 1975, 127.
33 On the subject, see Kasbekar, Asha, 'Hidden Pleasures: Negotiating the Myth of the Popular Female Ideal in Popular Hindi Cinema' in Dwyer Rachel, and Pinney, Christopher, ed, *Pleasure and the Nation: The History, Politics and Consumption of Public Culture in India*, SOAS Studies on South Asia, London, Oxford University Press, 2003, p. 295.
34 Mulvey has not been able to quite clarify the problem visual pleasure when it comes to female audience, especially on the subject of how this pleasure is generated in women. For a discussion see Mulvey, 1988.
35 Mulvey, 1975, p. 129.
36 Thomas, Rosie, "Sanctity and Scandal: The Mythologization of Mother India" in *Quarterly Review of Film and Video* 11:3, 1989, pp. 11–30, p. 11.
37 R. Vasudevan, 'The Melodramatic Mode and the Commercial Hindi Cinema: Film History, Narrative And Performance In The 1950s,' in *Screen* 30, 3: 29–50.
38 I find it extremely interesting that she reassures Raj that he does not have to give up his socially sanctioned relationship to satisfy her needs and at the same time demonstrates no interest in other male characters in the film.
39 Prasad 2003, p. 2.
40 Neale 1980, p. 19.
41 Cooke 1985, p. 58.
42 Prasad 2003, p. 7.

Chapter Five. Globalization and the Cultural Imaginary: Constructions of Subjectivity, Freedom & Enjoyment in Popular Indian Cinema

1. A version of this paper titled 'Globalization and the Fantasy of Enjoyment: The Mythopoiesis of Individuality and Freedom in Two Recent Indian Films' was presented at the Annual Global Studies Association Conference on 'Contested Terrains of Globalization' held at California, Irvine; May 17 – 20, 2007.
2. For a more detailed exploration of this issue see Lacan 'Kant avec Sade' in Lacan, J, *The Complete Écrits*, Tr. B. Fink, New York: Norton, 2006; Zizek, s, *The Metastases of Enjoyment: Six Essays on Woman and Causality*, London/NY: Verso, 1994.
3. 'India Poised', [http://www.indiapoised.com/video2.htm] (accessed September 25th 2007).
4. [http://www.indiapoised.com/outline.htm] (accessed September 25th 2007).
5. Ibid.
6. Prasad, Madhav M, *Ideology of the Hindi Film: A Historical Construction*, Delhi: Oxford U. Press, 1998, p.107.
7. Throughout the essay I use enjoyment and jouissance interchangeably.
8. McGowan, T. *The End of Dissatisfaction? Jacques Lacan and the Emerging Society of Enjoyment*. Albany: SUNY Press 2004.
9. [http://ibnlive.com/news/basu-favoured-nuke-power-not-ndeal-karat/49187-3-2.html] (accessed September 22, 2007).
10. [http://www.ibnlive.com/news/nuclear-deal-is-best-thing-to-have-happened-to-india/47490-7.html] (accessed September 22, 2007).
11. To give two slightly different examples, in *Jo Jeeta Wohi Sikander* (1992) where the young hero is censured for pursuing his ethical position as a subject of desire when he uses the money saved for buying his brother's cycle to buy instead an expensive necklace for his girlfriend; or in *Qayamat Se Qayamat Tak* (1988) where the ethical position of two families is shown as morally harmful and destructive to all possibilities of reconciliation; or in the endless Sunny Deol films where the unscrupulous businessman or industrialist is finally destroyed by the hero standing up for the rights of the common people.
12. McGowan, 2004, p. 11.
13. McGowan, 2004, p. 3.
14. Zizek, 1994, p. 69.
15. See, Prasad, 1998, Chapter 3 for example.
16. Lacan, 2006.
17. [http://hindimoviereviews.blogspot.com/2006/08/review-yun-hota-to-kya-hota.html] (accessed September 23, 2007).
18. Interview with Buddhadeb Bhattyacharya, Feb 25, 2007, IBN-LIVE; [http://www.ibnlive.com/news/some-farmland-has-to-go-buddha/30957-3.html] (accessed September 25, 2007).
19. Ibid.
20. Bartaman, April 13, 2006. Also see, Interview with Chaitanya Kalbag, Hindustan Times, July 19, 2007.
21. Zizek, S, *Tarrying with the Negative: Kant, Hegel, and the critique of Ideology*, Durham: Duke University Press, 1993, p. 217.
22. Zizek, S, *The Zizek Reader*, Eds. Elizabeth Wright & Edmond Wright, Oxford: Blackwell 1999, p. 13.

NOTES 181

Chapter Six. *Rang De Basanti*: The Solvent Brown and Other Imperial Colors

1 Aamir Khan plays DJ/Chandrasekhar Azad, Siddharth plays Karan/Bhagat Singh, Sharman Joshi plays Sukhi/Rajguru and Kunal Kapoor plays Aslam/Ashfaqullah Khan in this 2006 Bombay film which went on to become a runaway hit that grossed over 345.5 million Rupees worldwide in its very first week.

2 In 'Autonomy and Comparability: Notes on the Anticolonial and the Postcolonial', Manu Goswami points out that Indian economics began as an anticolonial disciplinary formation rooted in the everyday experience of colonial evenness. In the present Indian context however, this impulse is slowly and agonizingly giving in to an economism that must reside on a single lane of regularities with the universalizing drive of capitalism.

3 Mark Sanders, in 'Postcolonial Reading' writes that postcoloniality urges a training of the agent as reader in the literary. For Sanders, 'the literary' evokes and invokes an elsewhere, and an other, and constantly performs disruptions between aesthetico-epistemic and ethico-affective codings of representation. I follow Sanders' reading in this respect, attempting to understand how the ecology of images in *Rang de Basanti* in fact forecloses such disruptions, instead violently yoking all elsewheres and others to reside on one uninterrupted continuum of globally resonant desires.

4 A largely forgotten revolutionary of the Indian freedom movement of the 1920s and later, Durgavati Devi died at age 92 in 1999. On Decmber 17, 1928, when Bhagat Singh and Sukhdev arrived at the Durga Bhabi's doorstep after having slain J.P. Saunders, it was she who arranged for their escape from Lahore to Calcutta, an event that was acclaimed as nothing short of miraculous. It is said that Bhagat Singh's plan to bomb the Central Assembly in Delhi, evolved during this stay in Calcutta. After the spectacular bombing was finally carried out on April 08, 1929, Bhagat Singh courted arrest, and when along with Sukhdev and Rajguru, he was condemned to die, Durga Bhabi came out of hiding to plead with Mahatma Gandhi to intervene on behalf of the martyrs. Durga Bhabi was herself arrested and awarded three years confinement after her thwarted attempt to assassinate Lord Hailey, an ex-governor of Punjab, and her involvement in Chandrasekhar Azad's frustrated arrangements to attack the very jailhouse where his revolutionary comrades were being held.

5 Developed in roughly the 9th and 10th centuries, Hindi was first known to the Turks who overran Punjab and the Gangetic plains in the early eleventh century by the Persian name Hindvi i.e. the language of the Hind (the land of the River Indus). Hindvi was constructed from the Indo-Aryan Prakrit languages, as well as from Sanskrit loan words, 'softened' for everyday use. It also absorbed Persian, and through Persian, Arabic loan words, and developed as a mixed or broken language of communication between the newly arrived immigrants and the native population of North India. Written in the Devanagari script, it became 'the official language of the Union' on January 26, 1950, even though the Indian Constitution still recognizes English as well as 21 other regional languages as official. After independence, the Government of India undertook the standardization of the language through a publication entitled, 'A Basic Grammar of Modern Hindi' (1958), the result of the work of a government appointed committee. This not only involved cleansing the language of its dialectical variants – Brajbhasa, Maithili, Bundeli, Awadhi, Marwari, Maithili, and Urdu – but also standardizing Hindi spelling and regularizing the system of transcribing the Devanagari script, such that Hindi was could be proudly displayed as one of the many faces of a successful Nehruvian, pan-Indian nationalism.

6 In his seminal essay 'Postcolonial Criticism and Indian Historiography,' Gyan Prakash argues that postcolonial criticism must undo the implacable opposites of colonial thought – east-west, traditional-modern, primitive-civilized – yet in *Rang de Basanti* there is not attempt to either dialectically resolve or radically undo such contentious opposites. Instead, the lexis of national becoming in the film generates India as the effect of aphoristic, fragmentary and discrete intimacies between precisely such ancien binaries as those between primitiveness and civilization, nation and empire, and self and other.

7 Grant Farred, in 'A Thriving Postcolonialism: Toward an anti-Postcolonial Discourse' points out that both Homi Bhabha's and Gayatri Spivak's critique of postcolonial temporality is not satisfied with reducing postcolonialism to the marking off of the colonial from the postcolonial based solely upon chronology, a strategy required and undergirded by the unsettling implication that the residues of colonial rule have seeped not so imperceptibly into the postindependence state.

8 At this point, I refer readers to Vinayak Damodar Savarkar's 1909 magnum opus *The Indian War of Independence, 1857* where the author reads a constellation of local, fragmentary, and aphoristic expressions of insurgency as the first signatures of a cohesive national struggle for independence.

9 Khan had also recently starred in Asutosh Gowarikar's 2001 film *Lagaan*, which despite being recognized as a 'patriotic' film, I choose to leave out of this list because it is pitched at something of a fantastic, even absurdist, rather than realist register. The film begins in the year 1893 when the farmers of Champaneer, a small, non-descript village tucked away in the heart of central India, despairingly search hard, blue skies for signs of evasive monsoon clouds. In the midst of their woes, the local British officer, Captain Russel (played by Paul Blackthorne) demands *dugna lagan*, or double tax, and willfully, even capriciously decides that he will forego the tax only if the villagers can beat his men at a game of cricket. The unlikely heroes are led by an enigmatic young peasant named Bhuvan (played by Aamir Khan) who thrillingly stimulates the villagers to learn this strange, foreign pastime and the film climaxes in a game that is on the one had perhaps the most colonial of subcontinental legacies and on the other, at the centre of a newly liberalized global economy for which cricket is perhaps the most treasured money-spinner. Like *Rang de Basanti* after it, *Lagaan* had also clamorously jingled the cash registers at the box offices worldwide.

10 One of the leaders and founders of the Hindustan Socialist Republican Association, Bhagat Singh has been labeled by the Communist Party of India (Marxist) as one of the earliest Marxists in India. He had read the works of Marx, Engels, and Lenin and believed that with such a large and diverse population, India could only survive under a socialist regime. Introduced to these considerations during his days at the National College in Lahore, Singh also believed that India should re-enact the Russian Revolution; and it was this and his thoughts on violence that positioned him at odds with Gandhi and at least one section of the Congress. Bhagat Singh served on the Hindustan Socialist Republican Association with Chandrasekhar Azad, Ram Prasad Bismil and Ashfaqullah Khan and on the Naujawan Bharat Sabha (Youth Society of India) with Durga Bhabi or Durgavati Vohra. It is known that he was aware of the plans for the Kakori Train Robbery, even though he was not actually a part of that event, but he did actually collaborate with Sukhdev and Hari Sivaram Rajguru in the assassination of J.P. Saunders. Several popular Bombay films have already been made on the life and times of Bhagat Singh – of these, the 1965 film, *Shaheed* starring Manoj Kumar in the lead role was particularly successful. In 2002, two films were released side by side, one entitled, *23 March 1931: Shaheed* and the other named, *The Legend of Bhagat Singh*, but neither obtained much popular success.

11 Despite knowing that the boys and Sonia are apprehensive of his links to a rather volatile Hindu nationalist organization, Sue chooses Laxman Pandey (played by Atul Kulkarani), to essay the role of the fifth revolutionary in her cast, Ramprasad Bismil. Bismil was a revolutionary poet who wrote in Hindi and a major protagonist of the Indian Independence Movement, put to death in December 1927, along with Bhagat Singh and Hari Sivaram Rajguru for his role in the Kakori Train robbery. Pandey, the young man who Sue chooses to play Bismil, is himself a student and in fact a rather important character in *Rang de Basanti*, for we see him early on in the film, distinguished very sharply from the other four boys, and visually proposed as something of a foil to them. Unlike DJ, Karan, Sukhi, and Aslam in their rugged jeans and timberland gear, Laxman sports the traditional kurta-pajama complete with his forehead smeared in red vermillion, and is critical not only of the western attitudes of Daljit's group, but also, in particular of their closeness to Aslam, who is after all Muslim, and therefore not to be trusted. Indeed, even when Laxman and the group must bury their overt differences in order to come together for Sue's film, and Laxman joins the cast in their capers, he remains the perpetual outsider, tainted by the mark of Cain. He cannot take part in the hedonistic surfeit that his colleagues seem so comfortable with, and even though he no longer dresses in the traditional style, his stuffy, close-button shirts, formal trousers, and altogether awkward body language prevent him from actually being a part of the group. In fact, Laxman is perhaps the only figure who cleaves the consolidated lifestyle of the protagonists, for no matter how selective his historicizing may be, he is, like Sue, not devoid of a 'sense of history'. Yet, after the death of Ajay Rathod and the event of paramilitary forces opening fire on the gathering at the candlelight vigil Laxman becomes an integral part of the group and of the fight against the Ministry of Defence. This is also the occasion in which Aslam and Laxman's differences dissolve into a haze of melodramatic friendship through which it is easy to view the zone of indistinction between the tenets of the Hindu Right and those of a newly liberalized and technologistic state.

12 The Jallianwala Bagh Massacre is named after the Jallianwala Garden in Amritsar, Punjab, where on April 13, 1919, soldiers of the British Army in India under the command of Brigadier General Reginald Dyer opened fire on an unarmed gathering of men, women, and children. As a conversation between young students in *Rang de Basanti* reveals, while official sources placed the casualties at 379, private numbers recorded 1000 dead and more than 1200 wounded. This massacre followed upon the events of April 10, 1919 when government fired on a procession advancing towards the residence of the Deputy Commissioner of Amritsar to demand the release of two popular leaders who were on the brink of being deported for sedition against British Raj. In response, property emblematic of British rule was set on fire or otherwise destroyed and Europeans were attacked and killed. For the next two days, Amritsar was quiet, but since violence continued in other parts of Punjab, a decision to place most of the state under martial law was taken by April 13. Despite the resulting confinement, thousands of Sikhs gathered to celebrate the Baisakhi festival in Jallianwala Bagh, partly because those who had traveled from rural areas were unaware of the recent violence in Amritsar, and partly because it had become a tradition for Sikhs to gather at Jallianwala to celebrate this particular religio-agrarian festival. Indeed, the title song in *Rang de Basanti* commemorates this same religio-agrarian occasion, and thus the fact that it is immediately after that carnival that Sue's camera moves from Kakori to Jallianwala Bagh is particularly relevant.

13 The death of Lieutenant Ajay Rathod is based loosely on the life of Flying Officer Abhijit Gadgil who was killed in an MIG crash in September 2001. In the decade before that 120

young pilots of the Indian air force died in 290 non-combat accidents, most of them involving Russian made MIG aircraft. Indeed only two months after the death of Gadgil, two more IAF pilots were killed when their MIG-21 crashed into a tea estate in West Bengal. At this time, Defence Minister George Fernandes had suggested, in the face of growing scandals around the quality of the aircraft that the accidents had in fact resulted largely from human error. The controversy however took a difficult turn when Kavita Gadgil, Abhijit Gadgil's mother launched the Abhijit Air Safety Foundation in Mumbai, creating a foundation from which Indian citizens could unify to demand better safety standards in the air force and ask the Defence Ministry necessary, but uncomfortable questions. Given that *Rang de Basanti* quite recognizably dabbles in this scandalous episode, it was viewed prior to the release by current Minister for Defence, Pranab Mukherjee himself, in the company of Air Marshall S.P. Tyagi, General J.J. Singh, and Admiral Arun Prakash. All four cleared *Rang de Basanti* with the requirement that the Producer clearly declare his film a work of fiction.

14 In 1992, almost a decade and a half before *Rang de Basanti* was to be released, Sara Suleri had in *The Rhetoric of English India* already developed a line of thinking that relentlessly foregrounded such disquieting liaisons between obsolescence and novelty in terms of the complicities between distinct actors on the colonial stage, whether they be oppressor or oppressed, colonizer or colonized, victor or vanquished.

Chapter Seven. Between *Yaars*: The Queering of *Dosti* in Contemporary Bollywood Films

1 Ruth Vanita, '*Dosti* and *Tamanna*: Male-Male Love, Difference and Normativity in Hindi Cinema' Diane P. Mines and Sarah Lamb (eds.), *Everyday Life in South Asia*, Bloomington: Indiana UP, 2002, pp. 146–158.
2 Vanita '*Dosti* and *Tamanna*: Male-Male Love, Difference and Normativity in Hindi Cinema', p. 146.
3 K. Moti Gokulsing and Wimal Dissanayake, *Indian Popular Cinema: A Narrative of Cultural Change*, New Delhi: Orient Longman, 1998, pp. 7–22.
4 *Sholay*, Ramesh Sippy, 1975. *Kal Ho Naa Ho*, Nikhil Advani, 2003. *Masti*, Indra Kumar, 2004.
5 *Whipped*, Peter M. Cohen, 2000.
6 *Yaar* translates as close friend.
7 Eve K. Sedgwick, *Between Men: English Literature and Male Homosocial Desire*, New York: Columbia University Press, 1985.
8 *Dude, Where's My Car?* Danny Leiner, 2000. *Harold and Kumar Go to White Castle*, Danny Leiner, 2004. *Hot Fuzz*, Edgar Wright, 2007.
9 I refer to the behaviors as 'innocent' due to the fact that viewers are expected to imagine the scenarios resulting in mistaken impressions of gayness are 'freak' coincidences such as Aman and Rohit wrestling over a cordless phone or Amar kneeling before Prem's waist trying to fix his pants zipper.
10 Sigmund Freud, *Jokes and Their Relation to the Unconscious*, London: Routledge and Kegan Paul, 1960, p. 14.
11 Freud, *Jokes and Their Relation to the Unconscious*, p. 98.
12 Freud, *Jokes and Their Relation to the Unconscious*, p. 151.
13 Sedgwick, *Between Men*, p. 21.

14 R. Raj Rao, 'Memories Pierce the Heart: Homoeroticism, Bollywood-Style' in A. Grossman (ed.) *Queer Asian Cinema: Shadows in the Shade* (Binghamton: Harrington Park Press, 2000), p. 299.
15 Marriage and reproduction are reified in nearly all national cultures as primary life goals. However romantic/sexual codes of ethics very greatly from region to region. Homosexuality, premarital, non-monogamous sexuality and extramarital sexuality all fall outside of the norm of monogamous marital heterosexuality but are tolerated to differing degrees in different cultural contexts. All of the above mentioned behaviors are either not legal or not encouraged but nevertheless they are widely practiced with more visibility and with fewer negative consequences in the West than in India.
16 The four stages of life for Hindu men are *brahmacharya*—which is essentially youth and young adulthood. *Brahmacharya* (walks with/teacher of brahma) is associated with schooling and knowledge and is often thought to be a time of celibacy in a young man's life though in reality this may not be the case. *Grhastha* is the householder stage during which a man marries and has children. The two later stages are *vanaprastha* and *sannyasa*. The last two stages indicate the latter half of life during which time he begins to renounce his earthly attachments in a quest to attain *moksha* (an end to reincarnation). *Vanaprastha* is concomitant with the onset of adulthood for one's children and *sannyasa* traditionally meant leaving one's family to become a *sadhu*.
17 Freud, *Jokes and Their Relation to the Unconscious*, p. 97.
18 Freud, *Jokes and Their Relation to the Unconscious*, p. 97.
19 Freud, *Jokes and Their Relation to the Unconscious*, p. 100.
20 Freud, *Jokes and Their Relation to the Unconscious*, p. 97.
21 This is particularly true of Amar in *Masti*. His first exchange with Dr. Kapadia takes place inside of an elevator immediately after an effeminate man wearing full make-up brazenly checks out Amar's buttocks. It is after Amar and Dr. Kapadia leave the elevator and continue their conversation about love that Dr. Kapadia first begins to think that Amar may be gay. Clearly a number of men pick up 'gay vibes' from Amar.
22 Ashok Malik suggests, Admittedly, there is some rhetoric about the cultural aspects of globalization. This is inextricably linked to fears of 'Westernization' of 'Indian values' being wiped out. Such political reflexes are, to be fair, scarcely unique to the BJP and its allies. There have also been occasional protests against 'Western-style decadence' and 'American-style consumerism,' omnibus phrases that really mean whatever one wants them to mean.
Ashok Malik, 'The BJP, The RSS family and globalization in India' in *Harvard Asia Quarterly* 7:1 Winter 2003. [http://www.asiaquarterly.com/index] (24 Aug. 2007).
23 Jyoti Puri, *Encountering Nationalisms*, Oxford: Blackwell Publishing, 2003, p. 142.
24 The term *desi* is a colloquialism used to describe people of South Asian descent. *Desi* derives from the Hindi word for country *desh* as well as the word/concept of *swadeshi*, which translates roughly as Indian self reliance/self rule.
25 Leela Gandhi, 'Loving Well: Homosexuality and Utopian Thought in Post/Colonial India' in R. Vanita (Ed.) *Queering India: Same-Sex Love and Eroticism in Indian Culture and Society*, New York, Routledge, 2002, p. 89.
26 Indira Gandhi proclaimed the Emergency in late June of 1975 as a response to political opposition. The Emergency basically amounted to a declaration of martial law through which Gandhi granted herself the power to indiscriminately jail those who dared to publicly oppose her. The Emergency only came to end during the 1977 national election during which an overly confident Gandhi was ousted from her position as prime minister in favor of Morarji Desai. For more information about the

Emergency see K.R. Sundar Rajan, 'Indira Gandhi and her advisers were surprised by the ease with which they could silence democracy' in *Rediff on the Net* [http://www.rediff.com/freedom/30rajan.htm] (30 Aug. 2007).

27 *Brokeback Mountain*, Ang Lee, 2005.
28 Fareeuddin Kazmi, 'How Angry is the Angry Young Man? 'Rebellion' in Conventional Hindi Cinema' in A. Nandy (Ed.) *The Secret Politics of Our Desires: Innocence, Culpability and Indian Popular Cinema*, London, Zed Books, 1999, p. 143.
29 *Yeh Dosti* was the first male-male duet (recorded by playback singers Kishore Kumar and Manna Dey) in Bollywood history.
30 The English translation of the *Yeh Dosti* lyrics is taken from Thomas Waugh's essay 'Queer Bollywood or I'm the Player, You're the Naïve One' in M. Tinkcom and A. Villarejo (Eds.) *Keyframes: Popular Cinema and Cultural Studies*, New York, Routledge, 2001, p. 292.
31 Perry Brass,'India's Pioneer: Ashok Row Kavi Interview by Perry Brass,' in *Gay Today: A Global Site for Daily Gay News*. [http://gaytoday.badpuppy.com/garchive/interview/050399in.htm] (30 Aug. 2007).
32 **Kothi-**'A self-identifying label for males who feminise their behaviours and state that they prefer to be sexually penetrated anally, and, or, orally.' Naz Foundation International. *Fact File 1: Defining terms used in working with male-to-male sex*. Naz Foundation International, 2004.
[http://www.nfi.net/NFI%20Publications/NFI%20Fact%20Files/NFI%20fact%20file%201.pdf] (30 Aug. 2007).
Panthi is by definition a man who penetrates, whether it is a woman, and, or, another male (Naz Foundation International 2004). Naz Foundation International. *Fact File 1: Defining terms used in working with male-to-male sex*. Naz Foundation International, 2004.
[http://www.nfi.net/NFI%20Publications/NFI%20Fact%20Files/NFI%20fact%20file%201.pdf] (30 Aug. 2007) **Giriya**s– '[M]en who have sex with *kotis*, dress and act like 'real men' and perform the role of husbands to their *koti*.' Ninad Jog,'*Kotis* and *Giriyas*' in *Workstations at Maryland*. University of Maryland. January 15, 2001. Ninad Jog, 2001. [http://www.wam.umd.edu/~ninad/gay/Kotis.html] (30 Aug. 2007).
jiggery dost–'young unmarried males, who, in a homosocial and homoaffectionalist environment find themselves sexually aroused through physical contact, either through play or sleeping next to each other.'
Shivananda Khan, 'Risk and Needs Assessment amongst Males who have Sex with Males in Lucknow, India' in *NAZ Foundation International. Lucknow Report*, 1998.
[http://www.nfi.net/NFI%20Publications/Assessments/Lucknowrpt.pdf] (30 Aug. 2007).
33 Shivananda Khan and Omar Khan define *masti* as 'nonpenetrative sexual behavior.' Shivananda Khan and Omar A. Khan, 'The Trouble with MSM' *American Journal of Public Health*. 96:5 (2006), pp. 765. According to M.A. Nazi, '*Masti* has two meanings. One is the *masti* of a bull elephant, which is its state when in heat. Then there is the *masti* of the *Sufi*, which is supposed to be for the select few a state of spiritual enhancement.' *The Nation on the Web*. [http://www.nation.com.pk/daily/july-2006/28/columns1.php] (30 Aug. 2007).
34 My own reaction to *Yeh Dosti* being a case in point.
35 Shivananda Khan, 'Male 'Homosexualities' In India & South Asia: Culture, Sexualities, and Identities: Men who have Sex with Men in India' in *Journal of Homosexuality*, Vol. 40 (2001).
[http://www.globalgayz.com/g-india.html] (30 Aug. 2007).
36 Heretofore non-resident Indian will appear as NRI.

37 *Purab aur Paschim*/East and West (1970) is a classic example of a prototypical anti-nonresident Indian film. Gurinder Chadha's film *Bhaji on the Beach* (1993) involves a delightful parody of *Purab aur Paschim*'s over the top depiction of diasporic *desis* gone wild.
38 *Hijra* is a term used to refer to intersexed men who choose to dress and live as women. They often live in *hijra* communities which function as surrogate families. *Hijras* are thought to be an auspicious presence at engagement parties and baby naming ceremonies and often earn money for singing at such events. However many *hijras* are also involved in sex work in order to make ends meet.
39 The Law of Manu or *manusmriti* is thought to have derived from the Vedas and is essentially a manual dictating Hindu codes of living. The Law of Manu regarding the relationship between a husband and wife is commonly cited as the basis for the idealization of the chaste and dedicated Hindu wife worshipped in mythological figures like Sita, the wife of Lord Ram of the *Ramayana*.
40 *BenGAYliz Times* August 2007, No. 2 [http://bengayliz.com/news.aspx] (30 Aug. 2007).
41 Jawaharlal Nehru, *The Discovery of India* (New Delhi, Penguin Books India, 2004), p. 62.
42 Western values are also perceived as at odds with Islam, the largest minority religion on the subcontinent. However the Bollywood films of the mid 1990s and 2000s are so thoroughly Hinducentric that I cannot think of any recent Bollywood films in which the protagonists are practicing Muslims—or non-Hindu for that matter.
43 Muraleedharan, T. 'Queer Bonds: Male Friendships in Contemporary Malayalam Cinema' in R. Vanita (ed.) *Queering India: Same-Sex Love and Eroticism in Indian Culture and Society*. (New York, Routledge, 2002), p. 183.
44 Muraleedharan, 'Queer Bonds,' p. 181.

Chapter Eight. Imagined Subjects: Law, Gender and Citizenship in Indian Cinema

1 Jaikumar, Priya, *Cinema at the End of Empire: A Politics of Transition in Britain and India*, Durham: Duke University Press, 2006, p. 34.
2 Sahlins, Marshall, *Islands of History*, Chicago: University of Chicago Press, 1985, p. 146.
3 The paired oppositions of 'anthropology' and 'history' – from which emerge the further dichotomies of 'structure' and 'event' respectively – are to be found in structural anthropologist accounts of the social and cultural real. Of these accounts, the most influential for me has been Marshall Sahlins' work. See especially his *Islands of History*. Work on South Asian societies has been influenced by this debate; see especially Bernard Cohn, *An Anthropologist Among Historians and Other Essays*, New York: Oxford University Press, 1998. As will be seen, this essay concerns itself with historical memory via the paired oppositional hermeneutics of a 'structural' versus 'eventful' or 'evenementielle' discourse upon the historical nation.
4 Sahlins 1985, p. xiii.
5 Sahlins 1985, p. vii.
6 Sahlins 1985, p. xiv.
7 See Turner, Victor, 'Frame, Flow, and Reflection: Ritual and Drama as Public Liminality,' in *Performance in Postmodern Culture*, Ed. Michel Benamou and Charles Caramello, USA: Paj Publications, 1977, pp. 33–55, and Turner, Victor, "Liminality and the Performative Genres" in *Rite, Drama, Festival, Spectacle, Rehearsals toward a Theory of Cultural Performance* Ed. John J. McAloon, USA: Inst for the Study of Human Is, 1984, pp. 19–41.

8 See John H Mansfield, 'The Personal Laws or a Uniform Civil Code?' in Baird R, Ed. *Religion and Law in Independent India*, Delhi: Manohar, 1993, p. 141, with regard to the question of how law, politics and violence have been inseparably etched on the canvas of religious identity in India.
9 Turner, 1977, p. 36.
10 Patel, *Film India*, 1952, p. 9.
11 Raman, Shankar, *Framing 'India:' The Colonial Imaginary in Early Modern Culture*, Stanford: Stanford University Press, 2002, pp. 30–1.
12 See Menon, Ritu. 'Reproducing the Legitimate Community: Secularity, Sexuality and the State in Postparition India,' in Patricia Jeffery and Amrita Basu, Eds., *Appropriating Gender: Women's Activism and Politicized Religion in South Asia*, London: Routledge, 1998, pp. 15–32; Aiyar, Swarna. "August Anarchy': The Partition Massacres in Punjab, 1947,' in *South Asia:Journal of South Asian Studies*; special issue on 'North India: Partition and Independence,' pp. 13–36; Butalia, Urvashi. *The Other Side of Silence: Voices from the Partition of India*. Durham: Duke University press, 2000; Menon, Ritu and Kamla Bhasin, *Borders and Boundaries: Women in India's Partition*, New Delhi: Kali for Women, 1998; Menon, Ritu and Kamla Bhasin, 'Abducted Women, the State and Questions of Honour: Three Perspectives on the Recovery Operation in post-Partition India,' in Kumari Jayawardena and Malathi de Alwis, ed., *Embodied Violence: Communalising Women's Sexuality in South Asia*, London: Zed Books, 1996, pp. 1–31; and Menon and Bhasin, 'Recovery, Rupture, Resistance: Indian State and the Abduction of Women During Partitiion,' *EPW* xxviii no. 17, April 24, 1993.
13 Menon, 1998, p. 31.
14 Menon, 1998, pp. 27–9.
15 Menon, 1998, pp. 21, 29.
16 Menon, 1998, p. 22.
17 Derrida, Jacques. 'Signature, Event, Context,' in *Limited, Inc.*, Evanston, Ill: Northwestern University Press, 1988, pp. 1–23.
18 Cited in index but not covered in Rajadhyaksha Ashish and Paul Willemen. *Encyclopedia of Indian Cinema*. London; Oxford: British Film Institute/Oxford University press, 1994.
19 As in the Shah Bano (1986) case, discussed below.
20 The issue of indeterminate and incomplete citizenship and rights reappears in the post-nineties in legislation such as the POTA or Prevention of Terrorism Act and the TADA or Terrorist Activities Disruption Act (1993; 1994).
21 Bhagwati, in Baird, R., Ed. *Religion and Law in Independent India*, Delhi: Manohar, 1993, p. 9.
22 Khory in Baird 1993, pp. 134–5 details how under Jawaharlal Nehru and his grandson Rajiv Gandhi, prime ministers respectively in the fifties and the nineties, the state faced and defaulted on this identical question: 'how does the state reconcile group interests with the demands of common citizenship' (p. 135). As to what religion in the Indian context itself means, and how it overlaps with lived tradition, the literature is enormous. Consult, however, Bhagwati in Baird 1993, 17; Peter Van der Veer, *Religious Nationalisms*; Christophe, Jaffrelot, *Hindu Nationalist Movements in India*; Thomas Blom Hansen, *Wages of Violence*; Cohn, *An Anthropologist*; Lloyd and Susan Rudolph, *In Pursuit of Lakshmi*; and Ashutosh Varshney, *Ethnic Conflict*.
23 Coward in Baird, 1993, p. 32. See also Larson and Mansfield in Baird, 1993.
24 An earlier draft was proposed in 1944, but was shelved temporarily (Virdi, 2003, pp. 68–9).

25 Dhagamwar in Baird, 1993, p. 215; Virdi 2003, pp. 67-9.
26 Dhagamwar in Baird, 1993, pp. 235, 241; Virdi, 2003, p. 68. This anticipated, as I have stated above, the riskiest political fallout of the important Shah Bano controversy in 1986.
27 Virdi, 2003, p. 70.
28 Virdi, 2003, p. 73. For another indispensable commentary on religious 'communities' as being 'undemocratic' regarding women, see Kumkum Sangari, 'Politics of Diversity: Religious Communities and Multiple Patriarchies,' in Bidyut Chakraborty, Ed., *Communal Identity in India: Its Construction and Articulation in the Twentieth Century*, USA: Oxford University Press, 2003, pp. 181-213.
29 Virdi, 2003, pp. 71-2; Agnes, Flavia, *Women and Law in India: An Omnibus*, Oxford University Press, 2004; Lateef, Shahida, *Muslim Women in India – Political and Private Realities: 1890s-1980s*, New Delhi: Kali for Women, 1990.
30 Geeta Kapur, 2000, 267.
31 Also see Mishra, 'The Texts of 'Mother India," 2001, p. 63.
32 Vasudevan, 2000, p. 115. See also Rosie Thomas, 1989, pp. 14, 15, 19, 27; Ashish Rajadhyaksha, 2003; and Mishra, 2001.
33 Vasudevan, 2000, p. 115.
34 Perhaps less obvious, and thus necessitating this note, is the fact that Radha and Lakshmi are both names of Hindu goddesses who are, at different times, consorts of Lord Krishna the saviour, also known as Shyam, a diminutive form of which name is Shamu, the name of Radha's husband. Shamu has abandoned Radha, who faces her inverted reflection in Lakshmi, the goddess of fortune, across the chasm of psychic and sexual horror opened up by the disappearance of all former authority and faith.
35 Radha's faith is illusory, of course; in the end Radha's husband never returns, and her beloved younger son dies at her own hands.
36 See Mishra, 2001, pp. 65, 81-7.
37 Rajadhyaksha, 2003, p. 35. Identifying the film's address constitutes filmic spectatorship for Metz; identifying the state's address constitutes political citizenship for Rajadhyaksha, Ritu Menon and the constitutionalists and critics represented in Baird, 1993.
38 In this context, Vijay Mishra writes 'Bombay Cinema is self-consciously about representing, in the context of a multicultural and multiethnic India, the various disaggregated strands of the nation-state – political, social, cultural, and so on' (2001, pp. 65, 77).
39 Ravi Vasudevan reviews the form and content of Hindi 'socials' of the 1950s as an essentially 'social' form of reprising the realistic through the melodramatic in an attempt to re-establish the sacred premises of social relations in a chaotic 'modern' world via cinematic technique that perforce mixed realism and melodrama; see Vasudevan, 2001.
40 For the colonial and anticolonial nationalist antecedents of this postcolonial legal enterprise see Virdi, 2003, pp. 67-73.
41 Mishra, 2001, p. 63.
42 See Thomas, 1989; and Parama Roy, *Indian Traffic: Identities in Question in Colonial and Postcolonial India*, University of California Press, Berkeley, 1998.
43 The review in *FilmIndia* characteristically declaims: 'because this picture succeeds in bringing home their shame to the butchers of human brotherhood, it has been summarily banned in Pakistan' (July 1949, 47).
44 Thomas, 1989, 23. This story might be apocryphal, but it no doubt contributed to the creation of Nargis' star text as the Muslim woman of dubious sexuality who came to embody the chaste Mother India later.

45 Vasudevan 2001, p. 105; See also Rajadhyaksha, 2003, pp. 34–5, and Vasudevan, 2001, p. 113.
46 pp. 108–109.
47 Director Guru Dutt.
48 Virdi, 2003, pp. 75–6, discusses the 'infamous' appearance of the Hindu Code Bill's clause granting divorce to Hindu women as a severe blow to Hindu patriarchal 'tradition': 'The film turns the Hindu Code Bill on its head…referring to it as the 'divorce bill' – a term assigned to it in popular parlance' (76).
49 'Guru Dutt's 'Mr. And Mrs. 55' Is A Polished Musical Comedy,' *Filmfare* 27 May, 1955, p. 21.
50 'Retired Hurt,' and 'Hindu Code Debate?' *FilmIndia* November 1951, pp. 15, 33.
51 For a good review of the parliamentary debate on these terms see Dhagamwar in Baird, 1993, pp. 236–4; Virdi, 2003, pp. 69–71, 79–81.
52 Coward in Baird, 1993, pp. 24–32.
53 Director Mohan Segal.
54 In fact, the Punjabi father is the Tamil father's boss at work.
55 Director Anil Sharma.
56 Deepa Gahlot 2004, pp. 110–1.
57 Gahlot 2004, p. 111.
58 On trains and partition massacres, see Menon, 2004, chapters 2 and 3, and Aiyar, among many others. Trains were sites of traumatic and prolonged violence at the time of partition.
59 Director Yash Chopra.
60 Menon, 2001, p. 24.

Chapter Nine. 'It's All About Loving Your Parents': Liberalization, Hindutva and Bollywood's New Fathers

1 This title is derived from the tagline of Karan Johar's 2001 blockbuster *Kabhie Khushi Kabhie Gham* (*KKKG*).
2 Jameson 1998, p. 60.
3 Narayan Shankar in *Mohabbatein*.
4 For example, see Rajagopal, A. *Politics after Television: Religious Nationalism and the Reshaping of the Indian Public*. Cambridge: Cambridge University Press 2001, who charts the contours of Hindu nationalism over three fairly distinct phases.
5 'If liberalization and privatization had already been words in vogue until this time, they attained the status of gospel truths, containing both diagnosis and cure'. Rajagopal 2001, p. 39.
6 Rajagopal, 2001.
7 For a range of scholarship that has attempted to analyze the historicity, the constituent components and the peculiar force garnered by Hindu nationalism, see Basu, T, et.al., *Khaki Shorts and Saffron Flags: A Critique of the Hindu Right*. New Delhi: Orient Longman 1993; Nandy, A. *Creating A Nationality: The Ramjanmabhumi Movement and Fear of the Self*. Delhi: Oxford University Press 1998; Ludden, D. *Contesting the Nation: Religion, Community, and the Politics of Democracy in India*. Philadelphia: University of Pennsylvania Press 1996;

and Sarkar, S. *Beyond Nationalist Frames: Postmodernism, Hindu Fundamentalism, History.* Bloomington, Indiana University Press 2002.
8 Rajagopal 2001, p. 34.
9 Rajagopal 2001, p. 34.
10 For instance, Virdi 2003.
11 See Kaur, R, and Sinha, A J. *Bollyworld: Popular Indian Cinema Through a Transnational Lens.* New Delhi: Sage Publications 2005, p. 19.
12 For instance, it has been suggested that in recent years, the aesthetics of MTV has had a profound influence on Bollywood's image. Through increased incorporation of steadycams, filters, diffusers, and highly sophisticated digital image and sound construction, Bollywood's products became suffused with a sensuousness that did not so much mean increased realism as a heightened 'realism effect.' A virtuoso performance of technology brings a new kind of aesthetic into being—where the film image operates as a media-text, one among others—evoking/mimicking the gloss and sensuality of music videos and television advertisements.
13 One could read the dyad's impact on cinema in multiple ways. Since it became absolutely crucial to re-imagine a reconfigured Hindu nation, 'threats' to the national space and boundaries became charged with new significance. In fact, rarely has the materiality of national borders been more obsessively fetishised. Thus, a series of violent, rabidly anti-Pakistan—and thus anti-Islam in Bollywood's shorthand—films, such as J.P. Dutta's *Border* (1997), Rajkumar Santoshi's *Pukar* (2000), John Matthew Matthan's *Sarfarosh* (1999) and *Gadar: Ek Prem Katha* (Anil Sharma, 2001), became huge commercial successes at the box office. I am not suggesting any direct causal link between the rise of Hindutva and the popularity of anti-Pakistan/anti-Muslim films. What I am trying to describe however, is an atmosphere where certain discourses—which were perhaps subliminally present in earlier decades—came out in the open, finding in Hindi cinema a novel forum for elucidation. It is the generation of this space—where the fantasy of national plenitude can only be configured as a particular 'mythic' struggle—that begs interrogation.
14 By underscoring the massive reach of the rhetoric of Hindu nationalism and neo-liberalism, I do not mean to belittle or elide dissenting voices—for there were many. I am however, trying to describe the sheer power of an overarching ideological machine that constitutively transformed the nation-state—to a large degree effectively marginalising other, resistant discourses.
15 For a discussion of melodrama as a mode of excess, see Nowell-Smith, G, 'Minnelli and Melodrama,' *Movies and Methods: An Anthology*, Ed. Bill Nichols, Berkeley, University of California Press, 1976; B Brooks, P, *The Melodramatic Imagination: Balzac, Henry James, Melodrama and the Mode of Excess*, New York, Columbia University Press, 1985; and Elsaesser, T, 1995, 'Tales on Sound and Fury: Observations on the Family Melodrama', *Film Genre Reader II*, Ed. B K Grant, Austin: University of Texas, 1995, pp. 350–380.
16 Virdi 2003, p. 7.
17 Virdi 2003, p. 178–204. See also, Uberoi, P, 2001, 'Imagining the Family: An Ethnography of Viewing Hum Apke Hain Kaun!' in R Dwyer and C Pinney eds. *Pleasure and the Nation: The History, Politics and Consumption of Public Culture in India.* Delhi: Oxford University Press 2001.
18 Films like *KKKG* do not simply fetishise consumption, they also clutter the cinematic frame with a plethora of consumer products, which are offered to the spectator as aspirational items.
19 A notable exception is Vijay Mishra's reading of Bachchan's recent avatar. Mishra 2002.

20 Prasad 1998.
21 For example, Vijay's compelling presence in *Deewar* is significantly aided by the contrast between hyper-kinetic action sequences of violence and scenes of absolute stillness. Bachchan replicates the stillness and grace of movement in more recent films like *KKKG* and *Mohabbatein*.
22 Mishra 2002, p. 153.
23 In other words, Aditya Chopra's *Dilwale Dulhania Le Jayenge* (*DDLJ*)with very similar ideological propensities was released earlier in 1995, but the film did not feature Bachchan. Here, I am arguing for a character consolidation that is best embodied by the Bachchan star text at this time.
24 The massive Longleat House in Wiltshire masquerades as the exterior of Gurukul. Other scholastic locations include Queens College in Oxford and The American University at Bushey, Hertfordshire.
25 For example, he sports on his forehead a *tika*—a mark of his devotion to Hindu gods; he chants Sanskrit *slokas* on several different occasions; he has erected a temple to Lord Shiva on the lawns of Gurukul, where *havans* and prayers are regularly held and attendance of all students and staff are deemed mandatory. Presumably, then, Gurukul does not admit non-Hindu students or teachers, a disturbing vision in India's fraught political present.
26 It is crucial to note that the Shahrukh Khan persona signifies globality, freedom and the consumer's fundamental right to choice; in this instance these qualities and his friendship with the three young students—whose worlds seem chock-full of global logos—speaks for and to the ethos of a newly liberalised India.
27 In this instance, Aryan mirrors that other Raj Malhotra who sought a similar acceptance and recognition from the Phallic patriarch in *DDLJ*.
28 Of course, the development of high capitalism in the subcontinent has been uneven at best. This patchy, incomplete transition to capitalism and now an equally uneven transition to an even more intangible form of modernity make the national parallel particularly poignant. *Ek Rishtaa* does not, however, address these structural problems in any significant manner. The choices and alternatives faced by characters remain highly individualistic.
29 See Harvey, D, *The Condition of Postmodernity*, Oxford: Blackwell, 1990.
30 For example the workers and their leader join the festivities at Preeti's wedding and act as hosts, a task that they interpret as duty, because Preeti is like their daughter as well.
31 The film marks Nisha, from the beginning of their courtship as spoiled and 'too modern'. She is rude, wears bold, revealing clothes and enjoys the attention of other men. Ajay however, soon teaches her the error of her ways and marriage temporarily transforms her into a silent, submissive homemaker.
32 Interestingly, the police—the arm of the state—do appear a few times in the film. However, they are clearly more invested in aiding Kapoor's rehabilitation than in exercising their duty. The police inspector spends much time in reprimanding Rajesh for troubling the Kapoor clan, but does not do anything to stop Ajay from using extra-legal means to bring the former to heel.
33 As is obvious in this brief introduction to the plot, *Baghban* generously borrows from Ozu's classic *Tokyo Story* (1953), which was in turn a loose remake of a Hollywood film, *Make Way For Tomorrow* (Leo Mc Carey, 1937). The resonances only get stronger over the course of the film. To my knowledge, there has been no acknowledgement of these multiple sources from the makers of *Baghban*. Given the Bollywood industry's propensity

for appropriating plots and narratives freely and with scant regard for copyright regulations, this does not come as a surprise.

34 Julia Kristeva, in *Powers of Horror*, has undertaken the most compelling initial work on abjection. For her the abject is a figure that inhabits a plethora of things—it is a source of horror, it is that which does not 'respect borders, positions rules', it is the excluded, the ejected, filth, bodily wastes, menstrual blood, perversions, the corpse 'the place where meaning collapses'. Kristeva's abject is, 'the place where 'I' am not. The abject threatens life; it must be 'radically excluded' from the place of the living subject, propelled away from the body and deposited on the other side of an imaginary border which separates the self from that which threatens the self.' Creed, B, 'Horror and the Monstrous Feminine: An Imaginary Abjection', *The Dread of Difference: Gender and the Horror Film*, Ed. B K Grant, Austin, University of Texas Press, 1996, pp. 37–38. This metaphor of ejection and expulsion is especially resonant with the Father's place in Baghban. He comes to be that which must be violently excluded, even jettisoned, for the generation and maintenance of life. He is the waste, the corpse, and the excess that 'must nevertheless be tolerated, for that which threatens to destroy life also helps to define life.' Creed 1996, p. 38.

35 For instance, Payal's desire for a love life free from her grandmother's interference is pitched by the film on the same register as Reena and Sunju (Sameer Soni) not leaving any food for Raj to break his fast with on *karvachauth*. The term describes a north-Indian Hindu ritual of wives fasting for their husband's long lives. As a signpost of his own modernity and 'progressive' views, Raj fasts along with Pooja. When Pooja and Raj decide the break their fast together on the phone, she realizes that he has been left no food to eat. Similarly Reena as a working mother quite reasonably demands rest that is uninterrupted by Raj's noisy typing, and *Baghban* ascribes to this expectation the same cruelty that, for example, Kiran (Suman Ranganathan) embodies in relegating Pooja to the maid's room. In other words, Payal's perfectly legitimate demand as a modern, adult subject to conduct an autonomous social existence and Reena's equally legitimate expectation that she be allowed rest after a long day, are nullified by the film in one fell swoop.

36 This lack and incompleteness is echoed by Rahul (Shahrukh Khan) and Anjali (Kajol) in *KKKG* once they are banished from the patriarch's home and hearth. The deep desire to surrender to the father's law also inflects Johar's film.

37 Bachchan has continued to embody abjection in more recent films. Particularly interesting performances include those in *Nishabd* (Ram Gopal Varma 2007) and *Eklavya* (Vidhu Vinod Chopra 2007). While the latter recuperates the feudal Father somewhat, the former traces his complete annihilation within the ambit of the nuclear family.

SELECT BIBLIOGRAPHY

Appadurai, Arjun, *Modernity at Large, Cultural Dimensions of Globalization*. Minneapolis, London: University of Minnesota Press 1996.
Baird, R, ed, *Religion and Law in Independent India*. Delhi: Manohar 1993.
Basu, T, et.al., *Khaki Shorts and Saffron Flags: A Critique of the Hindu Right*. New Delhi: Orient Longman 1993.
Brass, Paul R, *Language, Religion and Politics in North India*. Delhi: Cambridge 1974.
Brooks, P. *The Melodramatic Imagination: Balzac, Henry James, Melodrama and the Mode of Excess*. New York: Columbia University Press 1985.
Chakrabarty, Bidyut ed, *Communal Identity in India: Its Construction and Articulation in the Twentieth Century*. USA: Oxford 2003.
Chakravarty, Sumita S. *National Identity in Indian Popular Cinema, 1947–1987*. Austin: U. of Texas Press 1993.
De Alwis, Malathi ed. *Embodied Violence: Communalising Women's Sexuality in South Asia*, Durham: Duke University Press 2006.
Dwyer Rachel, and Pinney, Christopher, ed, *Pleasure and the Nation: The History, Politics and Consumption of Public Culture in India*, SOAS Studies on South Asia, London, Oxford University Press, 2003.
Goswami, Manu. "Autonomy and Comparability: Notes on the Anticolonial and the Postcolonial", *Boundary 2* 32:2, 2005. pp 201–225.
Guha, Ranajit, ed, *A Subaltern Studies Reader, 1986–1995*. Minneapolis: University of Minnesota Press 1997.
Pandey, Gyanendra, *Remembering Partition: Violence, Nationalism and History in India*. Delhi: Cambridge 2002.
Gupta, Charu. *Sexuality, Obscenity, and Community: Women, Muslims, and the Hindu Public*. New York: Palgrave 2002.
Harari, R. *Lacan's Seminar On "Anxiety"*, Tr. Jane C. Lamb-Ruiz, New York: Other Press 2001.
Harvey, D. *The Condition of Postmodernity: An Enquiry into the Origins of Cultural Change*. UK: Blackwell 1990.
Jaffrelot, Christophe, *Hindu Nationalist Movement in India*. New York: Columbia University Press 1996.
Jaikumar, Priya, *Cinema at the End of Empire: A Politics of Transition in Britain and India*. USA: Duke University Press 2006.
Jameson, Fredric et al. ed. *The Cultures of Globalization*. Durham: Duke University Press, 1998.
Jha, Priya, "Lyrical Nationalism: Gender, Friendship, and Excess in 1970s Hindi Cinema", *The Velvet Light Trap* 51 (2003) 43–53.
Kaur, R, and Sinha, A J. *Bollyworld: Popular Indian Cinema Through a Transnational Lens*. New Delhi: Sage Publications 2005.

Kristeva, J. *Powers of Horror: An Essay on Abjection.* trans. L S Roudiez, New York, Columbia University Press 1982.
_____ *The Complete Écrits,* Tr. B. Fink, Norton: New York 2006.
_____ *The Ethics of Psychoanalysis,* (1959–60), Seminar Book VII, Tr. Dennis Porter, London/New York: Norton 1997.
_____ *The Other Side of Psychoanalysis,* Seminar XVII, Tr. R. Grigg, New York: Norton 2007.
Lal, Vinay and Nandy, Ashis ed. *Fingerprinting Popular Culture: The Mythic and the Iconic in Indian Cinema.* Oxford: Oxford University Press 2006.
Lateef, Shahida, *Muslim Women in India – Political and Private Realities: 1890s–1980s.* New Delhi: Kali for Women 1990.
Ludden, D. *Contesting the Nation: Religion, Community, and the Politics of Democracy in India.* Philadelphia: University of Pennsylvania Press 1996.
Majumdar, Neepa, "The Embodied Voice: Song Sequences and Stardom in Popular Hindi Cinema." *Soundtrack Available: Essays on Film and Popular Music.* Ed. Pamela Robertson Wojcik and Arthur Knight. Durham, NC: Duke UP 2001: 161–81.
McGowan, T. *The End of Dissatisfaction? Jacques Lacan and the Emerging Society of Enjoyment.* Albany: SUNY Press 2004.
Menon, Ritu et al. *Borders and Boundaries: Women in India's Partition.* New Delhi: Kali for Women 1998.
Miller, Jacques-Alain. (2005). 'Introduction to Reading Jacques Lacan's Seminar on Anxiety', in *Lacanian Ink 26,* Ed. Josefina Ayerza, Wooster: New York; pp. 8 – 67.
Mishra, V. *Bollywood Cinema: Temples of Desire.* London: Routledge 2002.
Mufti, Aamir, 'Secularism and Minority: Elements of a Critique', *Social Text,* 45:14, No. 4, 1995.
Mulvey, Laura, "Visual pleasure and Narrative Cinema", *Screen,* Vol. 16, No.3. Autumn,
Nandy, A. *Creating a Nationality: The Ramjanmabhumi Movement and Fear of the Self.* Delhi: Oxford University Press 1998.
Nayar Sheila, "The Value of Fantasy: Indian Popular Cinema through Western Scripts", *Journal of Popular Culture,* Summer 1997 vol. 31: 73–90.
J. Sinclair, E. Jacka and S. Cunningham (eds.). *New Patterns in Global Television.* Oxford: Oxford University Press, 1996.
Penley, Constance ed. *Feminism and Film Theory.* London: Routledge, 1988.
Prasad, Madhav M, *Ideology of the Hindi Film: A Historical Construction,* Delhi: Oxford U. Press, 1998.
Prasad, Madhava, 'This thing called Bollywood' *UNSETTLING CINEMA* a symposium on the place of cinema in India May 2003.
Ragland, E, *Essays on the Pleasures if Death: From Freud to Lacan,* Routledge: New York/London, 1995.
Rajadhyaksha, Ashish, and Willemen, Paul, *Encyclopedia of Indian Cinema,* British Film Institute/Oxford University Press, London, Oxford, 1994.
Rajagopal, A. *Politics after Television: Religious Nationalism and the Reshaping of the Indian Public.* Cambridge: Cambridge University Press 2001.
Raman, Shankar. *Framing 'India': The Colonial Imaginary in Early Modern Culture.* Stanford: Stanford University Press, Stanford 2002.
Roy, Paroma, *Indian Traffic: Identities in Question in Colonial and Postcolonial India,* Berkeley; University of California Press 1998.
Rudolph, Lloyd, and Susan, *In Pursuit of Lakshmi: the political economy of the Indian state,* University of Chicago Press, Chicago, 1987.

Sarkar, S. *Beyond Nationalist Frames: Postmodernism, Hindu Fundamentalism, History.* Bloomington, Indiana University Press 2002.
Savarkar, Vinayak Damodar, *The Indian war of Independence, 1857*, Delhi: Phoenix 1947.
Roach, James R. ed, *India 2000: The Next Fifteen Years.* Maryland: Riverdale 1986.
Suleri, Sara. *The Rhetoric of English India.* Chicago: University of Chicago Press 1992.
Thomas, Rosie. "Sanctity and Scandal: The Mythologization of Mother India" *Quarterly Review of Film and Video* 11:3 (1989): 11–30.
Uberoi, P, 2001, 'Imagining the Family: An Ethnography of Viewing Hum Apke Hain Kaun!' in R Dwyer and C Pinney eds. *Pleasure and the Nation: The History, Politics and Consumption of Public Culture in India.* Delhi: Oxford University Press 2001.
Van der Veer, Peter, *Religious Nationalism: Hindus and Muslims in India.* Berkeley: University of California Press 1994.
Varshney, Ashutosh. *Ethnic Conflict and Civic Life: Hindus and Muslims in India.* New Haven: Yale University Press 2003.
Vasudevan, R. "The Melodramatic Mode and the Commercial Hindi Cinema: Film History, Narrative And Performance In The 1950s." *Screen* 30, 3: 29–50.
_____ ed, *Making Meaning in Indian Cinema.* New Delhi: Oxford University Press India 2000.
Virdi, J. *The Cinematic ImagiNation: Indian Popular Films as Social History.* New Brunswick: Rutgers University Press 2003.
Wojcik, Pamela Robertson and Arthur Knight eds. *Soundtrack Available: Essays on Film and Popular Music.* Durham: Duke University Press 2001.
Zizek, S. *For They Know Not What They Do: Enjoyment as a Political Factor*, Verso: New York 1991.
_____ *Tarrying with the Negative: Kant, Hegel, and the critique of Ideology*, Durham: Duke University Press: 1993.
_____ *The Metastases of Enjoyment: Six Essays on Woman and Causality.* London/New York: Verso 1994.
_____ *The Zizek Reader*, Eds. Elizabeth Wright & Edmond Wright. Massachusetts: Blackwell: Oxford 1999.

www.ingramcontent.com/pod-product-compliance
Lightning Source LLC
Chambersburg PA
CBHW021828300426
44114CB00009BA/368